"SHAKIN' UP" RACE AND GENDER

Chicana Matters Series

DEENA J. GONZÁLEZ AND ANTONIA CASTAÑEDA, EDITORS

Chicana Matters Series focuses on one of the largest population groups in the United States today, documenting the lives, values, philosophies, and artistry of contemporary Chicanas. Books in this series may be richly diverse, reflecting the experiences of Chicanas themselves, and incorporating a broad spectrum of topics and fields of inquiry. Cumulatively, the books represent the leading knowledge and scholarship in a significant and growing field of research and, along with the literary works, art, and activism of Chicanas, underscore their significance in the history and culture of the United States.

"Shakin' Up" Race and Gender

INTERCULTURAL CONNECTIONS IN PUERTO RICAN, AFRICAN AMERICAN, AND CHICANO NARRATIVES AND CULTURE (1965–1995)

Marta E. Sánchez

UNIVERSITY OF TEXAS PRESS
Austin

Illustrations in this work are by David Avalos, Professor of Visual Arts, California State University San Marcos

⊗ The paper used in this book meets the minimum requirements of ANSI/NISO z39.48-1992 (R1997) (Permanence of Paper).

Library of Congress Cataloging-in-Publication Data

Sánchez, Marta Ester.
  "Shakin' up" race and gender : intercultural connections in Puerto Rican, African American, and Chicano narratives and culture (1965–1995) / Marta E. Sánchez. — 1st ed.
      p.   cm. — (Chicana matters series)
  Includes bibliographical references and index.
  ISBN 0-292-70693-6 (cl. : alk. paper) — ISBN 0-292-70965-x (pbk. : alk. paper)
  1. American literature—Minority authors—History and criticism.   2. American literature—20th century—History and criticism.   3. Puerto Ricans—United States—Intellectual life.
4. African Americans—Intellectual life.   5. Mexican Americans—Intellectual life.   6. African Americans in literature.   7. Mexican Americans in literature.   8. Puerto Ricans in literature.   9. Ethnic groups in literature.   10. Minorities in literature.   11. Sex role in literature.   12. Narration (Rhetoric)   13. Race in literature.   I. Title: "Shakin' up" race and gender.   II. Title.   III. Series.
  PS153.M56S26   2005
  810.9'920693'09045—dc22

                                                    2004030274

For my students

CONTENTS

AGRADECIMIENTOS

This book is the product of several years of research aimed at establishing intercultural connections among three literatures and cultures. The immediate time period on which it focuses is 1965 to 1973, eight crucial years in the historical evolution of modern Puerto Rican, African American, and Chicano literature. I look back at these literatures from the perspective of the events that transpired during the past thirty years and in the belief that to understand the historical evolution of Puerto Rican, African American, and Chicano literatures and cultures in the United States, it is crucial to study them in relation to each other and to U.S. ethnic white cultures as well.

Every book emerges out of collective effort and support. This one is no different. Just as the literatures and cultures I am examining did not develop as discrete units, so this book was not conceived or written in isolation. I received sustained encouragement and support from my colleagues at the University of California, San Diego (UCSD), my intellectual home for twenty-five years where I taught and researched Chicano and Chicana literature. The germinal form of this book probably took place in the classroom, with my undergraduate students. My two-quarter stay at the University of California, Irvine (UCI), Humanities Research Center allowed me time to delve into the topic more deeply. There I had the opportunity to share my ideas with scholars from other University of California campuses. In ways I could not know then, my discussions with Jeffrey Belnap, Karen Christian, Raúl Fernández, Katherine Kinney, Shirley G. Lim, George Lipsitz, and Vince Raphael shaped the intellectual direction of my book. They directed me to useful sources and offered me exciting ideas. I deeply appreciate the generous sharing of their time, knowledge, and expertise.

The University of California awarded me a President's Research Fellowship in 1992–1993 that afforded me valuable release time to continue the research I began at UCI. I thank the UCSD Humanities Research Center for a grant to advance the writing of the book. The Academic Senate at UCSD provided funding to prepare my book manuscript for final submission to the University of Texas Press. I am grateful to Provost Gabriele Wienhausen for the opportunity to contribute to the founding of Sixth College at UCSD. I also thank Provost Cecil Lytle at UCSD for the opportunity to serve and contribute to the Preuss Charter School. It is my hope that strong leaders will emerge from Preuss to lead future generations.

All the material in this book, with the exception of chapter 2, is published here for the first time. Chapter 2 is a revision of "La Malinche at the Intersection: Race and Gender in Piri Thomas's *Down These Mean Streets*," published in *PMLA* in January 1998. It is reprinted here by permission of the Modern Language Association of America.

I thank all my undergraduate students for keeping me rooted in the importance of teaching, itself an intercultural experience. Their questions, curiosity, and fresh responses to the texts we studied in class taught me more than they will ever know. Ed Avila, Jo Brinkman, Dolores C de Baca, Lillian Carrazco, Mai Nasif, Rachel Pimental, George Ramírez, and Linda Yaron were especially important in my exploration of the ideas presented here. I am indebted to my graduate students who shared ideas with me about teaching and subject matter: Adrian Arancibia, Juli Barry, Jewell Castro, Yu-Fang Cho, Norienne Fauth, Carlton Floyd, Martha Gonzáles, Jason Homer, Hellen Lee, Rubén Murillo, Elva Salinas, Gregory Stephens, and Filemon Zamora-Suchilt. My thanks to Hellen Lee and Jake Mattox, also a doctoral candidate at UCSD, for their help in the last stages of the computer preparation of the manuscript and for being meticulous and engaging editors in both form and content.

The friendship and support of my colleagues in the Spanish section of the Department of Literature at UCSD—Carlos Blanco, Jaime Concha, Susan Kirkpatrick, Misha Kokotovich, Jorge Mariscal, Max Parra, and Rosaura Sánchez—has been priceless. I am also grateful for the support of Linda Brodkey, Charles Chamberlain, Steve Cox, Michael Davidson, Stephanie Jed, Todd Kontje, Fred Randel, Kathryn Shevelow, Nicole Tonkovich, Don Wayne, Donald Wesling, and Ana Celia Zentella, who have been outstanding colleagues. Carlos and Iris Blanco have a special place in my heart for making it possible for me to come to UCSD as a graduate student in 1970.

I owe a debt of gratitude to Beatrice Pita, one of the most astute readers I know, who provided enjoyable and stimulating conversations in the early but crucial phase of my research. Rosaura Sánchez, an intellectual giant in

Chicano and Chicana matters, gave me unwavering support, and I salute her leadership, courage, and fearless commitment. The questions, comments, and creative suggestions of Stephanie Jed, Susan Larsen, Kathryn Shevelow, and Nicole Tonkovich saw me through what seemed at times an endless endeavor and provided a safe haven to explore and try out ideas. I am proud that their voices accompany mine in this book. Muchas gracias, compañeras! Abrazos y solidaridad!

I am grateful to the reviewers for the University of Texas Press whose suggestions helped to make the ideas in this book clearer and sharper. Theresa May, my editor at the press, graciously and patiently answered all my emails.

I also thank Frances Aparicio, Rina Benmayor, Arnaldo Cruz-Malavé, Emory Elliot, Deena González, Frances Foster, Mary Louise Pratt, Diana Tey Rebolledo, and Marc Zimmerman for their support and belief in my work.

I shall forever cherish and remember Lisa Hirschman's loving guidance and support. Antonia Meltzoff provided me with loving comfort and support and showed me the way to a healthy distance and sense of humor about my life in academia.

Thanks also to the staff of the Literature Department at UCSD—Nancy Hesketh, Thom Hill, Gretchen Hills, Nancy Ho-Wu, Heather Fowler, Suzie Melad, Ana Minvielle, Lucinda Rubio-Barrick, Patricia Valiton, and Diane Wells—for taking care of my research needs. Karen Linvall-Larson's expertise in navigating the UCSD library was invaluable for my research. I thank Cecilia Ubilla, a longtime friend, wise person, and sharp reader of texts. I thank Barby Reyes and Steve Potts, with whom I had stimulating conversations about *Down These Mean Streets* and *The Autobiography of a Brown Buffalo.*

I thank David Avalos, the well-known Chicano artist, for the striking images in this book and the cover design. He put into visual form my intercultural theme. I am proud that the heart and passion of his creative talent accompanies my words.

Finally, my deepest love and gratitude to Paul Espinosa, my husband, friend, and lifetime supporter, and to Marisa Espinosa, our daughter, who is making her parents proud in her pursuit of learning, her energetic idealism, and her work and dedication to social equity and justice.

PRELUDE

All the faces are brown, tinged with brown, lightly brown, the feeling of brown.
—OSCAR ZETA ACOSTA, *The Autobiography of a Brown Buffalo*

Langston Hughes wrote what became his most famous poem, "The Negro Speaks of Rivers," on a train trip from St. Louis, Missouri, to Mexico.[1] In this poem, Hughes mentions the Mississippi, the Euphrates, the Congo, and the Nile, a gesture, I believe, to situate African Americans within international culture. Although he does not name the Rio Grande in the poem, Hughes crossed this river many times on his travels to and from Mexico. These frequent crossings suggest that Hughes's experiential relationships extended to Mexico and the Southwest and that these territories for him were more than touristic geography.

Hughes writes in his autobiography, *The Big Sea*, that on one of his many train trips between the two countries—in this case from Mexico into Texas—some white Americans mistook him for "Mexican." Hughes's self-description might provide a clue why: "I am of a copper-brown complexion, with black hair that can be made quite slick and shiny if it has enough pomade on it in the Mexican fashion" (50). When he arrived in San Antonio, where he was to change trains, this African American turned saboteur of taken-for-granted racial indicators that he knew would consign him to Jim Crow waiting rooms. He emphasized one of the many stereotypes already banked in the U.S. popular imagination for Mexicans—the "greasy" hair. He added another characteristic to make himself more convincing to his "white" audience: he ordered his ticket in Spanish and reserved a comfortable Pullman berth for the journey home to Cleveland. Most important, Spanish was a language that would set him far enough from "Negro" to allow him to pass for "Mexican." In other words,

"Mexican," even in the 1920s, contained an ambiguity that would bring him, in the perception of those around him, closer to "white." Hughes felt compelled to perform an identity "trick," to perform an intercultural[2] transaction, in order to pass as "Mexican," so that he might claim in his native country the equal rights enjoyed by "white" people.

This anecdote about Hughes intrigues me because it concerns an African American's surpassing the black/white binary[3] of white supremacy, not by rising above it or dismissing it but by confronting it head-on and working through it in an intercultural contact zone.[4] Hughes was able to play up his appearance as a "Mexican-looking" man in Texas because of the state's history encompassing Mexican, Native, Anglo, and African Americans.

In 1845 the United States conducted its invasion of Mexico, at least in part to satisfy the interests of those who would extend the enslavement of the black population in the Texas territory, at that time owned by Mexico, in which Mexicans and Native Americans were the indigenous peoples. In this historical contact zone, more than half a century after the U.S.-Mexico war, Hughes created imaginative and real cross-cultural meaning the day he took advantage of the ambiguity offered him in a "Mexican" identity. He "shook up" the one-drop theorem and drew a line to connect African American and Mexican American peoples, bringing both into a simultaneous conjuncture of belonging.

In this book I use a key Puerto Rican literary text, *Down These Mean Streets* (1967), to link three literary cultures—Puerto Rican, African American, and Chicano—at the time of the Civil Rights movement in the United States. *Down These Mean Streets* is an autobiographical novel by Piri Thomas and the point of departure or metaphor of my book. Although not as well known to a general audience in the United States as Hughes, Thomas knew as well as Hughes that racial identification was a messy business. A New York–born writer, he captures in *Down These Mean Streets* what it meant to be an adolescent, Puerto Rican male on the U.S. mainland in the 1940s. Thomas's protagonist, like the author,[5] was born in a Harlem hospital in 1928, twenty-six years after the birth of Hughes, and he grew up in East (or Spanish) Harlem, the Puerto Rican neighborhood adjacent to Black Harlem. Outside his home "turf" of East Harlem, the autobiographical and fictional character, also named Piri, was called every name in the racist lexicon for black people because he was dark-skinned, had nappy hair and an Anglo-sounding surname, and knew and liked the walk and talk of black men in Harlem. Confused about his racial identity and feeling compelled to find out what it meant to be

Puerto Rican, he decided to leave New York and travel to the South with his black American friend, going as far as Galveston, Texas.

Both the author Thomas and the character Piri, like Hughes, rejected the hierarchical absolutism in the black/white racial binary that gave no room in which to claim a rightful humanity as Puerto Rican men. Like Hughes, they did not evade it but confronted it head-on. Angry and resentful of the white world that hemmed him in, Piri was determined by the end of his trip in *Down These Mean Streets* to release years of stored-up rage. He devised a plan to gain entry into a white bordello in Galveston, where, as he put it, he could fuck a white woman. A fluent English speaker, he pretended to be able to speak only Spanish. As Hughes had done years before, Piri camouflaged himself as "Mexican." In a brief, revenge-driven scene, Piri deliberately misrepresents himself to the brothel owner as "Mexican," lays with a white prostitute, and immediately after unmasks himself to her as a "nigger." However tactically different, however self-inventive—or, as in Piri's case, self-destructive—their "stunts" may have been, Hughes and Piri—and also implicitly Thomas—subverted social practices of white supremacy by playing upon a linguistic difference to establish themselves as "Mexicans" and thus sabotage the black/white racial dyad. These men of color, far from being bereft and rudderless, resisted the systems of control set up to secure racial "purity" and turned the perceptions these systems uphold to their advantage.

A Puerto Rican in Texas passing himself off as "Mexican" is somewhat of an anomaly when one considers that the migration of the Puerto Rican diaspora has been primarily from the island to East Coast cities, especially New York. Thomas defamiliarizes Texas as a geopolitical space made up of a Mexican American and African American minority population. Texas represents the disputed boundary over which the United States went to war against Mexico, a war that enabled Texas to do to Mexico what the white segregationist South did to the Union North. In other words, Texas seceded from Mexico in 1845 just as the South seceded from the North fifteen years later. In 1848 the Treaty of Guadalupe Hidalgo ended the 1846–1848 war and sealed the fate of the Mexican borderlands. Texas entered the Union as a slave state, altering the balance of power between the North and the South, and forever became aligned with the South in the U.S. imagination. But the historical memory still holds: Texas in a Chicano imaginary is "Mexican" and is claimed by Chicanos to this day as part of the Mexican Southwest, or Aztlán.[6] In the nineteenth and especially the twentieth century, the city of El Paso became the southwestern Ellis Island of Mexican immigration to the United States. Hughes and Thomas not only expand the range of our imaginings of Texas; they also help to connect the dots between two of the peoples whose histories are intricately tied to this geographic space.

What would happen, then, if to the list of rivers that Hughes mentions in "The Negro Speaks of Rivers" we would respectfully add the unspoken river of his poem? Today, I allow myself to imagine a Spanish-speaking, "Mexican-looking" Hughes "speaking of" the Rio Grande (would he call it by its Mexican name, the Río Bravo?), a symbol of the intercultural contact zone where Mexicans, African Americans, Mexican Americans, Native Americans, and ethnic white Americans have met for almost two centuries. Thomas shows us that a Puerto Rican in Texas can also shake up the racial, gender, and linguistic categories that have been negotiated in this U.S.-Mexico border region. His protagonist traveled into Jim Crow territory and learned that if one drop of black blood can make one black, one drop of white blood can make one white. I add the Rio Grande/Río Bravo, then, to Hughes's international geography as a marker of the interethnic, intercultural activity I locate in this book. Let my grafting of the Rio Grande/Río Bravo to Hughes's poem stand as a space of symbolic possibility for an intercultural history among Puerto Rican, African American, and Chicano ethnic groups that has yet to be written.

"SHAKIN' UP" RACE AND GENDER

INTRODUCTION: INTERCULTURAL CONNECTIONS

1. THE PLAYERS

In the prelude, I began with two anecdotes—one about Langston Hughes, another about Piri Thomas—in the spirit of inviting my readers to entertain connections among continental Puerto Rican, African American, and Chicano (Mexican American) cultures.[1] These three cultures are the points of the intercultural triangle that this book aims to build. Since new populations took their place in the citadel of higher education in the 1970s and 1980s, a period in higher education that stands out for its "diversification,"[2] these cultures have been locked into separate domains, so that a pattern of relation to each other and to yet other cultures has remained in the background of intellectual inquiry. My objective is to make visible through literature a fuller picture of the interculturalism—the complex movement and interplay—among these three so-called minority[3] cultures during the years they began to emerge into our national consciousness. I aim to show hidden yet real ties that connect ethnic peoples of color to each other and to white ethnic peoples in a shared intercultural history.[4] Interculturalism is the theme of this book.

The beginning of the second phase of the Civil Rights movement (1965) and the formal closure of the war in Vietnam and the beginning of Watergate (1973) frame the period of this study. This sliver of history is a crucial turning point in the development of these three cultural groups and of the United States as a whole. Events since 1973 allow me to see sets of relationships in literature and history that were not visible, or as visible, then or immediately thereafter. New generations and new audiences have asked new questions, brought to the fore new understandings and approaches, proposed and pursued different ways to think about race and gender, ethnicity and sexuality, that make it possible to revisit this period with fresh eyes. More accurately, then, the span of this book encompasses more than eight years: it is a retrospective of 1965 to 1973 from the perspective of the past thirty years.

I engage Chicano, African American, and Puerto Rican cultures in conversation by way of three literary narratives—one from each of the three cultures and all published between 1965 and 1973. *Down These Mean Streets* (1967) by the Puerto Rican Piri Thomas, *Manchild in the Promised Land* (1965) by the African American Claude Brown, and *The Autobiography of a Brown Buffalo* (1972) by the Chicano Oscar Zeta Acosta are my windows for viewing clusterings of these cultures. I use these narratives to shake up the compartmentalization that keeps Puerto Rican, African American, and Chicano cultures apart in the historical record. It is in this spirit that I have used the expression "shakin' up" in my book's title, a motif I take from a chapter in *Down These Mean Streets,* "Gonna Find Out What's *Shakin'.*" *Down These Mean Streets* was a unique text for its time because it made explicit interracial linkages when the dominant trend in ethnic cultural movements was toward singular identities. I take *Down These Mean Streets* to represent the first moment of the intercultural approach to literature and culture that I am committed to validate. It is the paradigmatic text of my book.

In history's public record, the relationship of the three ethnic groups of color—Puerto Ricans, African Americans, and Chicanos—to white ethnic groups, the "dominant" cultures—is arranged along a subdominant to dominant axis. In chapter 1, I show how each ethnic group of color, for example, is keyed to a particular prominent and public intellectual who wrote what I call narratives of "family" about them: the Mexican Octavio Paz and his landmark book of essays on Mexican culture, *The Labyrinth of Solitude,* is linked to Chicanos;[5] the Irish American Daniel Patrick Moynihan and his influential government document on the black American family, *The Negro Family: The Case for National Action* (more simply called "the Moynihan report"), is tied to African Americans; and the Jewish American Oscar Lewis's best-selling ethnographic "life stories," *La Vida: A Puerto Rican Family in the Culture of Poverty—San Juan and New York,* about an extended Puerto Rican family, is associated with island and continental Puerto Ricans. Our way of organizing the study of these cultures has been to maintain these dual and hierarchical—subdominant/dominant—relationships.

Although the ideas these thinkers proposed about these populations were part of a broader constellation of thought and writing about racially marked and disenfranchised communities, I choose to concentrate on Paz, Moynihan, and Lewis for three reasons. First, they wrote specifically about these groups, and their writings were probably the most contentious published during this period. Second, what they wrote received significant attention in the popular press and scholarly communities, and their writings, at least those of Paz and Moynihan, provoked a strong critical response from the groups themselves.[6] And third, but no less important, the authors analyzed the life habits and practices of these groups in a way that contributed to their racialization. The controversy surrounding these men and their writings, especially the debates about Moynihan's *The Negro Family*, kept the national discussion on a black/white axis and distracted from the possibility of envisioning these groups as participants in an intercultural history. By "racialization," I mean the social practice of placing particular ethnic groups farthest from an accepted "norm," casting them in dangerous and disorderly roles. Social dysfunctions, such as violence, juvenile delinquency, crime, excessive male virility, prostitution, and single motherhood, were attributed to these racial groups as though an ability to engage in these practices had been handed down to them, and only to them, by divine decree. In the chapters and the interludes that follow them, I read the three literary texts against the voices of Paz, Moynihan, and Lewis in a way that goes against ethnic purity and sees them and the populations they emerge out of as participants in a shared intercultural history.

Puerto Ricans, African Americans, and Chicanos disputed in written and oral venues their displacement by the intellectual mainstream. They disputed images of themselves as "victims," helpless subordinates, unable to find their way without the help of dominant white society. The literary texts too suggest that the groups did not perceive themselves as "victims" and that they strove to obtain interpretive power in relation to other ethnic identities. By "interpretive power," I mean the access of cultural citizens[7] to become agents, or brokers, in social processes of meaning and knowledge, not simply carriers of cultural interpretations others see fit to bestow on them. Different groups may do this in different ways, as power looks relatively different to those who stand at different places along the social periphery. However, all ethnic groups are part of the broader social processes in which knowledge is produced about them. All cultural groups play a role, no matter how small, in the constitution of their histories and identities.

Except for a few brave women who broadened the discussion in the 1970s, most of the initial responses to the statements of the three thinkers came from men.[8] Almost all respondents of the 1960s and 1970s, however, consolidated ethnic separatism; that is, they followed the path of establishing singular group identities. They responded in opposition to the intellectuals who attempted to speak for them and thus stayed within the terms of the subdominant to dominant spectrum. This strategy was necessary, important, understandable, and even inevitable, given the constraints of that time. I believe, however, that the events between *then* and *now*, the events of the intervening years since 1973, enable us to reshape this vertical arrangement—that is, Chicano men and women to Paz, African American men and women to Moynihan, and Puerto Rican men and women to Lewis—in favor of a horizontal arrangement that brings the ethnic "minority" and white "dominant" cultures inside the same historical frame and allows us to see them in relation to one another.

In my pursuit of intercultural connections, I privilege concrete scenes from the literary texts because I believe that the built-in capacity of narrative to engage audiences with stories can frequently illustrate more effectively than abstract theory what happens when people from different cultures coexist and interact in the busy and noisy spaces of daily living. These literary texts are based on individuals' memories of lived, once spontaneous experiences, the feature that makes personal writing and storytelling so powerfully alluring. Herein lies the power of these texts. People, cultures, and their values and perspectives converge in these texts to share the same space at the same time, an impossibility in physics but not in literature. Cultural encounters are messy phenomena. Conflicts ensue, misunderstandings occur, especially when there is competition for purportedly scarce resources. The texts illuminate intercultural convergences suppressed in the rhetorical circuit of arguments that took place when the groups responded to the writings of the corresponding intellectuals. In the process of narration, or "storytelling," these texts show the rich texture of interculturalism.

2. RACE, GENDER, AND LA MALINCHE

As my title states, race and gender are the two primary categories of lived experience that precipitated my exploration of the interrelationships of these cultures. The intersection of race and gender is summed up in a megatrope of Chicano literature and culture, La Malinche.[9] In my "home" Chicano Mexican culture, this is the name of the actual historical Indian woman who accompanied Cortés in the Spanish conquest of Mexico (1516–1520). La Malinche (her real name was Malintzin Tenépal;

she was known as Marina to the Spanish) fulfilled a multiplicity of social roles. She was a native Indian informant, a talented linguist, a translator, and a mediator (she understood and spoke Mayan and Nahuatl languages and learned Spanish) between Spanish and indigenous peoples. She was also a military strategist, the companion and concubine of Cortés, and the presumed symbolic mother of Mexican *mestizos* and *mestizas*.

It is nearly impossible to invoke the name La Malinche without conjuring up the image of a flesh-and-blood woman. However, I use the trope in this book less to refer to the actual woman (or women) than to enlist it as a metaphor in the service of interculturalism. The metaphor of La Malinche lifts a veil: it makes manifest the connections among the three cultures. The metaphor is important to me for three reasons. First, it offers a way to organize the intercultural scenes and themes enacted in the literary texts of this book. The action of labeling, for example, calling someone a name, stereotyping them, especially when it carries pejorative connotations, occurs often in the texts and is captured in the traditional meaning of this trope. The woman behind the name La Malinche has been most labeled and relabeled in Mexican and Chicano cultures and studies. In common parlance, to call someone "malinche," a term inseparable from La Malinche, implies betrayal of self, of group interests—selling out, in other words. It implies an act that betrays one's group, country, even one's sex or gender, whether by a woman or a man. Indeed, when *malinche* appears in lowercase, without the feminine adjective "La" preceding it, the term may refer, depending on the context, to either a man or a woman. Since the emphasis is understood to be a condemnation of the action of betrayal rather than the person, the term in many ways becomes gender-neutral. Transgression, exposing one's culture to outsiders, even through writing, a public act; the crossing of prescribed ethnic, cultural, and linguistic borders; violating "purity" by engaging in racial mixture and miscegenation; the theme of woman as *puta* (whore) and single (abandoned) motherhood; migration from "home"—these themes, and others, radiate out from the name and meanings of La Malinche. No categorical divide separates the themes; they are interrelated, mixed, and never singular, like spokes on the wheel of interculturalism.

Second, the trope of La Malinche allows me to make visible what would not be visible if I did not use it in my analysis. I am fully aware that there is no figure of La Malinche explicitly represented in African American and Puerto Rican cultures, an absence that is testimony to the fact that the three cultures are different. Nor am I suggesting that every Chicano and

Chicana writer has spoken or written with one voice about La Malinche. But the absence of a female figure so named in African American and Puerto Rican cultures does not mean that the same properties encased in the Mexican and Chicano trope are not used to configure images of black and Puerto Rican women and men, or white ethnic women and gay men. The gender neutrality of lowercase *malinche* is important because it suggests that the trope may encompass heterosexual as well as homosexual men. My objective is to show how acts of so-called betrayal, treason, and deceit—actions argued to be uniquely specific in my Mexican and Chicano "home" cultures—may have applicability in other cultural contexts, which makes us reframe the debilitating nature ascribed to these actions in the first place. We see these actions differently, primarily because we see them through the prism of another culture. In other words, can one or ought one use a cultural icon intimately connected to one cultural group as a hermeneutic filter through which to read and give meaning to texts of other cultural groups? This is one of the central questions of this book, and my answer to this question is affirmative. We can then return to the "home" context with fresh eyes and "revision" acts said to be "betrayals." Familiar elements reappear in unfamiliar ways.

Third, the conceit allows me to reveal my own identity as a Chicano woman in relation to the other two cultures that have no specifically named La Malinche figure. In other words, this trope is indigenous to Mexican and Chicano cultures and therefore situates me in relation to these cultures. Like the character-narrators of these literary texts, like the writers Piri Thomas, Claude Brown, and Oscar Zeta Acosta, I too am both inside and outside my home cultures, situated also in the larger "dominant" culture. My life and scholarly experiences as a Chicano woman make me aware of the trope and the purposes in history to which it has been put. Knowledge about the trope enables particular kinds of insights into the literary and extraliterary texts, such as those by Paz, Moynihan, and Lewis. My use of the trope signals that I consider my readings partial, in the sense that my experiences as a Chicano woman and scholar circumscribe my interpretations. I wish the migration of this metaphor into different cultural contexts to convey that I do not see myself as disembodied of ethnicity and gender or as someone who makes her own ethnicity and gender the ultimate criteria of social existence.

My contribution to the history of this trope, then, is to make it "travel" into other cultural domains. Historically, this figure of La Malinche has stayed inside Mexican and Chicano cultures. Invoking it in different cultural settings is not intended to force comparisons where they do not exist. It is to establish links among these cultures and to show how they interconnect—at times supporting one another, at other times entering into conflict with each other. La Malinche is the mantra of this book.

3. THE INTERCULTURAL

I call my comparative approach "intercultural."[10] This word signals a relatively recent rubric of social and literary analysis that posits cultures in contact. Rather than the more common label "multicultural" that characterizes contemporary discussions about racial and cultural diversity, I prefer "intercultural" to describe the approach I take to the three core literary texts and the writings of the intellectuals who initiated controversial discussions about the groups.[11] While *multi-* suggests a "plural" array of cultures, *inter-* emphasizes the dimension of cultural contact I want to stress—that cultures are relational, that cultures are interdependent and interactive, and that cultures are neither discrete nor pure. Exchange between cultures is reciprocal, though seldom symmetrical in terms of social power and perceived status. Culture is ever in movement, not only from the top down, but also from the bottom up, between, around, and across society, itself part of culture. This means that people act out their identities and affiliations through ongoing tensions and conflicts, in spaces where they engage in negotiation about values, ideas, and norms.[12] Better than "multicultural," "intercultural" bespeaks the way communities situate themselves and the ways they are situated by each other and by the dominant Anglo communities. It also highlights textual space as a contestatory site where readers negotiate meaning in the context of literatures and cultures other than their own.

The path of compartmentalized ethnicities is more traveled, but I have opted for a wider view on these cultures. Using the three literary texts, I make visible intersections excluded from the official historical record. I think it is important that we see these cultures in reciprocal and copresent arrangements because such an approach can show how, when, and why common interests are established and differences negotiated. An intercultural configuration goes against one popular mainstream perception that the 1960s produced a balkanized society—too much "me-ness" and not enough "we-ness"—that those who struggled in the 1960s have helped to produce a "disunited" United States, that we have chosen "pluribus" over "unum." I do not want to reinforce "me-ness" or identity politics—that is, the idea that one ethnic group's interests should override those of all others, or that one single element of our group identity is absolute. However, neither do I want to reinforce "we-ness" or abstract notions that suggest wishful togetherness and social harmony, as do the frequently used metaphors "melting pot," "salad bowl,"[13] "can't-we-all-get-along," and the imagined community of "the American people," which promotes the illusion that the United States is politically and culturally a homogeneous whole. I want to enable us to envision a shared history, one that includes the challenges and the conflicts that result from the encounters of people at the gateways of different cultures. My vision of a shared history posits connection through difference, not difference as an end in itself. To make cultural difference an end in itself is ultimately to be indifferent to the very difference I aim to grasp. Differences are real and actual because ethnic cultures are different and because social and economic inequalities abide in our world.

For me, culture is a field of struggle, where people of distinct racial, gendered, and linguistic backgrounds adjudicate truths and values to obtain some degree of interpretive power about their lives and place in the social body. The theme of this book, then, is intercultural relations resulting in specific areas where people of different cultures come into contact and oppose the strict boundaries and borders imposed on them by socioeconomic injustice.

4. THE PERIOD 1965–1995

The 1954 Supreme Court ruling in *Brown v. Board of Education* and significant social shifts in the 1960s and 1970s laid the basis for audiences to become conscious of what perhaps we always were, since our beginnings, but did not officially acknowledge: an interracial country.[14] By the 1960s and 1970s there were shifts in immigration patterns, no longer dominated by Europe but by Latin America and Asia; in demographic migration of African Americans and Puerto Ricans to the urban industrialized centers of the East and Midwest; in differential birthrate patterns, with higher birthrates among populations of color; in legislative orders, such as the 1967 Supreme Court's decision in *Loving v. Virginia* declaring unconstitutional the outlawing of interracial marriage (at that time legal in many states outside the South) and the Civil Rights and Voting

Rights Acts. Yet the familiar retrospective story about these tumultuous decades is that they were characterized by identity politics, absolute value commitments, pulls of separatism from the Anglo-American heritage, reinscriptions of bipolar frames (white/black, Anglo/Chicano, Anglo/Puerto Rican, male/female, dominant/subdominant), singular identities, broken alliances, and ideological zealotry. Reviewers, journalists, and academic scholars across the political spectrum attribute agendas of "identity politics" and group insularity to these years.[15] These political positionings of identity politics and strict criteria for group inclusion have become categories for organizing our knowledge and memory of these years, and they keep us from finding new ways to think about them. They would seem to rule out this period as historical ground for interculturalism.

I want to offer an ironic twist to this by now familiar interpretation: I propose to find zones of intercultural contact in an era now perceived to have nurtured unified and separate identities. It is no accident, I think, that these eight years (1965–1973) are also the bookend years of the Vietnam War. They mark a historical transition from the "Old Order" of the 1950s to the "New Order," if you will, that begins with the end of the war and the shock of Watergate, when a political and moral system broke down. I take 1965–1973 as a liminal period, an in-between time, when identities chosen and identifications imposed—whether individual, ethnic, racial, or social—were supple, in flux, not yet solidified into the rigid blocs of identities we now associate with this span of time. These are years of possibility, where I propose we turn to find signs of intercultural connections. Today, we are a visibly more mixed population. One reason for this is the more numerous and varied cases of intermarriage across the racial-ethnic array of peoples. Another reason is the even more intense shifts in (im)migration than those of the 1960s, especially in geographic areas where this was hardly expected in the 1960s—Catholic Latinos in Utah, Latino immigrants in the South, Latinos outnumbering African Americans in Watts, and Hindu Mexicans in the Imperial Valley of southern California.[16] We are also more overtly self-conscious about our racial and gendered diversity. The increase in the numbers of avowedly mixed-race individuals and families, for example, challenged not only the once seemingly immutable categories of the census but also the prohibition against selecting more than one identity box on federal and state census forms.[17] The increased numbers of men and women of color, along with white women, in the workforce has led to gendered and racially diverse areas of employment. The social reach of the university has widened to include new populations of color, although its doors, for reasons of asymmetrical access to preparation and opportunities, remain more open to some than to others.

Even so, the histories and literatures of diverse cultural groups are, I believe, more often than not presented in college and university curricula in disconnected ways, taught and researched as separate areas of study, quarantined into separate camps, as though their populations had participated in history in ethnic isolation, or only in relation to a presumably homogeneous dominant white population. New paradigms and dramatic shifts in old ones in the past twenty years make it possible, in hindsight, to revisit these years, texts, histories, and cultures—with racial and linguistic roots reaching long and deep into the Spanish-speaking Latin and Afro-Caribbean Américas—in different and exciting ways. For example, there are now studies on Euro-American white ethnicities; on white, African American, and U.S. Latino forms of masculinity; and on Latino diasporas of men and women. Women's studies has been expanded to include the histories of men and women of color as well as culturally specific re-interpretations of women's roles and rapprochements between men and women of the historically marginalized groups. More generally, academic departments and curricula now include the study of working-class communities along with gender, gay, ethnic, and cultural studies. All these new modes of intellectual inquiry offer potential for a richer, more nuanced social analysis of the era Todd Gitlin in his book *The Sixties* so aptly called "years of hope [and] days of rage."

The 1960s and 1970s posed potent challenges to the legal, political, and social establishment of that time, challenges that brought fundamental changes to American society. With a force and drive not seen before, constituencies challenged social and institutional racism on the legal front at private, governmental, and educational levels. They dismantled the black *or* white model of a white supremacist society. New titles appeared during the 1980s and 1990s to propose more equitable and expansive models: black *and* white, not black *or* white. A few of these are Manning Marable's *Beyond Black and White: Transforming African-American Politics* (1995), Kenneth W. Warren's *Black and White Strangers: Race and American Literary Realism* (1993), Dana D. Nelson's *The Word in Black and White: Reading "Race" in American Literature 1638–1867* (1993), Werner Sollors's *Neither Black nor White Yet Both: Thematic Explorations of Interracial Literature* (1997), and Michael Omi and Howard Winant's *Racial Formation in the United States: From the 1960s to the 1990s* (1994). Rachel Moran, in "Unrepresented," an article about the affirmative action debate in higher education in California, and Deborah Ramirez, in "Multicultural Empowerment: It's Not Just Black and White Anymore," address the black-and-white paradigm in a legal context. These sources gesture to more expansive redefinitions of populations that go beyond black and white relations.

However, the majority of the books I name above, and also Eric Sundquist's prize-winning book, *To Wake the Nations: Race in the Making of American Literature* (1993), albeit no longer locked in a black *or* white paradigm, continue to frame the discussion in terms of black-and-white, with little or no attention to the cultures of people of color. Gender too has little if any play in these books. Piri Thomas, Claude Brown, and Oscar Zeta Acosta, the authors of the literary texts I focus on here, are men, but race and gender are at the heart of my discussions of the stories they tell and that I transcribe. In fact, gender is indispensable to a mapping of an intercultural approach to literary and cultural studies.

In this book, I have created points of mediation, what we might call "third terms," at various levels: the trope of La Malinche is one, the text of *Down These Mean Streets* another, and Puerto Rican culture yet another. These "third terms" will help to navigate the extremities of black and white. The flexible term "interculturalism" invites relation, which always implies some other entity. Its open-ended quality makes it easier for me to place gender in relation to race and ethnicity. I want to contribute to a contemporary conversation about "difference," "hybridity," and "heterogeneity"—at the level of both race and gender—that can enable us to move "beyond black and white" by focusing specifically on intersections where people of "dominant" and subdominant cultures bump into each other—participating, engaged, never passive, often in asymmetrical relations of power.

5. THE LITERARY TEXTS

I sought out the three books discussed here specifically because their authors made dangerous connections outside their "home" communities. Risk-taking ventures are an essential ingredient of the intercultural. Thomas, Brown, and Acosta, in different ways, stepped into "foreign" terrains and incurred the stigma of suspicion of their "native" reading communities. Insider groups deemed these authors traitors to their race; they allegedly had sold out and betrayed group interests. Unlike other texts published during this time, these books were more readily accepted by the mainstream, a gesture that only increased the degree of resistance and distrust of the insider groups. I turn the odd-man-out status of these books—a clear drawback in their moment—into a strength by making them my doors of entry into intercultural zones of contact.

Down These Mean Streets was published in 1967, two years after *Manchild in the Promised Land,* but for two reasons I think it appropriate to begin my intercultural discussion with the former rather than the latter, which was the defining text of the 1960s and 1970s for cultures of color. First, I want to shake up the black and white imaginings of our history, to see the experiences of cultural groups against the grain of the stark black and white categories that informed our public debates about our racial history in the 1960s. In the late 1960s, reviewers classified *Down These Mean Streets* as a Puerto Rican *Manchild.*[18] At that time black Americans constituted the most familiar and largest "minority" group for a national audience. But the dust jacket of the most current Vintage edition of *The Autobiography of a Brown Buffalo* (1989), originally published eight years after *Manchild,* is proof that the black/white dualism dies hard. The cover touts *The Autobiography of a Brown Buffalo* as a "Chicano *Manchild.*" The point is that *Manchild,* the black text, provided the measure against which the other two texts were marketed: *Down These Mean Streets* on its first publication and *The Autobiography of a Brown Buffalo* to this day. Second, I intend the placement of these texts in this book to underscore the fact that the racial and demographic composition of the United States has changed since the 1960s and that the shift in the nature and numbers of the population necessitates new ways to think about our history and these literary texts.

The initial text, *Down These Mean Streets,* opens a window onto the intercultural dimensions of *Manchild in the Promised Land* and *The Autobiography of a Brown Buffalo. Manchild in the Promised Land* has only been studied, when it has been studied at all, in terms of black and white, but Claude Brown, a contemporary of Thomas, showed that ethnic diversification was part of the vibrant life of Harlem. Brown represents an intra-Harlem divide of West Indians, black Americans, mainland Puerto Ricans, and Italian and Jewish Americans. Although he places the first four ethnic groups on the periphery of his narrative, the important point is that these groups were present enough in his experience to have impinged on his autoethnographic canvas.[19] In the center of the text's action, the protagonist moves to define his manhood in relation to white Jewish American and black African Coptic religious and cultural values. Reading *Manchild in the Promised Land* through the intercultural lens offered by

Down These Mean Streets forces us to reconsider the bifurcated reception of *The Autobiography of a Brown Buffalo,* which was seen as either a purely countercultural or a purely Chicano text. Embedded in *The Autobiography of a Brown Buffalo* are Native American, black American, and white ethnic cultural contexts.

As important as it is now in hindsight, *Down These Mean Streets* received little written press in the Puerto Rican community. Only one or two brief reviews by mainland Puerto Ricans appeared when it was published in 1967, and these were in sociological journals.[20] Thomas, I speculate, touched a few nerves having to do with race and class in the Puerto Rican community of his day. Since Thomas's dark-skinned, "kinky"-haired narrator-character voluntarily affiliated with a "Negro" community, his avowal of "blackness" would have created unease among some Puerto Rican readers who were accustomed to seeing themselves through the prism of Puerto Rico's white European Hispanic tradition—a tradition that historically has disavowed the island's African heritage.[21] However, what these Puerto Ricans resisted, some African Americans embraced. Thomas's identification as a "Negro" attracted the attention of reviewers writing for Negro American journals (Luther P. Jackson in *The Crisis,* John O. Killens in *Negro Digest,* and Lennox Raphael in *Freedomways*) who applauded this identification and his journey into the South in search of the meaning of his "blackness." In contrast to the Spanish-sounding "Nĕgro" (short e) of the island, a pronunciation that many mainland Puerto Ricans would have been accustomed to hearing at home or in the larger Spanish-speaking communities of the cities to which Puerto Ricans migrated in the 1940s and 1950s, the English "Nēgro" (long e), used commonly at the time, was charged with emphatic racist meanings and connotations of inferiority. It is this English pronunciation that would have stood out in the mainstream reception. The Spanish-sounding "Negro" of the island is a more varied linguistic unit; it has diverse usages in Puerto Rico but not in white communities on the mainland. Mainland Puerto Ricans knew well what the English-sounding "Negro" meant, and many would have tried to distance themselves from it.

In addition to racial identification, class divisions proved a barrier to the reception of *Down These Mean Streets.* Middle-class Puerto Ricans, from both the mainland and the island, would have rejected the representation of ghetto life.[22] Working-class Puerto Ricans from *el barrio* with middle-class aspirations also would have wanted to distance themselves from the book's portrayal of violence, drugs, and gangs. Nicholasa Mohr's *Nilda,* the first Puerto Rican novel about and by a woman who grew up in *el barrio*,[23] represents an attempt to transcend a "ghetto life" narrative. In *Nilda*, Mohr offered a female representation of barrio life that centered on topics of family and the quotidian, on the world of art as an alternative to violence, on the artistic ambitions of a young girl and her desire for self-improvement, upward mobility, and education.[24] Publishers, Mohr said, wanted books that detailed "great escapades: a little bit of robbing, shooting, swearing; men going around like Puerto Rican John Waynes and women who are either morons or prostitutes devoid of any real depth or substance."[25] Although she respected Piri Thomas's experience as "authentic" for him, she was critical of publishers and audiences who wanted the sensational aspects of ghetto life—in other words "more Piri," the supposedly "authentic" barrio experience of drugs, crime, gangs, sex, and so on. In this sense, *Nilda* may stand as an alternative narrative that implicitly testifies to the power of class—the desire to leave behind, or deny in some cases, the ghetto environment of many Puerto Ricans.

The third reason that explains Puerto Rican unwillingness to embrace Thomas's book is the lack of public forums to discuss and raise issues of interest and importance, a textual space where Puerto Ricans could disagree on the ways race and class operated in the Puerto Rican community. I say more about this topic in chapter 2.

Manchild in the Promised Land too encountered resistance on the "home" front. While Claude Brown presumably had gratified his white audience with his individual story of rehabilitation—"bad boy" turned "good boy"—his Harlem audience expected more. They expected a Black Harlem writer to challenge the fundamental views dominant society held about the larger body of black working families and folk. For these readers, Brown was, in fact, a white people's "boy": the successful exception that proved the mainstream expectation of black failure. Underpinning the reviews were suggestions of having betrayed the group interests of a black community by taking on middle-class values. This perspective implied that middle-class values were "white" and that black Americans should not desire or aim to achieve them. While Thomas was too Negro for his Puerto Rican audience, Brown, it seems, was not Negro enough for his black audience.

To begin with, Claude Brown, its author and narrator, did not express an explicit ethnic nationalist group consciousness. Neither did he see himself (nor was he seen) as voicing the urgent political and social agenda of the period. His contemporaries—James Baldwin, Malcolm X, and Eldridge Cleaver—had strong political voices and made strong political statements. While no reviewers took him to task for it, Brown exposed an uninformed white mainstream audience to black insider codes (such as his frequently used "bad-ass nigger") at a time when the racist implications of this and other offensive names were being exposed by a vociferous black contingency. In other words, some things are best left unsaid in front of white audiences. Elsewhere in the black community, the book annoyed one black Muslim critic who, writing for *Muhammad Speaks,* deemed it "not fit for Muslim reading" because, he argued, it misrepresented the Muslim faith and practices of the Nation of Islam.[26] Brown's portrayal of the Black Muslims in Harlem was presumably inaccurate and negative. The book also upset non-Muslim Harlem citizens who thought Harlem's black writers should have stopped the book's publication. "Why'd you guys let that man [Claude Brown] put out that book?" they asked, and they urged them "to hit that cat—and hard" in their reviews.[27]

Black readers objected because Brown had revealed "what the Establishment wants to hear" (Mitchell 537). This meant that Brown had presumably confirmed the usual associations whites held of populations of color who had moved into the nation's urban areas by the 1960s: poverty and crime, school truancy and lack of education, drugs and juvenile delinquency—everything that white and some black middle-class people had flown from in the post–World War II era and that the Moynihan report had helped to foment. Another black reviewer-writer saw in it a piece of social science fiction that "dramatize[d] the stereotypes of urban sociology."[28] Reviewers like this one were tired of seeing blacks represented as "victims," bereft of agency, as Moynihan had portrayed the black family and black men, of hearing that the causes for poverty and everything that came with it stemmed from individual deviant behavior rather than from institutional systemic and economic causes. Although this particular reviewer did not mention the Moynihan report, he found the individual (in this case, Brown) to blame for having dramatized black poverty and family life in a tradition of a racial liberal philosophy. This black reviewer's response is ironic considering that Moynihan too blamed the individual for social problems.

Manchild in the Promised Land and *Down These Mean Streets* were immediate runaway best-sellers. Their reception was fueled in part by the controversy about "the black family" that had been ignited by the Moynihan report. The report was published the same year as *Manchild in the Promised Land* and two years before *Down These Mean Streets*.[29] Acosta's *The Autobiography of a Brown Buffalo* had a different publishing history. First published by a small press, it was not taken up by a mainstream press until seventeen years later.[30] Although available at the time of the Chicano movement and the founding of Chicano studies programs in southwestern colleges and universities, it was not, for example, among the founding texts of Chicano studies, as were *Pocho, . . . y no se lo tragó la tierra,* and *Bless Me Ultima,* all narratives that focused on pubescent boys. Issues of manhood were more easily side-stepped in these novels because of the youth of their protagonists. *With His Pistol in His Hand,* by Américo Paredes, the Chicano "statesman" and "father" of Chicano studies (appropriately named in the Spanish masculine rendition of the English "America"), focuses on Gregorio Cortez, an adult border hero, but it does not directly or explicitly question his masculine identity. In my view, Paredes's book is a classic warrior story—the building of a masculine hero—and not the ironic portrait of a Chicano hero that we find in *The Autobiography of a Brown Buffalo.* In other words, Gregorio's masculinity is not to be questioned. *Down These Mean Streets, Manchild in the Promised Land,* and *The Autobiography of a Brown Buffalo* concentrate on grown men who are hardly the poster children that Chicano, African American, and Puerto Rican ethnic nationalist movements wanted dominant and subdominant audiences to behold, an understandable desire and need for the time.

6. THE THREE CULTURES

This project grows out of my experiences as a Chicano woman and my twenty-five years of teaching and researching Chicano literature at the University of California, San Diego. Twenty-five years ago, minority cultures were researched and represented in isolation and in reference to a white dominant master narrative. Since then, the founding of ethnic studies programs, the renaissance of comparative studies of race and ethnicity, and the use of interdisciplinary approaches to gender and sexuality have encouraged research that integrates rather than separates the experiences of different white ethnic and racial groups of color. Through my study and teaching of Chicano literature in an academic context that favors comparative work, I became aware of the importance of intercultural communication, which now leads me to add a comparative dimension to my field of expertise and to expand my focus into other ethnic literatures of populations of color. Chicano literature took me into mainland Puerto Rican literature, and this move led me to draw on African American culture and literature. The Puerto Rican cultural practices embedded in *Down These Mean Streets* make the novel a kind of "third term," a passageway and building block into an intercultural perspective that offers a new way to look at *Manchild in the Promised Land* and *The Autobiography of a Brown Buffalo* other than through the standard mono-cultural black/white and Chicano/Anglo frames.

Although Chicano and Chicana literature is my specialty and is always the starting point of my research, the conceptualization of this study actually began with my reading and analysis of the Puerto Rican text *Down These Mean Streets*. I want in this section to summarize and anticipate some of the linkages that I found in my analysis of *Down These Mean Streets* and to contextualize them in terms of some broader historical connections that characterize the three cultures. *Down These Mean Streets* offered me an opportunity to develop an intercultural and interethnic perspective that connects Chicano and African American cultures. These cultures might seem at first very different and distant from each other, but *Down These Mean Streets* shows in very concrete terms the histori-cal intercultural situation of the 1940s, when "Piri Thomas," the novel's protagonist, "shook up" the black/white binary on the streets of Har-lem. Thomas wrote about the Harlem of the 1940s, the same Harlem por-trayed by Claude Brown in *Manchild in the Promised Land*.[31] *Down These Mean Streets* suggests that Harlem, the historic capital of black America, the "black Paris" of the 1920s, became a racially diverse space as early as the 1940s.

In *Down These Mean Streets,* Harlem has porous geographic borders: Spanish Harlem merges to become Black Harlem; African Americans and Puerto Ricans run into one another in Harlem, and also into Irish, Ital-ians, and Jews. The text's intercultural spaces capture the common pat-terns of housing and settlement and of urban migration that make up part of the history and culture of working-class mainland Puerto Rican and African American families. Puerto Ricans, more than other nonwhite Hispanic groups, have shown less resistance to establishing residence near African Americans.[32] *Down These Mean Streets* demonstrates that African Americans and Puerto Ricans must coexist in urban areas. Although there is no guarantee that the coexistence will always be harmonious, they have to negotiate physical space, ideas, and behaviors. Perhaps the most com-pelling factor is socioeconomic circumstance, which results in residen-tial segregation and confines working-class people of these two cultures to live side by side in crowded tenement buildings and to populate, as Thomas shows, the welfare offices, employment agencies, and metropoli-tan schools.

Down These Mean Streets also represents a black American urban cul-ture that has served as a close frame of reference for Puerto Ricans—

sometimes to disavow a Puerto Rican relationship to black culture, sometimes to avow it.[33] Once on the mainland, the mulatto segment of the Puerto Rican population became locked into the dominant U.S. racial binary in a way that Mexicans usually did not. Hard as he tries to mark his Puerto Rican racial and cultural difference away from a black existence, to avoid the stained arena of white people's (and his Puerto Rican father's and brother's) racial hatred of "Negroes" and to boost his status as a non-black man, Piri could not escape his geographic and cultural relationship to African Americans. The text's references to Puerto Rican blackness serve as a reminder to us that both island and mainland Puerto Rican populations have had strong historical connections to black Caribbean and African American cultures. Puerto Rico (unlike Mexico, the country of origin for Chicanos and Chicanas) had a long history of slavery and a large ex-slave population. In this respect, its racial extremes are "European white" (conquest first by the Spanish, then by North Americans) and "African black," similar to the racial polarities that have dominated U.S. history and culture. But unlike the United States, it did not fight a civil war to abolish slavery, and it has a *mestizaje* paradigm: it has officially recognized a mulatto (black-and-white) racial category and population, and it has a tripartite Spanish, African, and Indian identity. All three have been traditional emblems for its racial *mestizaje*.[34] The origins of Puerto Rican culture, therefore, have always been embodied in a range of "Latin," "tropicalized," and "Caribbean African" identities. Even when Puerto Ricans grow up in U.S. cities without ever visiting or living on the island, as is true of the main character in *Down These Mean Streets,* they maintain symbolic and cultural ties to a Puerto Rican homeland, despite physical absence, through memories imparted to them by their parents or grandparents and through the consciousness-raising strategies of the Puerto Rican movement in the 1970s. Just as Chicanos and African Americans during the Civil Rights period developed national collective imaginaries, the reclaiming of Aztlán and Africa as utopic homelands, for example, so mainland Puerto Ricans returned symbolically to their *borinquén* (the indigenous name for Puerto Rico), Taíno, and black Caribbean roots.

Down These Mean Streets uses a rich hybrid Puerto Rican dialect. The linguistic nuances of this dialect spark interesting intercultural lexical analogies among Puerto Rican, African American, and Chicano cultures. The text's miscegenated vernacular resisted assimilation into the "pure," standard linguistic system of the dominant aesthetic of the English-language canon and maintained ties with Chicano, black, and white popular usage. One reviewer called the creolized language "an electric amalgam of Negro hipster jive and a kind of Puerto Rican bop,"[35] and another characterized it as "a gutsy idiomatic blending of Puerto Rican and Afro-Americanese."[36] Linguistic deviation gives the text its charged power of perlocutionary effects that resonate with Puerto Rican and African American language systems. But since Chicano and Puerto Rican cultures share commonalities of the Spanish language, of *caló*, or street slang, and of vernacular expressions, resulting from contact with the English language, it is not difficult to find linguistic linkages between Puerto Rican and Chicano cultures as well. For example, Piri unselfconsciously uses the term *moyeto* to refer to African Americans, a slang term that Chicano and Chicana readers familiar with *caló* recognize as a linguistic proxy for their own term *mayate* for African Americans.[37] Then too the terms "Negro" and "Indian" extend beyond their English-speaking contexts to encompass cultural and linguistic meanings in Spanish-speaking Puerto Rican circumstances. For example, "Nĕgro," a Spanish homonym for the English "Nēgro," is not intelligible to Anglophone readers but has a wide variety of ironic meanings to Puerto Ricans and Chicanos. In this way, the book showcases "blackness" in its differentiated cultural and linguistic forms. Puerto Rican racial differentiation is more flexible in terms of skin color; there are degrees of whiteness and degrees of blackness. This malleability is caught in the plethora of words of its racial nomenclature—*trigueño, moreno, negrito, clarito, mulato,* and *blanco*—sprinkled throughout the pages of *Down These Mean Streets*. The term "nigger" appears in *Down These Mean Streets, Manchild in the Promised Land,* and *The Autobiography of a Brown Buffalo* and means different things in each text. It is a polyvocal term.[38]

Finally, my attention to gender in the analysis of *Down These Mean Streets* enables me to make my study intercultural and comparative. Though the authors and protagonists of the three texts constitute different racial identities, they have all inherited traditional definitions of what it means to be a man in their respective cultures. The problem spot of their male gender has eluded literary commentary, but it, more easily than their racial identification, provides me with an entry into a gender paradigm, a common denominator that, albeit momentarily essentializing, is nonetheless necessary and productive to make intercultural connections. Piri's fancy footwork in his high-stakes drama of interracial negotiation mirrors nicely the traits of the La Malinche trope as it had operated in Chicano literature in the 1960s. Seeing gender through the central conceit of La Malinche in this high-level intercultural text that relies heavily on interaction with one mode of African American masculinity, I am able to highlight structural connections among Puerto Rican, Chicano, and African American cultures in a certain moment in time that a monocultural lens would not permit. I am also able to highlight my reading of this Puerto Rican text as a Chicano woman reader. Setting this central conceit in texts produced outside Mexican and Mexican American cultures allows me to emphasize the trope's positive and energetic power. My study reaffirms the importance of gender to studies of race and ethnicity.

7. LOOKING AHEAD

Four chapters and three chapter interludes constitute the heart of this book. In chapters 2, 3, and 4, I develop the theme of interculturalism in each of the three literary narratives. Each chapter is followed by an interlude, in which I explore related subthemes of interculturalism. The epilogue, "La Malinche Comes Home," concludes my discussion.

In chapter 1, I consider representations of "family" and the "feminine" as they interlock in the visions of the three cultures offered by Octavio Paz, Daniel Patrick Moynihan, and Oscar Lewis. I show how these men implied that the "feminine" is responsible for the breakdown of the family in the three cultures. These men did not strike isolated notes in their analyses of these cultures. The three cultures share a common historical link in the way they were seen by those who spoke in a dominant voice.

Although the literary texts are the center of this book, throughout I allude to the three intellectuals Paz, Moynihan, and Lewis because it was they who kicked off the ball that the subdominant groups caught and then ran with. To provide a fuller appreciation of these men's relation to the literary texts, in the first half of chapter 1, I discuss in some detail who they were, the relation to state power they enjoyed, and what they wrote. Chapter 2 is a sustained and concrete examination of interculturalism in a literary text that tells the experiences of the New York–born, Anglo-sounding surnamed, dark-skinned, Spanish- and English-speaking Puerto Rican Piri Thomas. In the interlude that follows, I propose that we consider the protagonist of *Down These Mean Streets* as a Puerto Rican male *malinche* figure to show that the trope is not gender-specific and that it has liberating functions. The trope looks different, in other words, when seen against a culture "foreign" to it. In chapter 3, my discussion of interculturalism moves to *Manchild in the Promised Land*. I explore *Manchild*'s responses to the issue of the flawed masculinity proposed by Daniel Patrick Moynihan about black men. The responses take us into black American affiliations with Jewish and Pan-African heritages. The interlude that follows explores primarily the different responses of African American women to their subordination in ways unforeseen by Moynihan. I also explore here the subtext of La Malinche in these responses. In chapter 4, I discuss Acosta's Chicano road narrative, *The Autobiography of a Brown Buffalo*, in its broad context. In interlude 4, I show how Brown Buffalo establishes his cultural identity in relation to other ethnic groups, and I bring La Malinche home to its Chicano-Mexican terrain.

I revisit the period 1965–1973 neither with nostalgia nor with condemnation, neither to rewrite nor to alter the past; I do it because I believe with Walter Benjamin that "every image of the past that is not recognized by the present as one of its own concerns threatens to disappear irretrievably" (*Illuminations* 255). My book, then, is an attempt to retrieve images from the past that merit retrieval because they make denser, richer, and more complex a contemporary conversation about cultural and ethnic diversity. My book goes against ethnic isolation and moves toward a glimpse of the shared history these authors forged in the challenging, sometimes dangerous, cultural intersections they decided to cross. I redirect our direction away from viewing cultures—minority and nonminority—as discrete and isolated toward viewing them as inextricably bound, by history, place, time, and the high stakes of participating in an increasingly multiracial, multilingual, and multiethnic society. We are all "in it" together.

One   "IN BED" WITH LA MALINCHE:
          STORIES OF "FAMILY" À LA
          OCTAVIO PAZ, DANIEL PATRICK
          MOYNIHAN, AND OSCAR LEWIS

Almost forty years ago, three mainstream intellectuals—
Octavio Paz, Daniel Patrick Moynihan, and Oscar Lewis—provided cues
for how the American public should think about Puerto Ricans, Mexican Americans, and African Americans. When Paz looked at Mexicans
in Mexico and pachucos[1] in Los Angeles, when Moynihan looked at the
African American family in a national context, and when Lewis looked
at the Ríos family in San Juan and their kin in New York City, they saw
people who lacked the right stuff to compete in middle-class capitalistic
society.[2] They noted similar and in their estimation counterproductive
characteristics of these groups that, they argued, left them ill equipped for
succeeding in white middle-class society. Fatalistic attitudes toward life,
self-perpetuating cycles of poverty, family instability, matrifocal families,
illegitimate offspring, nonintegration and participation in the mainstream,
and a flawed manhood were all on the list of unresolved problems they
saw in the histories of these groups. Assuming the white heterosexual nuclear family as the norm against which to measure them—in a time, says
Adrienne Rich, "when the selling of the nuclear family with the mother
at home at its core" came to the foreground—all three men offered tidy
systems for understanding why these groups were not "making it" in U.S.
society (171). Paz, Moynihan, and Lewis believed the people they wrote
about should become middle class and take on the values (economic am-
bition, work ethic, etc.) generally assumed by social scientists to lead to
success. The problem was that these men implied that the culture of these
populations—their way of life and values—stood in the way of middle-
class achievement. Organizing their analyses around the normative conjugal unit of the "white" family and household, they denied agency and
"healthy" culture to the groups whose life habits and practices they analyzed, and they implicitly slighted the women of these groups.

Although each man used a different approach, trained in a different discipline, and cast his assertions in a different mode of writing, they all tended to pathologize the cultures they studied.[3] All wrote in terms of foundational stories, or stories of origin, to explain the root cause of a cultural group's deficiency. For Paz, the root cause of the "failure" of Mexicans in Mexico and in the United States was to be found in the conquest and colonization of Mexico; for Moynihan, the root cause of the failure of working-class black Americans was located in the institutions of slavery and the Jim Crow de jure laws of segregation; and for Lewis, the underlying reasons for the failure of Puerto Rican families living on the island and in New York City emanated from Spanish colonization and the development of U.S. capitalism in Puerto Rico. Their analyses, however, ultimately gave insufficient weight to the impact of these historical and institutional macro-events and their legacies of social inequality on the performances of these groups. Instead, they chose to emphasize individual and family responsibility. They wrote what I call "narratives of family." The central kernel of their discourses is the conjugal unit of the family.

I refer to these narratives throughout the book, but here I want to highlight in them the theme of family and the logic specific to each one. The trope of La Malinche, the mother/betrayer of the Mexican people, is explicit in Paz but an occult presence in Moynihan and Lewis.[4] I want to make it visible to show how it lies at the bottom of the explanation these men gave to justify their claim that women-as-mothers/mothers-as-women led to what they considered flawed masculinity. But first I want to say something about who these men were, their relation to state power, and what they wrote.

1. OCTAVIO PAZ

Unlike Lewis and Moynihan, who had sociological and anthropological backgrounds, Paz was a man of letters, a social thinker, and a philosopher. He became Mexico's first Nobel Laureate in Literature (1990). He was born in 1914, during the years of Mexico's Civil War. He came from a family of liberal and progressive political intellectuals. His grandfather had been a prominent liberal intellectual and an active political journalist, and his father, a lawyer, joined the struggle of Emiliano Zapata, the peasant leader for agrarian reform during the Mexican Revolution. Paz was foremost a poet (he published his first book of poems at the age of nineteen) and an essayist, but he also embarked on a career as a diplomat in the Mexican Ministry of Foreign Affairs in the 1940s, serving in France and Japan. From 1962 to 1968 he was Mexico's ambassador to India. Notably, he resigned this post and withdrew from diplomatic service in 1968 in protest against the government's massacre of Mexican students at Tlatelolco in this year of the Olympic Games in Mexico City. It was during his tenure in the diplomatic service that he wrote *The Labyrinth of Solitude,* a collection of essays about what he called "the character of the Mexican" (71), in essence a study of the Mexican national character. The book became a landmark treatise in Mexico during the 1950s, and on its translation into English in 1961, it became a pivotal text during the Chicano intellectual and social activist movement of the 1960s and 1970s.

Paz's *Labyrinth* in English, widely read and reviewed, served to interpret to the Anglophone world the culture, history, and people of modern Mexico. In the United States, this cultural exchange took place between Paz and the English-speaking monocultural and literary audience. In Aztlán, a subdominant audience of English-speaking Chicano men and women, the generation that came of age in the 1960s, also read the translation and knew *they* were implicated in the U.S.-Mexico exchange of Paz's unflattering images of the pachuco, the *macho,* and La Malinche, Paz's representation of the treacherous Mexican mother. Paz had traveled to the United States on a Guggenheim Fellowship in 1943 and had visited Los Angeles, where, he says in *Labyrinth,* he encountered the pachucos, or youths "identified by their language and behavior as well as by the clothing they affect" (Paz 13). However, Chicanos and Chicanas also knew they were not considered participants with interpretive power in this conversation about Mexican and Chicano identity, attitudes, and behaviors. Anglophone Americans accepted Paz as *the* interpreter of Mexican and Chicano participation, or lack of it, in U.S. society. Paz, they felt, had represented men with no productive male agency,[5] and Chicanas in the 1970s objected to his belittling of Mexican women and themselves.[6]

Let me offer a metaphor about this configuration of audience that also applies to the reception given by the other two groups to the ideas of Moynihan and Lewis. It was as if Paz and a receptive mainstream Anglo audience were in a room talking about Mexicans and Chicanos, and a group of Chicano men and women accidentally stepped into this room. They realized that those in charge of this international reading "event" had never thought about inviting them, the subjects of the event, into the room to participate in the conversation. But on overhearing the buzz of talk—about "the pachuco," "the Mexican," "the macho," La Malinche, and other figures of Paz's Mexican and Chicano literary landscape—Chicano men and women decided to "interrupt" the conversation. They decided to exercise interpretive power. Paz may have imagined Chicanos, but Chicanos and Chicanas were ready to reimagine the images Paz offered of them.

Paz was not the first Mexican to talk about the masculine stereotypical figures. Samuel Ramos had anticipated Paz's stereotype of the pachuco and the macho with his character-type of the *pelado,* an uncouth and aggressive urban man who compensated for his alleged inferiority complex with disagreeable agonistic male behavior.[7] But Paz was the first Mexican commentator to make a sophisticated literary presentation of the Los Angeleno pachuco: he presented a buffoonish hybrid character—neither Mexican nor American, "floating" (his word) in limbo, a man he feminized with the traits he himself attributed to the Mexican woman. The mainstream audience had the luxury of listening to Paz without feeling negatively implicated in his troublesome mythopoetic history. Chicanos and Chicanas, however, felt deeply implicated, though not all in the same way.[8] However they felt, whatever they thought, few were lukewarm about *Labyrinth.*

2. DANIEL PATRICK MOYNIHAN

Moynihan was a political scientist by training who by 1965 had accumulated considerable experience in New York politics. According to Lee Rainwater and William Yancey in *The Moynihan Report and the Politics of Controversy,* Moynihan "was one of a new breed of public servants, the social scientist–politicos, who combine in their background both social science training and experience and full-time involvement in political activity" (17–18). He became particularly interested in the sociological study of urban life. The Washington portion of his political career began when he joined the Kennedy administration in 1961 as special assistant to Arthur J. Goldberg, then secretary of labor. In 1963 he became President Lyndon B. Johnson's assistant secretary of labor in charge of the Office of Policy Planning and Research. In this high-level post, he wrote the landmark seventy-eight-page government document officially titled *The Negro Family: The Case for National Action.* Of the three intellectuals, Moynihan was the closest to state power. As Rainwater and Yancey point out, "Only a person in this position would have been able to write a report relatively free of the long review process typical of government reports or to ensure that it received high-level distribution" (19). To gather previously unpublished information, Moynihan "had available to him not only the vast range of published and indexed government statistics but also the services of Labor Department economists and of the Bureau of Labor Statistics" (25–26).

The report was social science data intended to produce "white" knowledge and make "white" policy about the "Negro problem."[9] Released for public consumption during the summer of 1965, a few months before the publication of *Manchild in the Promised Land* and two years before the publication of *Down These Mean Streets,* the report triggered one of the angriest, most passionate and bitter national disagreements on race relations of the twentieth century. Although the report's authorship had much to do with the attention it received, two major events also contributed to keeping the topic of the black family and culture within eye range of the press, even before the report's official release. The first was President Johnson's historic commencement address, "To Fulfill These Rights," at Howard University in Washington, D.C., the prestigious black institution of higher learning. Johnson delivered his speech in June 1965, four months after the assassination of Malcolm X and two months before the civil unrest in Watts. The speech, Rainwater and Yancey inform us, was codrafted by Moynihan and presidential adviser Richard N. Goodwin, and the two writers drew heavily from the report that, by the time of the speech, already had been drafted by Moynihan (4). The report hovered over the speech; press attention to the speech therefore led back to the report.[10]

The second event was the Watts riots of August 1965. As had *Manchild in the Promised Land,* the Moynihan report focused on Harlem, the epitome of the northeastern hard-core black ghetto and one of the main urban centers of African American migration. But now one of the ugliest civil disorders of the decade had occurred in Los Angeles. Consequently, the report and *Manchild in the Promised Land* were considered particularly relevant to those searching for knowledge to explain the ghetto puzzle.[11] There was pressure at the national level to address poverty, unemployment, and the sound and fury in the cities.[12] The press coverage of the report intensified in August and tended, as Rainwater and Yancey claim, to "exaggerate the already dramatic and sensational aspects of Moynihan's presentation" and to reinforce the impression that the "dysfunctional" Negro family was the cause of "the problems Negroes have" (153). Hence the media helped to create a prurient public's interest in the titillating details of the report—unwed mothers, illegitimate children, emasculated men, teenage pregnancy, urban and domestic violence, and so on.

3. OSCAR LEWIS

Of the three mainstream intellectuals, only Lewis was a trained ethnographer. Lewis went to the "site" of anthropological research; he did fieldwork, and he was the first among modern-day anthropologists to use the tape recorder to collect the "life stories" of his informants. He turned his attention to the study of poverty in urban areas in Mexico, and his fictionlike style of writing made his anthropological work accessible to a mass audience. To his credit, Lewis was an ethnographer who was exceptionally fluent in the language of his subjects, for he also translated and transcribed the life stories from Spanish into English.

When Paz's ideas were in the air in Mexico City, during the 1950s and 1960s, Lewis was doing the fieldwork that formed the substance of his *The Children of Sánchez: Autobiography of a Mexican Family*, a book about a lower-class urban family living in Mexico City's *casas de vecindad* (multi-family dwellings grouped around courtyards) that was published in 1961. It became a best-seller in the United States, but *Los hijos de Sánchez,* the 1964 Spanish translation by the government-owned Fondo de Cultura Económica, created an outcry in Mexico City because certain influential people did not want the failings and uncertainties of Mexicans and Mexico to be held up to scrutiny by outsiders, especially when the majority of those outsiders were U.S. audiences.[13] The book was censored, though many prominent Mexican academics, writers (Carlos Fuentes and Rosario Castellanos among them), and journalists defended its publication. The scandal coincided with Paz's ambassadorship in India. Paz did not participate in the controversy—as ambassador it probably would have been awkward for him to address the issue—but he certainly would have been aware of it.[14]

Mexico had made a big impression on Lewis; he loved the country, its people, and the language (Rigdon 288). After the scandal of *Los hijos de Sánchez,* however, and after being told by a few critics in Mexico to go home and study poverty in his own country, he decided to leave Mexico and make his next fieldwork site Puerto Rico, a middle ground between the "foreign" and his native country. According to Susan Rigdon, Lewis received major funding from the Department of Health, Education, and Welfare to conduct fieldwork in Puerto Rico and New York City. She states that Lewis had completed field research for years on shoestring budgets and that this grant, the largest he had ever received, allowed him to employ several dozen transcribers, field-workers, translators, and editors (73).

Although Lewis was an innovator in the field of anthropology, his assumptions about culture still rested on the disciplinary norms of classic ethnographic research. Taking for granted a white European moral starting point as a frame of reference for measuring any kind of difference, he coined, theorized, and popularized the methodological approach of the "culture of poverty"—a set of adaptive mechanisms identified, systematized, and revised by Lewis to explain how the urban poor coped with their displaced situation in capitalist societies.[15] He believed that the cultural practices of the poor were a "way of life" with its own "structure and rationale," handed down in families from generation to generation. Each core trait in his "culture of poverty" formulation implied a corresponding polar term on the "normative" scale of social mobility, or the presumed value of middle-class achievement and success. The polar relationship was never explicitly stated by Lewis, but it was always operative in his conceptual model. If poor families were matrifocal, middle-class families were patrifocal. If the former were fatalistic, the latter were future oriented. The relationship operated like a pendulum: the more people participated in cultures of health (meaning class mobility and patrifocality), the less they participated in cultures of illness (self-generating poverty and matrifocality). By the mid-1970s, when *The Autobiography of a Brown Buffalo* was published, the "culture of poverty" had been discredited, but one or another version of this interpretive blueprint for making "impoverished" cultures intelligible to the "developed" world had influenced almost every facet of the national conversation about poverty in the 1960s.

4. PAZ AND LA MALINCHE

From a tradition of Spanish and European existentialism, combined with Mexican historical and popular lore about the Spanish Catholic colonization of Indian Pre-Columbian Mexico, Paz creates a mythopoetic story of Mexico's "first" family, the triad of personages in the conquest of Mexico (ca. 1517): the Spanish father, the Indian mother (La Malinche), and the offspring, the mestizo, or hybrid, "illegitimate" male children.[16] Paz became the author, the progenitor, of what is probably the most influential interpretation of "the Mexican personality" in the Spanish-speaking Américas and the Mexican United States.[17] Since the 1960s it has been a story well known in Chicano Studies departments of universities and colleges. His narrative of family, whether deified, reified, or vilified, is almost always told in relation to Mexico (Indian vs. Spanish) and

the Mexican Southwest (Chicano vs. Anglo), with no connective tissue to
a non-Mexican cultural context.

In his family narrative about a contact zone of two civilizations, race
and gender are the two operative categories, but Paz primarily privileges
the category of gender: relations between father and sons, mother and
sons, men and women, and, less overt but no less important, relations
between men.[18] The nuggets of his story are seduction, rape, power, betrayal, and illegitimacy, all encased in the trope of the woman La Malinche.[19] The alleged symbolic mother of the Mexican mestizo people and
the ideological glue of Paz's story, La Malinche is the source of the family's,
and also Mexico's, ruin. Paz makes explicit his parallel between family and
nation: "And as a small boy will not forgive his mother if she abandons
him to search for his father, the Mexican people have not forgiven [the
Indian mother] for her betrayal" (86). Paz's simile equating "the Mexican
people" with "a small boy" does two things: it infantilizes the Mexican
national community, and it makes "the Mexican people" male. In another
passage, the "small boy" is a grown man: "The history of Mexico is the
history of a man seeking his parentage, his origins" (20). This simile too
makes "parentage" male, since the "man" searches for the father, the one
he lacks in life.

Paz's narrative about this native woman is built on a double irony: La
Malinche is Everything (the founding mother of a new civilization) and
Nothing (an "inert heap of bones, blood and dust") (85). To represent this
second meaning, Paz offers a second name—La Chingada.[20] La Malinche's
act of falling in love with, or aiding, Cortés, in the context of conquest and
possession, is powerful enough to generate an entire "nation"; and her
act of collaborating militarily and politically with Europeans, Christians,
and foreigners is powerful enough to topple a "nation." Her complicity
with the foreigner is her "betrayal" of the interests of Mexico's indigenous
communities.[21] For this betrayal, she is punished and transformed into
La Chingada, the "violated mother," the "inert heap of bones," and so
on. The paradoxical irony, then, is that La Malinche was simply "too"
active for her own good and the good of others. She betrays but is herself
betrayed by the Mexican people: "there is also nothing surprising about
the curse that weighs against *La Malinche*," "the Mexican people have not
forgiven [her]," and "[Cortés] forgot her as soon as her usefulness was
over" (86). She becomes the mother rejected by father, sons, and nation.
Paz turns the progenitor and caretaker of Mexico's mestizo population
into a victim.

All this, of course, has negative implications for Mexican women and homosexual men, two sets of people who are victims, predisposed by nature to play, in this system that Paz explains, the "passive" and "weaker" role in sexual and social, private and public, acts. Paz says that "we," the Mexican people, regard all women as sexually and socially passive by nature, that is, "open," receptive to penetration. In Paz's context, a woman is "penetrated" in the sex act, whether she is raped or a consensual participant; she is also "penetrated" socially because she is always by nature in the passive position. The same goes for the man who is "penetrated" in the homosexual act. The power, impact, and consequences of "opening up" or "being fucked" go far beyond the physical and sexual realms of experience. For practical purposes of self-image and dignity, women and homosexual men, in Paz's system, might as well consider themselves "castrated."[22]

The situation is only slightly optimistic for the fatherless male children (the *machos*).[23] Mothers pass the genetic flaw of openness—the "taint [that] is constitutional and [that] resides . . . in her sex" (85), the "unfortunate anatomical openness" (39)—down to their sons, whose masculinity is always tenuous, always in question, in danger of being taken away, tantamount to their emasculation. Paz's woeful narrative, maddeningly circular and contradictory, is built on a woman's power to seduce and at the same time her vulnerability to rape. His narrative also insinuates that it is the mother who emasculates, metaphorically, the male issue of the Spanish father and Indian mother. The macho's knowledge of his mother's rape mars his masculinity and habituates him to compensate, with exaggerated maleness, for the lack in the family (national) origins. Paz's macho operates on a compensatory model, always in deficit, always in a process of trying to catch up to the middle-class standard.

The machos, then, according to Paz, must always project the look of a self that is impenetrable, ready to wound, humiliate, and annihilate. They must constantly test the limits of their bodies and their ability to endure because they feel that their manhood is in constant peril of feminization.[24] For the most part, their acts of domination take place in sex and other activities involving the investment of physical force and power, never acts of ratiocination, persuasion, or any form of reflective display, which are generally associated with "civilized," "self-controlled," "intellectual" endeavors. The macho is outside the frame of Western rationalism. Acts of rape and violence frame the acts of the animal, the primitive and instinctive. Violence and force, then, are the tools of he who has nothing else. Violence is what the man who runs out of words or has no words commits.[25] The stakes are high. One false move and the machos may be turned into *chingados,* "fucked"—either literally, physically that is, or metaphorically, in a social, public space. The homosexual man, in this system, is a literal *chingado,* in the sense that he is anatomically penetrated.[26]

The result of this Pazian "family" narrative is a symbolic version of the controversial template of the "dysfunctional" family in subordinated cultures: a "raped" or promiscuous single mother, illegitimate children,[27] absent, unknowable fathers, vicious cycles of destructive behavior. La Malinche is allowed to represent "family" and "nation," but she, like the women she represents, is not permitted to speak for family and nation and is allowed only limited participation in them.

5. MOYNIHAN'S "MATRIARCH"; OR, LA MALINCHE IN BLACKFACE

If Paz created an imaginative, lyrical, quasi-historical scenario of the Conquest to stage the mother/malinche trope as the explanation for the flawed Mexican "family" and "nation," Moynihan, keenly interested in the study of urban life and public policy, used graphs, notes, and quantitative data in his report[28] to buttress his explanation of what he called the "breakdown" of the African American family and community (5, 12). Moynihan argued that this breakdown (he also used descriptors like "crumbling" [19] and "deteriorating" [5, 29]) of the Negro family was the "fundamental problem" keeping African Americans from achieving middle-class status. His yardstick for measuring the health of the black family was always the structure of the white, middle-class, nuclear conjugal family household, itself an invention of recent history. The dramatic core of the report and the central point of the full-blown controversy that surrounded it was the unflattering portrayal of the black family, especially the black mother, or "matriarch," at the family's helm. The fundamental binary that powered the report, however, was the white middle-class patriarchal family—a picture of health—and the black working-class matriarchal family—a picture of illness. Matriarchy was the pathology, the virus that had infected the black family.

The event analogous in the Moynihan report to Paz's Conquest is Slavery, the ultimate symbolic "castration" of black personhood.[29] Moynihan argued that slavery, and Jim Crow laws after the Reconstruction period, had damaged black family structure and life to such an extent that the black family would need no help from the white world to continue its downward path toward complete deterioration if the machinery of the federal government and public servants like himself did not intervene to remedy the situation. Moynihan represented black men as needy persons whom people like him could redeem, but his vision, like Paz's, is predicated on displacing blame and responsibility to black women for damage to the family. Black women, like La Malinche, must take the fall.

Two seemingly irresolvable strains of thought characterized the report. On the one hand, Moynihan asserted that the U.S. version of slavery had been the most inhumane in world history;[30] that the legacy of slavery—three centuries of exploitation, segregation, poverty, persecution, and unemployment—was the underlying cause of black economic inequality today; and that "the racist virus in the American blood stream still afflicts us" (précis).[31] On the one hand, Moynihan recognized centuries of structural racism and inequality, and he benevolently extended sympathy to the victims of this oppression. On the other hand, he proposed that the chief obstacle to "white" economic progress and "white" middle-class respectability was the matriarchal structure of the black family, thereby highlighting the role that black women had played and were playing in the black family. Although he recognized that the putatively mother-centered structure was a direct result of slavery, a concession that attenuated somewhat the message that black mothers were responsible for the damage to the family,[32] he claimed that the consequence of slavery—matriarchy—was the cause of black male failure at the moment.[33] In this way, Moynihan had his cake and ate it too.

The Moynihan report was a logical outgrowth of a long tradition of racial liberal philosophy in the United States. I use the term "liberal" to refer to a consensus of attitudes and programs on civil rights, integration, assimilation, and equal economic opportunity embraced by American intellectuals and socially progressive politicians from the 1940s through the 1960s.[34] As in Paz's case, there was a maddening circularity to Moynihan's argument. Negroes were entitled to real equality, but inherent defects in their family structure deterred them from achieving it. What Moynihan did was shift the responsibility from the macro-historical event of slavery and its legacy of systemic racism in the first part of the report to the modern black family in the second part of the report. He shifted responsibility to the people *in* the family, particularly the black mother, victimized by the institution of slavery.

Moynihan not only racialized poverty and inequality; he subliminally gendered his formulation about the black family.[35] As Paz does, Moynihan produces a gendered narrative. The predominance of female-headed households—a family structure with roots in slavery that Moynihan called "a matriarchy" (30)—was the reason, he claimed, that the "Negro" family was in crisis in 1965. Moynihan was invested in the protection of black manhood, which he said was in peril. That black women were the active family providers, the ones raising the children, instilling moral and social values in present and future generations, and, most alarming perhaps, in control of family finances, was a source of worry for him. Moynihan implied, in this much-circulated, much-commented-on government document, that black women prevented black men from assuming their rightful places as "mature bread winners" and effective agents of family and citizens of the nation-state. Unlike their white male counterparts, Moynihan's ideal social type, and some black middle-class men, the majority of black men did not own middle-class respectability, nor were they likely to achieve it, because with no employment they had no economic control and therefore no social status as heads of households.

The same triangle of characters in Paz's narrative appears in Moynihan's report, with slight variations: man, mother, and fatherless offspring. But whereas sexual power and fantasy imbue Paz's vision of the legacy of the Conquest on family and nation (romance, seduction, rape, *mestizaje*, or miscegenation, and machismo),[36] Moynihan's analysis of the legacy of slavery on the family is clearly based on economic value and power. If Mexican men have surplus sexuality, albeit rooted in weakness, black men have an inadequate supply of it.[37] This deficit in sexual, manly virility is linked to economic power. Moynihan seconded the words of the black social scientist Whitney Young when he quoted: "But in a society that measures a man by the size of his pay check, he [the black man] doesn't stand very tall in a comparison with his white counterpart" (80). The figure with excess sexuality in the report is the black woman, not only because she produces a supposed abundance of children, but also because, having more opportunities for employment than black men, she becomes the "matriarch" of the family, the one with economic and moral power.

One implication of all this is that the low-income black woman is out of control, beyond the boundaries of the acceptable and of what is socially and morally beneficial for the family: she is promiscuous, she is strong (coded negatively), she is either in the workforce or at home dependent on welfare, in comparison to the middle-class white woman, who knows that her place is near the hearth and that the public world belongs to her husband.[38] So with his representation of the white woman tucked safely away in the home, a positive domestic force, the "good" wife presumably doing everything right, and with his representation of a weak desexualized black man underpinning the report, Moynihan does away with the image of the lascivious black man, whom the white imagination holds as a threat to the white woman—sign of moral virtue and economic value, key to the white man's reputation and property. Moynihan ingenuously says that "the [African American] female was not a threat to anyone," in contrast to an African American male who would be perceived as a "sassy nigger" if he attempted to "strut" the way men should. To "strut," for Moynihan, is the "very essence of the male animal" (62). Moynihan suggests the image of a meek desexualized "mammy" during slavery; yet he suggests that working-class black women now are so strong that they impede the progress of today's black family. If not "mammy," then "Sapphire," the caricature of the iron-willed, "bossy," treacherous black woman whose behavior and words express contempt for black men.[39]

Moynihan's modern-day black woman is a variant of La Malinche, the overactive woman who does not contribute to the common good of the black family, given middle-class patriarchal social codes. Like La Malinche and La Chingada, "mammy," "Sapphire," and "matriarch" (the first two names are implied images in the report, the third is overtly stated) are generic and gendered labels that designate no one person's name. The black man, on the other hand, fits the description of Paz's *chingado:* weak, screwed, unable to assert himself to the matriarch. Both paradigms imply woman's emasculation of the male, whether husband or son.

6. LEWIS'S FERNANDA: "NEVER LET MEN DOMINATE YOU"

For Lewis, the development of capitalism had marginalized modern-day, low-income urban populations of "Third World" countries, such as Mexico and Puerto Rico.[40] During the 1950s, when doing ethnographic research in the *casas de vecindad* of Mexico City, and in the 1960s, when supervising his team of researchers in the "slum" of San Juan's La Esmeralda (an area "not more than five city blocks long and a few hundred yards wide, . . . [with] nine hundred houses inhabited by 3,600 people" [*La Vida* xxxii]), Lewis theorized, systematized, and constantly revised his conception of poverty. He termed this conceptual format the "culture of poverty," a corpus of traits that the urban poor developed to cope with their displaced situation in postcolonial societies within the capitalist orbit. The culture of poverty was the way the poor adapted to their environment, the strategies they used to cope with feelings of "hope-lessness and despair," a result of their "realization of the improbability of achieving success" in class-stratified societies undergoing rapid techno-logical change (*La Vida* xliv). At the center of the culture of poverty stood the unit of the family. This, Lewis believed, was the place to study the cul-tural and behavioral practices of low-income people, a kind of laboratory that would expose the psychological and social dynamics of the culture of poverty, no matter where it occurred in the developing world.

The hallmark of the culture of poverty, and a disquieting one to many of Lewis's readers, was its self-perpetuating quality.[41] It was a "subculture" with its own "structure and rationale" (*La Vida* xliii), handed down from generation to generation. He wrote, "Once it comes into existence it tends to perpetuate itself from generation to generation because of its effect on the children" (*La Vida* xlv). In Puerto Rico, in contrast to Mexico, Lewis found a predominance of mother-headed families going back sev-eral generations.[42] Matrifocality was the prevailing structure of the five households of the Ríos family Lewis studied in Puerto Rico and that he interviewed for *La Vida*. Basing his assumptions on the behavioral pat-terns of this extended family, Lewis generalized that mothers exercised the most influence in the lives of their children, whether living in San Juan or New York City. Since he took the five households of the Ríos fam-ily as his paradigmatic example of the culture of poverty,[43] not only of San Juan but of all lower-economic-status life in Puerto Rico,[44] it follows that mothers will necessarily assume the responsibility for passing on this "tenacious cultural pattern" (*La Vida* xxvii). Mothers, as though oper-ating outside social institutions or cultures as a whole, are the engines that propelled this problematical way of life. Children of subcultures of poverty, said Lewis, knew their mothers, as opposed to their fathers, and thus acquired a greater knowledge of maternal relatives. In his generalized descriptions of and abstractions about poverty, Lewis shows his aware-ness that the family existed in relation to larger social networks, but he portrayed the members of the Ríos family in *La Vida*, primarily Fernanda and her five grown children, as though they were living isolated from the historical forces and conditions that he himself acknowledged kept their poverty intact.[45]

In contrast to *The Children of Sánchez*, in which Lewis represented au-thoritative Mexican fathers and submissive Mexican women, in *La Vida* he represented weak Puerto Rican men and strong, even abrasive Puerto Rican women. In this sense Lewis's sketch of male-female power relations in Puerto Rico and New York is closer to Moynihan's portrait than to Paz's work, since Paz attributes a martyr complex to Mexican women. Fernanda Ríos, a "Negro" woman and the matriarch of the Ríos family, for example, is a steely and determined, earthy woman: "My *mamá* told me never to let men dominate me. 'If they do it to you, do it to them. Never give in. Don't bow down'" (*La Vida* 27). As a child, she was "like a fighting cock. . . . [N]obody [could] stop her [fighting with boys]" (29). She is as focused as the men, maybe more so, on bodily functions. Like her maternal ancestors and her own adult daughters, Fernanda has been married several (six) times, and when Lewis gets to know her, she is living with a nineteen-year-old boy named Junior. Fernanda asserts, "I'm forty now and I've had six husbands, and if I want I can have six more. I wipe my ass with men" (27). After raising her five children, Fernanda, like the other women of La Esmeralda, became a prostitute, seemingly with no moral scruples. She takes up "the life" to earn the money that more respectable jobs, such as taking in washing and ironing, cannot offer her.[46] The women prefer, Lewis says, common-law or free-union marriages because this option gives them the freedom and flexibility men have. It also gives them a stronger claim on their children should they decide to leave the fathers and makes it easier to obtain divorces. They are willing to part with the men, some fathers of their children, some merely consorts, but not the children whom they teach "to depend upon the mother and to distrust men." In fact, men, generally "more passive, dependent and depressed" (xxvii), are more likely to express a desire for stable family life, and wives are more likely to desire separation. While submissive Mexican women in *Children of Sánchez* do not worsen the culture of poverty, Puerto Rican women make it unbearable because they are more aggressive, more apt than men to use violent language and behavior (*La Vida* xxvi–xxvii), and more apt to "deprecate [men] and characterize them as inconsiderate, irresponsible, untrustworthy and exploitative" (xxvii). In his representation of Fernanda, Lewis creates a woman with some of the worst features of Paz's La Malinche.

Let me say that I believe none of these men intended to send such negative messages or for readers to draw such negative implications from what they wrote, but their works also have to be evaluated in terms of the effect they had on audiences who saw themselves implicated in the images these men drew of them. These men's narratives resonated with nineteenth- and twentieth-century elite discourses in the United States and Mexico that argued, explicitly and implicitly, that certain races were genetically and culturally inferior and, therefore, unable to achieve social betterment and progress without white society's intervention. A neopositivist inclination to see Third World peoples in terms of deficit models, predisposed to and responsible for their alleged failure, has been attributed to Paz's *Labyrinth* (Mexicans coping with the effects of conquest), Lewis's "life stories" (Puerto Ricans adapting to capitalism), and Moynihan's tract (the black family coping with the legacy of slavery).[47] These men saw white Europeans as productive citizens, thus placing them in a context of ethnicity. They saw blacks, Mexicans, and Puerto Ricans as dangerous and disorderly, a burden on society, draining its resources. They placed them in a context of race. For them, ethnicity, it seems, is a less threatening construct than race. All three men came out of traditions in which whiteness was the uninterrogated, undifferentiated norm, and, once normalized, Mexican mestizoness, "blackness," and Puerto Ricanness (especially when thought of in reference to black Puerto Ricans) could only be seen as the absence of "whiteness." But like all insidious binaries, the "superior" term depended totally on the "inferior" term for its claim to superiority.

Two

LA MALINCHE AT THE
INTERSECTION OF PUERTO
RICAN AND AFRICAN AMERICAN
CULTURES: PIRI THOMAS AND
DOWN THESE MEAN STREETS

In the prologue to *Down These Mean Streets,* the Puerto Rican protagonist stands on a tenement rooftop looking over Spanish Harlem. Exploding with frustration, feeling rage in his blood and bones, he cries out against a world that refuses to take note of his existence. *Down These Mean Streets* is Piri's cri de coeur. He is so invisible to people outside Spanish Harlem that he is not even, as a Puerto Rican, taboo—a sign of danger to whites, a threat—as are his black American friends. Through the persona of Piri, the Puerto Rican author Piri Thomas, in his novelized autobiography, attempts to correct this invisibility.[1] He speaks out as a Puerto Rican man, but he also sees himself and his community in explicit relation to African American, Native American, and Puerto Rican (Taíno) Indian, and ethnic white cultures, for example, Italian American and Irish American. In *Down These Mean Streets,* Piri Thomas intervenes in a dichotomized black/white racial space.

Although *Manchild in the Promised Land* was published two years before *Down These Mean Streets,* I have chosen to discuss the latter first because I want to stress the importance of conceptualizing the United States as an intercultural nation, rather than a black and white space. *Down These Mean Streets* is a more appropriate text to initiate my discussion about intercultural literature because it explicitly generates interracial linkages. Feeling caged inside the black/white division—"hung up between two sticks" (130)—Piri expresses his intercultural wish: "If there's anything in between [white and black], and it makes me belong, then that's what I want" (164). I intend to mobilize the intercultural elements in this text by focusing on sexuality and gender.[2]

Midway through *Down These Mean Streets,* in a chapter wittily titled "Barroom Sociology," Thomas showcases three unhappy and angry men. One is, of course, our hero Piri, a U.S.-born, dark-skinned mulatto of Puerto Rican descent traveling from Spanish Harlem to the Deep South

with his African American buddy, Brew. Brew is from Black Harlem, and he knows firsthand the trauma of racial oppression. Brew sometimes adopts the bravura of an angry black nationalist of the 1960s. Piri and Brew cross the Mason-Dixon line, and in a nightclub bar they encounter the third fellow, an African American named Gerald who, unlike Piri and Brew, is college educated and light-skinned. Gerald unabashedly admits to "passing" for a Puerto Rican to take "the next step to white" (191). He is bothered that whites allow him to be "Negro" but that "Negroes" do not allow him to be white. Brew openly scorns Gerald because he claims Puerto Rican heritage and demeans his Negro ancestry. In a voice with a threatening edge, Brew taunts him, "What kinda Negro is yuh?" (187).

Piri speaks both English and Spanish, but he does not know if he is "Negro" or "Puerto Rican." For the time being, he has decided to accept the gaze of the social system that blackens him and declares himself—momentarily at least—a "Negro" man. Brew is certain that Piri is "Negro": no matter how much Piri "rattle[s] off some different kinda language don' change [his] skin one bit" (132). Brew, however, considers Gerald an elitist-sounding "[d]amn p'lite prissy" (186). After several drinks, the tension rises, especially between Gerald and Brew, until Gerald caps the argument by articulating the central issue faced by this unusual social mix of men: "So I ask you, if a white man can be a Negro if he has some Negro blood in him, why can't a Negro be a white man if he has white blood in him?" (189). Though obsessed with the unfairness of the black/white binary, Piri and Brew are befuddled by Gerald's question. They retreat from the strained conversation and focus instead on what is for them unambiguous terrain: the traditional repository of sexuality and gender. With Lady Day (the jazz vocalist Billie Holiday) singing from a jukebox in the nightclub background, Brew shifts his attention from "prissy" Gerald and proposes to Piri that they go looking for women: "Le's go see what pussy's sellin' fo' by the pound." Piri assents. While Gerald walks off "a self-chosen white man mak[ing] it from a dark scene," Piri eyeballs the "broad" by the jukebox and thinks, "*pussy's the same in every color*" (191; original emphasis).

How does "prissy" become "pussy" in these men's conversation? How does a discussion permeated by ethnic, racial, linguistic, and class difference collapse into the essentialized sameness of female body parts? To present my intercultural reading of a Puerto Rican man who takes male privilege as a God-given right, I again bring to the fore a figure that has been the pivot on which the history of a Chicano woman's identity has turned. This figure is the intercultural trope of race, ethnicity, gender and sex—La Malinche. I rely on this trope for two reasons. First, as a woman of Mexican origin who is native to the United States and who developed political and cultural consciousness in the 1970s, I am familiar with this trope and its place in the cultural norms of Chicano ethnonationalism that galvanized the Chicano movement. Heterosexual men of color in the 1960s and 1970s redirected their struggle against their own racial abjection toward the subjugation of women ("pussies") and homosexual men ("prissies"). This strategy is not unique to Chicano men.[3] African American women, Chicanas, Puerto Rican gays, and others attest that this practice is not uncommon in nationalist and ethnic nationalist discourses.[4] My second, more important, reason for using this trope is to read *Down These Mean Streets* against the norms of Chicano ethnic nationalism because it reveals the interspaces that would otherwise remain hidden. The trope is my instrument to make my readings intercultural, a move that, in turn, subverts the idea that the elements encased in the trope are central only to Mexican and Chicano cultures.

Like his friend Brew, Piri is a victim of racism, but he compensates for the racialized and feminized abjection of black men in the United States by making the abjection of women the guarantor of his ethnic and masculine privilege. In other words, while Anglo society diminishes him, he takes comfort in his time-honored conviction that women—all women—exist to service men. For my intercultural interpretation, the variants of Chicana feminism are my lenses to expose Piri's presumably undebatable assumptions about male privilege and the subordination of women and homosexual men.[5] At the core of these variants of Chicana feminism is one salient feature: the retroping of La Malinche, a rhetorical figure of speech based on a historical woman.[6]

La Malinche, actually Malintzin, the native woman who was translator for the Spanish and the concubine of Hernán Cortés and mother of their son, was represented in Mexico during the 1940s and 1950s as the symbolic mother of the nation by artists and cultural thinkers. Because the Spanish language uses masculine forms generically, only her male symbolic offspring, the "sons of La Malinche," are recognized overtly.[7] In Mexican patriarchal culture, La Malinche is coded as a mother-traitor to the nation because she collaborated, sexually and politically, with the Spanish colonizers of Indian civilizations. The deep historical continuities between Mexican and Chicano cultures[8] made it possible for the Chicano movement to imaginatively transform La Malinche into a collaborator of the Anglo oppressors of Chicanos and Chicanas in the United States. The name suggests active power to betray perceived group or national interests. When lowercased, without the feminine article, *malinche* in modern-day Spanish can refer to either a man or a woman.[9] But even when applied to a man (as in "es un malinche," or he is a *malinche*), it contains a residual stigmatizing implication of femaleness. Another trope that usually accompanies it is La Chingada, or the fucked or violated mother (Paz 85). Therefore, La Malinche is La Chingada in the logic of the architect of this formulation.[10] As the "raped" or "fucked" mother, the trope embodies pure receptivity. The double-termed trope signifies the active mother-traitor as well as the forcibly raped mother of the Mexican nation.

In the late 1970s and the 1980s, Chicana feminist scholars and activists challenged the linkage of La Malinche with "betrayal" and of La Chingada with passivity. They restored the catalyzing power of speech embodied in the historical La Malinche—the woman with facility for languages whom Spaniards and indigenous peoples notably called La Lengua (the Tongue). They transformed La Malinche from a figure of destructive sexual agency (a traitor and a whore) and pure receptivity (fucked mother) into an icon of affirmative agency (a cultural bridge and communicator). I deviate from the Chicana feminist tradition of maintaining La Malinche in Chicano and Chicana cultural space by translocating this resemanticized trope to a cultural zone where neither historical woman nor trope appear explicitly.[11] I translocate La Malinche onto the Puerto Rican *Down These Mean Streets* to lay bare the arbitrariness of the black/white binary, to show the intercultural linkage among Puerto Rican, African American, and Chicano American cultures, and to make manifest how gender and sexuality mediate intercultural zones of race and ethnicity in this text. The La Malinche trope makes visible this nexus of relationships.

1. PUERTO RICAN: SOMETHING MORE THAN BLACK OR WHITE

A hybrid text of testimonial and imaginative literature, a text that combines the conventions of the novel of passing with those of the narrative of self-transformation, *Down These Mean Streets* initiates the *nuyorican* stage of continental Puerto Rican writing.[12] Thomas treats many of the subjects that society stereotypically associates with Latino minorities: poverty, educational failure, gang membership, drug addiction, welfare, petty crime, sexual "perversity," and prison life.[13] Piri moves in three bounded sites: the home, the school, and the street. His favorite place is the street because there he can *earn* his standing through physical strength, regardless of color. Physical stamina, cunning ingenuity, and the ability to respect the codes of street ethics are strategies of survival that he and other youths growing up in Harlem employ to contain interracial tensions. Italians, Polish, Irish, African Americans, and Puerto Ricans make up a "League of Nations" (229) in which boys of different ethnicities coexist harmoniously as long as they respect the boundaries of their neighborhood turfs. While physical violence takes place in both the barrio and the suburbs, the text primarily assigns acts of bodily violence to the street and acts of epistemic violence to the suburb. In the chapter, "Babylon for the Babylonians," set in Long Island,[14] the Italians unkindly remark that he is "passing for Puerto Rican because he can't make it for white" (92), implying therefore that he is really "Negro." Because for many whites at this time "Negro" was a racist category, those who used it on Piri perpetrated acts of mutilation on him by refusing him the possibility of self-representation.

Thomas appropriated the black/white racial signs of the larger metropolitan culture that dominated the period when *Down These Mean Streets* was published.[15] He opened up the two-toned racial economy to represent himself and his lifeways by generating intercultural linkages among Anglo-Americans, African Americans, and Puerto Ricans years before the concepts "hybridity," "heterogeneity," and "difference" gained academic and social repute. The book's initial reception in mainstream and black presses suggests that Thomas's bold attempt to undermine the black/white categories of U.S. racialization misfired. The audience replicated the racial polarization that renders the hero invisible in the world of the text and that he fought so hard to overcome. *Down These Mean Streets* was read and marketed as *either* a black cultural nationalist text in black journals *or* a white mainstream narrative of habilitation in mainstream newspapers and journals.[16] This bifurcated reception—black or white—was based on the common notion among dominant and subdominant audiences that race was a matter of looks, of phenotype, and, above all, of color. This binarized perception of racial identity prevented a reexamination of notions of cultural purity as well as the conceptualization of an autochthonous Puerto Rican culture.[17]

Not until the 1980s did sociologists and historians familiar with the racial and cultural nuances of Puerto Rican experience reevaluate this text as "Puerto Rican."[18] Scholars used Thomas's narrative to validate the cross-pollinated identity of the Puerto Rican population. By allowing for differences of language, religion, and history, they reframed Thomas's text as *something more* than black or white. These critics envisioned the dynamics of race as a continuum marked by both-and relations rather than by either/or polarities. They recognized that a Puerto Rican identity is simultaneously inside and outside the borders of the Caribbean isle and the U.S. mainland: both up here and down there, yet also in transit.[19] But since the 1980s the reception of *Down These Mean Streets* has remained locked in the three cultural areas it specifically invokes: Puerto Rican, white Anglo, and black American have remained discrete sites in its reception. This erroneously suggests that the text's audiences—Anglo-American, African American, and Puerto Rican—are insular units with no complex overlays or points of intersection.

Down These Mean Streets valorizes a black Puerto Rican man's encounters with different cultures, but readers have tended to overlook the book's cross-cultural dimension. This oversight is explained, in part, by the fact that Thomas's intercultural gestures are compromised by his reliance on the cultural practices of sexuality and gender that characterized the ethnic identity movements of the 1960s and 1970s. Piri and Brew take refuge in the belief that women and homosexual men are inferior to heterosexual men. In the scene that opens this chapter, Piri and Brew make homophobic comments to diminish Gerald. They do this to manage their racial anxiety about the subordinate status society assigns to them as men of color. For example, Gerald, a "Penn State man" (184)—an academic highflier and less likely candidate than Piri and Brew for the "state pen"—has a class and educational advantage, but Brew asserts manly status over the gentrified Gerald by calling him "prissy," and Piri attributes feminized behavior to him: Gerald "tenderly squeeze[s] the flesh of his left shoulder" (189). Piri and Brew make women and homosexuals, or men they perceive as homosexual, their sexual targets. Thomas's testimonial narrative faithfully represents the sexual politics of its time, namely the cornerstone equation of heterosexual masculine thinking: male = active; female = passive.

As enabling as this practice of sexuality and gender is for the constitution of Piri's (and Thomas's) sense of a masculine racial self, it has remained a taboo topic in post–civil rights discussions of how ethnic identity and identification work in this novel.[20] Sexuality and gender are nonstop background "noise" that would only upset a neat, relatively homogeneous interpretation of race and ethnicity in *Down These Mean Streets*.[21] But instead of silencing the "noise," I would like to bring these two variables into this discussion by highlighting my own familiarity with Chicano and Chicana gender debates of the 1970s and 1980s. Although Thomas does not use the name "La Malinche,"[22] or any variation thereof, the fancy footwork he uses to rework racial abjection into masculine strength replicates the familiar features of the traditional trope used by Chicano men for the same purpose in the 1970s. I recognize the trope's place in Chicano history because my reading is informed by a Chicana feminist re-creation of La Malinche. Incorporating a post–Chicano movement feminist re-creation of La Malinche enables me to establish intercultural relations among Puerto Rican, African American, and Chicano cultures without reinscribing the La Malinche trope (traitor and whore) of an ethno-nationalist Chicano movement. It also allows me to disturb the assumption that the traditional components of La Malinche/La Chingada—traitor, whore, violated and fucked woman—are unique to Mexican and Chicano cultures. If I did not bring the trope into my analysis, we would neither see the subtle nuances of race and gender in an intercultural context nor find the middle term that denaturalizes the black/white binary.

2. THE MIDDLE TERM: *MESTIZAJE*

The son of a dark-skinned Puerto Rican mulatto father and a white Puerto Rican mother who have migrated to New York from the island, Thomas's protagonist has dark skin, thick, nappy hair, and an Anglo surname. Born James Peter Thomas in Harlem Hospital in 1928, he is called "Petey" by his father and siblings, a nickname that his monolingual Spanish-speaking mother transforms into "Piri." Piri knows he is Puerto Rican, but he does not know what this ethnic label means. He is the only dark-skinned child in his family. While his two European-looking brothers pass for white in New York and his dark-skinned father lives a fantasy of desiring to be white, his own physical features reveal the blackness the other men in his family try to conceal. The father favors the other sons, who confirm the whiteness he desires, and slights Piri, who reminds him of the blackness society imputes to him. *Down These Mean Streets* thus exposes racialized differentiation among Puerto Ricans within their own families and communities.[23]

Piri decides to travel to the Jim Crow South to experience the materiality of being "Negro": he is called every name in the U.S. racist lexicon for African Americans, including "nigger" (92, 96, 201), "black bastard" (127), and "ape" (92). When he announces to his brother José his decision to be "Negro," a bloody altercation ensues between them over the forbidden subject of blackness. Piri argues that everyone in the family, including José, is "Negro." When José counters, "I ain't black, damn you! ... My skin is white," Piri retorts, "So what the fuck am I?" (155). José surmounts this problem by arguing that the darkness of both Piri's and their father's skin is traceable to "Indian" blood (155). Avowing "Indian" blood, José slips into a negation of blackness. While José's claim represents a distancing from the U.S. white/black binary, it also suggests a more nuanced Puerto Rican and Latin American system of racial categorization. In Puerto Rico, *indio* (Indian) may refer to a dark-skinned white man, thereby pointing to a difference in complexion—not in racial origin. A dark-skinned white man is a viable social category in Puerto Rico, where there are no ethnically marked Native Americans.

However, Piri spoils José's attempt to negate blackness in the family. He displaces José's comment into the multilingual, variegated context of the Greater Antilles, a site in the Hispanic Caribbean where the indigenous peoples were exterminated by the Spanish conquerors and replaced with a black slave population. He asks, "What kinda Indian? . . . Caribe? Or maybe Borinquén?" Then Piri presses on, "Didn't you know the Negro made the scene in Puerto Rico way back? . . . Poppa's got *moyeto* blood" (156).[24] By mentioning Native American populations that inhabited Puerto Rico at the time of the Spanish conquest, Piri questions his family's whiteness and insists on their difference as colonized Third World inhabitants. Piri's point is that in the United States the insidious racial binary subsumes the complexity of Puerto Rican *indio* and the mixture of European and African peoples, or mulattos and mulattas, into the sameness of the U.S. racial construct "Negro."[25] During the quarrel, José hints at miscegenation to explain the epidermal "stain" in the family, though miscegenation was legally prohibited and socially condemned in the United States.[26] Moreover, the historical construction "Indian" in the United States does not provide the biological mixture or the social mobility that José needs to erase the genetic "flaw" of his family's dark pigmentation. He needs a model that explicitly acknowledges racial and cultural mixing.

The term "Indian," which has many nuances in Puerto Rican usage, is a crucial shifting term in the novel. It is amenable to whatever referent a speaker wants or needs it to designate. Each brother angrily pulls toward one pole of the racial dichotomy—Piri toward darker oppressed shades, José toward lighter privileged skin colorings. This impasse occurs because both brothers have internalized U.S. black-white norms of cultural and racial intelligibility.

Piri chants the names "Caribe" and "Borinquén" (162) and the Spanish "Negro" to invoke the multiplicity of indigenous Puerto Rican populations and cultures, but he cannot make their subtle nuances fit the U.S. coding of racial identity. The one-drop rule petrifies the variegated Puerto Rican historical experience.[27] By contrast, José inverts the one-drop rule, claiming that one drop of white blood makes a person white. A mulatto or mulatta identity cannot register on a mainland racial scale in either Piri's or José's assumptions about race. Surface similarities between the mainland and Puerto Rico—white-black racial extremes, devastation of indigenous populations, and legacies of slavery—make it difficult for José and Piri to glimpse the complexity of their Puerto Rican mulatto identity.[28] What they need, I argue, is something akin to Mexican or Chicano and Chicana models of *mestizaje*, not U.S. constructions of racial apartheid.[29] Indeed, the third context of "Indian" implied in their argument is *mestizaje*, a Spanish American form of racial and cultural braiding. "Indian" is closer to the miscegenated identity José and Piri yearn for because Spanish American constructions of national and ethnic identity are explicitly predicated on miscegenation. "Indian" triangulates the ethnic model, driving a wedge into the racial binary.

3. LA MALINCHE/LA CHINGADA: A CROSSROADS OF RACE AND GENDER

The category "Indian" not only serves as the unassimilated racial and ethnic surplus of the category "Puerto Rican" but also disguises the anxieties Piri and his father feel about their gender when they are classified as "Negroes," and thus feminized, by white society. For if "Negro" is the reductive antithesis of the "normal" in U.S. culture (the only "real" man is a white man), then woman is the reductive antithesis of the "normal" in Puerto Rican culture; woman thus is the analogical equivalent of "Negro." Piri and his father achieve a sense of self that comes to them through a sense of what they seem certain they are not: women. They write gender over race to deal with the confusions of their uncertain racial position.

If the conjuncture of U.S. racial ideology and the Puerto Rican gender system (male = active, female = passive) is opaque, it becomes clear only through analysis of specific passages in the novel.[30] Woman as abject and degraded, as La Chingada, an appellation that cannot be dissociated from La Malinche in Chicano and Chicana discourse, is the notion that supports male displacement of racial anxiety to femaleness, specifically, to the female body as "the done-to" in zones of culture and ethnicity involving dominant and subaltern relations among men. In the four passages I examine, displacement of Piri's racial anxiety and its containment on the female body are Thomas's primary rhetorical strategies.

My first example involves Piri's father. Poppa is originally from an island mulatto and mulatta society where a person can have more apparent genetic traits of one racial heritage than another and yet partake of both. In Puerto Rico, Poppa protects himself against his ancestral black blood by marrying Piri's mother, whose white skin gives him racial privilege and cultural capital.[31] In the mainland United States, however, Poppa repeatedly confronts those who police the borders of the two-tiered racial hierarchy. To prove he is Puerto Rican and by default white, he performs society's Latino stereotype. He intentionally speaks with a Spanish accent "to make [himself] more of a Puerto Rican than the most Puerto Rican there ever was. [He] wanted a *value* on [himself]" (164–165; my emphasis). He obtains cultural "value" by deliberately pronouncing his English words with the Spanish accent that Anglo-Americans might expect of Latino Spanish speakers. He confides to Piri, referring to times when he entered New York nightclubs, "where a dark skin wasn't supposed to be" (164), or when society ascribed "Negro" status to him, "God, I felt like a *puta* [prostitute, whore] every time. A damn nothing" (165). Poppa feels injured: his choice of the words "puta" and "value" contains the connotations of a man who feels trapped into having to sell himself to appease his anxiety over his black racialized identity. Poppa displaces his anxieties about being racialized and contains them in a sexual simile.

Octavio Paz has written:

> If we compare [the Mexican] expression [*hijo de la Chingada*] with the Spanish *hijo de puta* (son of a whore), the difference is immediately obvious. To the Spaniard, dishonor consists in being the son of a woman who voluntarily surrenders herself: a prostitute. To the Mexican it consists in being the fruit of a violation. (79–80)

Paz's description applies, in particular, to the male offspring of the "forcibly opened," the Mexican mother, La Malinche, equivalent here to La Chingada (79). Poppa is neither Spanish nor Mexican, but his use of the word *puta* suggests that the semantic border between *puta* and La Chingada is not as fixed as Paz argues. Paz's argument suggests that Poppa's word choice conveys voluntary agency, but Poppa's attitude suggests a sense of "violation." The racial gaze of New York whites makes Poppa their passive target; it forcibly "opens" him like a woman, fucked. As a Puerto Rican man in the market of U.S. race relations, he feels devoid of exchange value.

In the second incident, a prospective white male employer in New York asks Piri how he acquired his Anglo-sounding surname "Thomas," insinuating that Piri is really "Negro" trying to pass for Puerto Rican. Piri replies, "My father told me that after Spain turned Puerto Rico over to the United States at the end of the Spanish-American War, a lot of Americans were stationed there and got married to Puerto Rican girls." He then thinks to himself, "*Probably fucked 'em and forgot 'em*" (107; original emphasis). Piri compensates for his tenuous Puerto Rican cultural identity by identifying with his imagined predatory mainland man. By implication, he affiliates himself with the imperial conqueror, the racially and sexually "superior" man who penetrates and colonizes the racially and sexually "inferior" woman. In recounting the 1897 colonization of Puerto Rico, Thomas does not indicate the racial or ethnic origin of Piri's mainland-born grandfather or Puerto Rican grandmother, nor does he specify whether Piri's black ancestor came from Piri's father's paternal or maternal line. But the penetrating male conqueror and the penetrated female conquered constitute Piri's version of a family romance of imperial racial conflict, a story that silences and suppresses yet again the presumably shamed grandmother. The image of the fucked mother perpetuates the imperial conquerors' attacks on the women of the conquered.

Unlike these two incidents, which are set in New York, the third is set in Texas, the southernmost point of Piri's travels. Annexed by the United States before the war of 1846–1848 and admitted to the Union as a slave state, Texas originally belonged to Mexico. In the 1960s Chicanos and Chicanas claimed it as part of the imagined homeland Aztlán.[32] By this stage of his journey, Piri has learned to adopt the colors of his environment and to use them to his advantage to disavow the racial binary. In Galveston, Piri, a rum-drinking Puerto Rican, bonds with a tequila-drinking Mexican man who consents to help him enter a brothel to "fuck a white woman." Posing as Piri's translator, this male malinche figure, "olive-skinned," hair "like silk," and a "straight and fine" nose, advises Piri to speak only Spanish, not English, and to speak Spanish only if he must. Translation is as much an act of withholding information as of releasing it. When asked where he is from, Piri says, "Puerto Rico," although he has never been to the island. "He ain't a nigger, is he?" (201), asks the manager, suspicious of Piri's skin color and features. The Mexican go-between authenticates Piri's nonblack status, which for all practical purposes in this context is equivalent to whiteness. Duped, the manager permits Piri and his "translator" to enter. Piri must mask himself as a Puerto Rican from the island to remove the black face society puts on him. He maintains his "brown" difference by speaking Spanish, a linguistic gesture reminiscent of his father's efforts to disavow blackness. But Piri once again dons blackface: "I just want you to know," he tells the prostitute, "that you got fucked by a nigger, *by a black man!*" (202; original emphasis). Piri turns the tables on his white oppressor through a white woman, thereby enacting his sexist maxim: "Pussy's the same in every color" (191). But he also entangles whiteness in blackness by sexually penetrating a lower-class white woman. To be sure, he inverts the positive Latin American encoding of racial mixing (*mestizaje*) into a negative notion of miscegenation, in which blackness presumably pollutes the "purity" of whiteness. But he endows the stigma "nigger" with powerful, destructive authority and thus displays the inherent instability of the racial binary, proving that its boundaries are indeed fluid and permeable. However self-destructive and demeaning, Piri's transculturating gesture manipulates the two-toned dominant culture that defines his identity. Piri thus resists that culture's representations of him.

Piri's actions in the brothel figuratively perform La Malinche and La Chingada but with a twist. Thomas here separates the stigma of feminization from the *malinche* function because he attributes it to a biological male who, seemingly, is confident that in this situation he will not be feminized. Thomas also separates the La Malinche trope from the La Chingada trope, for if the mediator, the Mexican male doing the translating, functions like La Malinche, the white prostitute, the target of Piri's masculinist mime, functions like La Chingada. Piri's revenge fantasy works precisely because La Malinche, in this scene the Mexican male, is not La Chingada, the white prostitute. The prostitute has negotiable cultural capital for Piri in his struggle against the white oppressor not only because she is white but also because she is female. Thomas resolidifies the link between maleness and activity, femaleness and passivity.

4. DRAG, ANOTHER TWIST IN THE TROPE

If the last example attributes a nonsexual active power to La Malinche, in other words, the Mexican man as translator, it preempts any move to dissociate female from La Chingada. For this we must look to the fourth and final example. In chapter 6, Piri and his male companions enter a New York apartment inhabited by transvestites. Their focus on the *maricones* (Thomas alternates between this label and its English counterpart, "faggot") grows out of the male bonding in Piri's community.[33] Ironically, their code of masculine behavior—never "punk out" (52, 60)—propels them into a homoerotic space that undermines their heterosexual masculinity. The experience with the transvestites is for them a test of that which presumably will affirm their masculine identity, just as Piri is empowered in blackness by his pretense of whiteness in the brothel. Piri and his companions pass themselves, self-consciously, as male homosexuals, whom they view as equivalent to women. They pretend that they have embarked on this adventure for the transvestites' money and that the situation will not compromise their manhood.

The transvestites are Puerto Rican with Spanish-sounding names. Their English is hyperfeminized with a deliberately Spanish sound associated with limited English speakers: "Oh, sheet," "thees needle" (61), and "thees pot" (63).[34] Thomas's distorted accentuation of Spanish pronunciation serves to suggest self-feminization. Just as Gerald transgressed the black/white boundary, the transvestites' feminine activities transgress the rigid boundary between male and female. Even more important, these are men who choose to dress as women. We could assume that in Piri's masculine code, betrayal of one's gender is worse than betrayal of one's race, since gender divisions are less negotiable than is racial identity.

It is important to understand that Mexican, Chicano and Chicana, and Puerto Rican notions of masculinity allow for a man to engage in homosexual acts if he takes the role of penetrator.[35] As long as Piri and his companions are not penetrated anally—and none of them is—they should be able to pass through this homoerotic zone with their maleness intact. However, the scene is so ambiguous that it is difficult to say whether the "real" men (Piri and his friends) feminize the transvestites or vice versa. It could be argued that the transvestites put Piri and his friends in the passive position of the ones soliciting action, rather than performing the action. Ordinarily, in a brothel money passes from clients to prostitutes, but here the transvestites are paying Piri and his friends, making Piri's group the prostitutes (*jotos* or *putos*).[36] In other words, the clients of prostitutes are usually men, and the men need money—exchange value—to pay them. But here the transvestites are paying the boys; it is the boys who need "spending money." So even while the boys go to "fool around" with the prostitutes and think that because they are so much men their masculinity cannot be jeopardized, in fact the opposite happens. The transvestites pay Piri and his friends for the use of their bodies and provide the liquor and marijuana to weaken their defenses. The economic overdetermines the sexual in this monoethnic zone. The transvestites are gendered "active" by their economic power. Social class challenges the traditional operations of the male/female binary.

Anxious about his anticipated feminization, Piri splits his heterosexual mind from his body, allowing his sexual organ to experience homoerotic desire. With the help of a "king-sized, a bomber" (a marijuana cigar), his mind escapes into the "mean streets," a place that *"takes, an' keeps on taking, till it makes a cat feel like every day is something that's gotta be forgotten"* (63; original emphasis). In his imagination, he places himself and his friends far from the transvestites' apartment, at a rooftop party filled with Latin music, girls, a rival gang, fighting, and blood, until the police or *haras*[37] enter his dream and interrupt the rapture (65). Awakening from his hypermasculine fantasy, he confronts the nightmare of a transvestite's "cold fingers [taking his] pee-pee out[,] . . . [pulling] it up and down. . . . [He] tried to stop [its] growth, but it grew independently. If [he] didn't like the scene, [his] pee-pee did" (65–66). His body provides the transvestite pleasure, but he too derives pleasure. He has to chant to himself to reaffirm his heterosexual manhood: "*I like broads, I like* muchachas, *I like girls*" (66; original emphasis). The bitter sweetness (62) of the "mean streets" exacts compromises that degrade even "real" men. Just as Piri must enact whiteness to reveal his blackness in the brothel, he must experience femaleness to affirm his masculine self. In that sense he reveals the continuum that the male/female binary denies between man and La Chingada and between active and passive functions.

The La Malinche trope exposes the negotiations of racial and gendered discourses in *Down These Mean Streets*. Thomas's text explicitly encodes woman as La Chingada, but reading the text cross-culturally against the trope of La Malinche as La Chingada provides full insight into what Chicana feminists have been saying since the 1970s: La Malinche is not La Chingada. The trope serves as a cross-cultural bridge, giving voice to the way that gender and sexuality mediate zones of culture and ethnicity, race and gender. My discussion of the operations of this trope in a Puerto Rican text is not meant to impose comparisons where they do not exist. In fact, the brothel incident shows that a Chicano and Chicana context does not precisely parallel a Puerto Rican one. If it did, Piri's black/white mimes would not reveal intercultural twists and turns, his efforts to displace race onto gender. The Puerto Rican backdrop also reveals the importance of directly confronting the abject passivity attributed to the second term of the trope.

A Chicana feminist reading recognizes Thomas's novel as divorced from the racial binaries of white supremacism yet implicated in upholding masculine privilege. It acknowledges that Piri's ability to see beyond binary racial oppositions is undermined by his commitment to sexual and gender hierarchies. In displacing the racial hierarchy, Thomas buttresses a gender hierarchy that reinvigorates the racism he challenges. Puerto Rican strategies of identity must reject either/or categories and typologies and instead embrace the articulating variables of race and gender as mutually constitutive and reciprocally informing categories.

Interlude 2 LA MALINCHE: SHUFFLING
THE PUERTO RICAN BORDER IN
SPANISH AND BLACK HARLEM

By the 1940s[1] African Americans and Puerto Ricans had settled in communities in New York and were living adjacent to each other in Harlem.[2] Piri Thomas's parents, for example, came to New York, as did many others, in the early 1920s, after the United States granted citizenship status to Puerto Ricans in 1917, facilitating movement between the island and the mainland. Many Puerto Rican families arrived by steamship, whose lines had a terminus in New York.[3] As a result of Operation Bootstrap[4] and the development of the modern airline industry, the numbers of Puerto Ricans increased substantially in New York and other cities where African Americans also had migrated: Philadelphia, Chicago, and Detroit. *Down These Mean Streets* was the first Puerto Rican narrative to bring these two ethnic groups into the same cultural and literary space.

In *Down These Mean Streets* Thomas tugged on the threads that bind the Puerto Ricans of East Harlem and the African Americans living in adjacent Black Harlem. Chapter 17, "Gonna Find Out What's Shakin'," unravels one thread of this special relationship. Here Thomas describes an encounter between Piri and two African Americans, Brewster (Brew) Johnson and Alayce, Brew's girlfriend. At the heart of this chapter stand the personal testimonies of Brew and Alayce.[5] Piri is a witness to Brew's and Alayce's "spoken" testimonies; he is a brown voyeur into blackness. Before hearing from Brew and Alayce about the torture inflicted on their black bodies, their flesh and blood, Piri observes a picture of a long-haired, kneeling, supplicant Christ. The testimonies of Brew and Alayce and Piri's reading of the pictorial image of the suffering Jesus represent one of the many contact zones in this Puerto Rican text. This particular contact zone occurs in the middle of the book's narrative progress, between the episode in which Piri and his "boys" are duped by the Puerto Rican male transvestites and the book's culminating episode of Piri's conversion in Comstock Prison.

Here I want to show how this Puerto Rican text enters into an intercultural relationship with African Americans and also how it offers a different way to look at the conventional troping of La Malinche in this intercultural context. Whereas the Pazian view has the trope stand for an active but negative agent (La Malinche) or passive victim (La Chingada), my reading of what happens in this scene shows how those coded as destructive agents or passive victims may be seen as agents with affirmative power. Paz moored his female La Malinche to three main areas: an anatomical female body, Mexican and Chicano cultures,[6] and a dominant Spanish versus a subdominant Indian hierarchical arrangement of social power. Using the fact that *malinche* is gender-neutral (equally applicable to men and women), I shake up Paz's neat definition of the La Malinche trope as uniquely Mexican and feminine by casting Piri in the role of a Puerto Rican male *malinche*.

Piri shares a cardinal feature of the La Malinche trope: he is a cultural liaison who negotiates not only in the classic *malinche* way—between dominant and subdominant (Anglo and Puerto Rican in this case)—but also between subdominant and subdominant (African American and Puerto Rican). Casting Piri, a male *boricua* (a person from Puerto Rico), as a *malinche* go-between enables me to upset Paz's argument on three levels: (1) it recontextualizes the M/*malinche* trope by locating it in Puerto Rican and African American situations, freeing it from the Mexican and Chicano contexts to which Paz tied it; (2) it loosens Paz's strict divide between dominant and subdominant; and (3) it disarms his apparently airtight separation, male = active and female = passive, the bedrock equation of his analysis.

Speaking in African American vernacular, Brew and Alayce recount stories of the racial and sexual atrocities they experienced in the apartheid South, before coming to Harlem. Brew's sexuality is almost compromised by a close call with rape (a case of attempted sodomy) in his hometown near Mobile, Alabama (143), but his story ends triumphantly as he overpowers his tormentors. Alayce's story also involves the double jeopardy of race and sex; however, hers ends tragically: she resisted a gang rape but lost the fight to maintain her sexual and bodily integrity. Together, this young man and woman offer firsthand evidence, via the Puerto Rican Piri of course, to indict racist U.S. society that granted to African Americans legal and moral status in theory and denied them protection of mind and body in practice.

In this scene, the complexities of gender and sexuality upset the black/white binary, and once this is done, the strict division between dominant and subdominant falls apart. The scene focuses on an interethnic contact zone (subdominant-subdominant) where Puerto Ricans and African Americans engage in ongoing communication about oppression and domination. Who is the most oppressed? Who has the most right to be angry? Whose "anger" is more important? Piri's? Brew's? Alayce's? Or the agonistic Christ represented in the picture in Alayce's apartment?

The juxtaposition of Brew's and Alayce's horrific stories with Piri's silent visual reading of the Christ picture, immediately preceding the telling of the stories, puts into play an ironic tension between two contrasting responses to a Christian-Catholic narrative of/about victimization. On the one hand, there is the black couple's firm disavowal of Christianity's potential to offer them salvation, rejecting the idea that the more one suffers in this life, the greater the reward in heaven. On the other hand, there is Piri's ambivalent reading of Christ's message. Piri is not so certain. Is the Milquetoast Christ he sees a victim? A dupe? A martyr? A savior? Is Christ male? Female? Whereas Brew and Alayce interpret the Christological model as a poison fed to black people by European Christianity, Piri uses the picture of Christ to mediate between the antinomies of the dominant mode of sexuality his culture has bequeathed to him—his own warrior masculinity—and the fragile femininity he presumes the Christ represents. Piri finds wiggle room in the fixed oppositions, active = male and passive = female. The contrapuntal call and response created by the two readings of the Christian narrative makes it possible for us to imagine intercultural connections between these two subdominant groups rather than reify the split that keeps them apart.

1. BREW AND ALAYCE "TESTIFYIN'" IN BLACK HARLEM

When the chapter opens, Piri is walking down to Alayce's apartment in the black section of Manhattan, looking for his *panna* (Puerto Rican slang for "buddy") Brew. Brew has agreed to accompany Piri on his projected trip to the South. Arriving at the doorstep of Alayce's building at 118th Street and Lenox Avenue, in Black Harlem, Piri whistles toward the window of her second-floor apartment. Brew comes to the window and motions to Piri to come up and join him and Alayce.

Inside the apartment, Piri explains that he has decided to cross the Mason-Dixon line to clear up once and for all the matter of his racial identity. Piri is not only daring; he is also a materialist: "*If I'm a Negro, I gotta feel it all over,*" he says (137; original emphasis). What better way to get in touch with the materiality of his "Negro-ness," reasons Piri, than to travel into Jim Crow territory.[7] He has gained a consciousness of his "Negro-ness" by association, namely, his relationship with Brew. Piri's plans spark an argument between Brew and Alayce. Are dark Puerto Ricans like Piri really "Negro"? Brew argues that Piri's dark skin "makes him a member of the black man's race." He caps his opinion with his own maxim: "When you're born a shoe, yuh stays a shoe." Alayce counters that Puerto Ricans "act different from us. They got different ways of dancin' an' cookin', like a different culture or something." Brew retorts, "What's culture gotta do with the color of your skin?" (171). He couldn't be more wrong, and by the end of the chapter we learn that the characters' social placement along lines of class and gender determines how they see skin color.

Alayce interrupts Brew's race = skin color presupposition by introducing the factor of ethnicity. She argues that she has never met a "Porto Rican"[8] willing to identify as "Negro." "An' I don't blame 'em," she adds, "I mean, like anything's better'n being a li'l ole darkie. . . . It's hard to be just plain black" (171). Like water in a kettle boiling too long on the fire, Brew's temper spills over on hearing Alayce's "li'l ole darkie" comment, and he accuses Alayce of being ashamed of her blackness and betraying the Negro race, turning her into La Malinche. He begins a chest-beating rant on the importance of black pride, ordering her to "be proud of being a Negro" (172). Alayce argues that pride gives no relief from the burdens of life when one is "just plain black" (171).

Brew's and Alayce's conflicting opinions modulate from race into gender. The couple launches into a confrontation over who—black man or black woman—is most oppressed. Brew argues that no one has a more legitimate basis than black men to be angry, whereas Alayce says that black women have it worse.

> Brew: "Yuh think Ah doan' know [that it's hard to be black]? Ah'm a black man, gur-ell."
> Alayce: "It's harder bein' a black woman[.]" (171–172)

The headstrong Brew insists that no matter how great the burdens, black people, men or women, must be proud of their blackness. Alayce digs deeper and jogs Brew's memory about the times he has had to act the happy-go-lucky, bowing-and-scraping "darkie" who licks "Mr. Charlie's" boots.[9] How can Brew, who she knows has had to demean himself as a black man, talk so cavalierly about black pride? She reminds Brew of what it means for a black man to live in an apartheid society: "How proud you feel, honey, smiling at Mr. Charlie from clear down yuh asshole?" (172). Insulted, his anger out of control, Brew "smack[s]" Alayce and catapults her "across the room on *her ass*" (172; my emphasis). Alayce has struck dead center at Brew's masculinity. Brew's violent act against Alayce in a domestic space serves as a transition to his own story of violence against him in public space. Underlying his anger at Alayce is his own experience with racial and sexual abuse. Alayce has put to him bluntly what he, at his young age, already knows: black men are as penetrable as black women. Alayce sharply criticizes Brew's mother, who believed in love and forgiveness modeled on "dear, sweet Jesus," who taught her children to comply with the "ABC's" of Christianity: A-accept, B-behave, C-care. Brew's mother wanted him "to care for the white man, not hate him." In turn, Brew has said that his mother's way of thinking is what makes "Negroes" internalize a self-image of themselves as victims and engage in self-loathing. It indoctrinates them to the point that blacks think they are to love and care for their white oppressors (144). Brew says that Alayce has internalized "what red-neck Mr. Charlie wants [black people] to feel" (172)—that they have no purpose in life other than the one their colonizers prescribe for them. But Alayce delivers a treacherous counterpunch. By stressing "asshole," she might as well have told Brew that he acted like the white man's "whore." Brewing mad, he tops off his punch with "You bitch!" (172), a label that stigmatizes an outspoken, independent-thinking Alayce as dangerous, aggressive, and "unfeminine" for daring to challenge male authority.

Now in command, Brew testifies to the veracity of his assertion that black men have it hardest. One day, walking home, he heard not the voice of God of Negro testimonials calling people to salvation[10] but the voice of two "motherfuckin' crackers": "Hey, niggah, whar yo'-all goin'?" The "crackers" want to participate in the privilege and power that they seize through whiteness. They hound Brew until they have him cornered like a dog straining on a leash. Brew recounts, "I smiled and smiled [to them] clear down to my ass, jus' like Momma said Ah should." He is ready to do anything they want in the hope of satisfying them and escaping whatever perverse fate they had in mind for him. In fact, he says, he smiled so hard and said "Yassuh" so many times to the "crackers" that "Ah almost tore my ass off, Ah wagged it so hard" (173). He plays the genial slave to perfection—to no avail. As narrator, Piri reports the story Brew tells:

> "One of the white boys," Brew continued, "put his hand on my haid and rubbed it jus' like he musta done a thousand time to one of his dogs, an' then he winked at the other white boy and said, 'You know, John, I bet heah's one of them good nigras. Ain't you, boy?'
> "Ah said through a smile, 'Yassuh.'
> "'An' bein' a good nigra, you-all won't mind doin' a favor for us . . .'
> "'Guess not, suh.'
> "'Fine, fine. Jus' take your pants down an' we jus' do a li'l corn-holin' with you-all.'"
> I looked at Brew. He was like one of those statues in Central Park. Only the tears running down his cheeks made him real. He went on talking. "'No, suh, Ah couldn't do that.'
> "'Why not, nigger?'
> "''Cose Ah'm a man.'
> "'Wal, nobody'll know, boy.'
> "'Ah'll know.'
> "'Ketch holt of him, John—.'" (173)[11]

Tense, angry, crying, and with a "big fist pressed against his palm," Brew tells how he wreaked havoc when his assailants penned him in. The point here is Brew's self-knowledge about his masculinity, even though the world knows nothing about his situation. Using language of metaphoric emasculation, Brew describes how he kicked one "daid in his balls" and "squeezed and squeezed" the other one's neck, "until [this one's] goddamn red face got redder and he went limper'n a motherfucker." Then he ran back to stand over the one named John, still on the ground, "holdin' on to his balls an' twitchin' all over" (174). The battle between persecutors and persecuted is fought on the terrain of the male sexual body. Finally, Brew explains how he redirected the menacing taunts of the white supremacists, who, now with the tables turned, claim to have intended the "corn-holin'" only as an innocent joke: "Damn boy . . . we's only funnin' with you-all" (174).

Brew redirects the original rape aimed at him. Retaliating with a vengeance, Brew forces John to endure the same physical and emotional terrorism earlier inflicted on him, ordering John to address him with "suh," an act of speech that reverses the feminizing and infantilizing epithets the attackers first used to cage Brew in: "nigra," "niggah," and "boy" (173). He also commands John to ventriloquize the words that he, Brew, speaks, but John refuses to speak Brew's climactic line—"*A black man's better'n a white man*" (174; original emphasis). Even with Brew standing on him, threatening to release a rock that he holds suspended in air, John refuses to mimic the words that would symbolically reverse the racial hierarchy of white supremacism. Brew restricts his assault to John's upper body, symbolically "penetrating" a different body orifice; he puts words in John's mouth rather than a penis in his anus, as the "crackers" wanted to do to him. He ups the ante by threatening to smash John's face with the rock if he does not speak the words. John refuses. Brew drops the rock "dead on his mouth and watched him spit out blood an' teeth." Brew then tells how he ran home: "An' next thing Ah was in a car with mah Uncle Stevens drivin' like hell ovah the state line an' on a train to New Yawk. That was three years ago" (174).

In a "fake voice," Piri says, "Goodness . . . that was a close shave, *amigo*. You almost lost your cherry" (174). This tops off Brew's story and diffuses the tension with ironic banter. Piri's commentary comes between the high drama of victory and Alayce's sad story that follows. The "fake voice" is Piri's self-conscious imitation of his version of a flaming drag queen. His falsetto accentuates exaggerated effeminate manners and language. For example, he uses an exclamatory "goodness," hardly fitting of a streetwise *hombre*.[12] Piri mocks the femininity that white racist society imprints on the bodies of men of color to stigmatize them as "penetrable," emphasizing their enforced absence of independent will. His choice of "cherry" is also ironic humor. "Cherry" is frequently used to refer to the virginity of either sex. I would paraphrase Piri's comment, "Gee, Brew, the crackers were treating you like the women they take us for, and you almost lost your virginity!" by which Piri really means "manhood." Piri's "cherry" remark is ironic, because virginity, generally, is something men are not supposed to hold on to or fret about; in fact, they are expected to lose it to become men. But here Piri suggests that if Brew had been penetrated anally, he would have lost his manhood by serving as a material receptacle for the "crackers'" will and pleasure, just as women are supposed to do for men in the heterosexual social hierarchy.[13] Thus we see in the novel the linkages between gender and sexuality in the face of sexualized and gendered oppression and exploitation.

Next is Alayce. She does not allow Piri's remark to sidetrack her from telling her story. Undoubtedly admiring Brew for his courage, she apolo-

gizes to him for "not having been proud of what we are." She now testifies
to her own "truth," that black women suffer more. In four brief sentences,
she tells how at fifteen four white men, twice as many as attacked Brew,
pulled her into the bushes and repeatedly raped her, "like Ah was one big
free-for-all pussy." She ends with, "Ah fought them as hard as Ah could,"
but they "hurt me an' hurt me an'—" (175).

Brew walks over to Alayce, bends down, picks her up "gently," takes
her face in his hands, and makes her look at him. He says, "Alayce, honey
... there ain't nothin' so bad can happen that'll make one ashamed of
what they is, if they's proud enough." Even *cara-palo* (stone-face) Piri
is surprised at Brew's behavior: "I'd never seen my boy so gentle" (175).
Brew's statement, although sincere, rings somewhat hollow in light of the
rage that colors *his* story of *attempted* rape. He demonstrates tenderness
for Alayce's feelings but expresses no rage or shame about the compromise of her bodily and sexual integrity.[14] The absence of rage suggests that
his masculine sexual and gendered integrity carries more value. I dare say
he would find little comfort in his own words if *he* had been raped. In the
retelling of what happened to him, Brew made clear that self-knowledge is
the point: "Ah'll know" (173).

No amount of pride would cancel the feelings of shame and loss that
are tied to his sexual and bodily integrity.[15] Nevertheless, Brew demonstrates an understanding of a shared experience of sexual assault despite
his insistence on gendered difference. And, as a result, he diffuses what
seems an aggressive masculinity for a more tender one. Embracing each
other, Brew and Alayce walk over to the windows covered with newspapers. They look out into the street. A mutual silence follows. This black
man and woman, formerly arguing about who is the more oppressed,
now stand together in a space of shared solidarity, with faith in their own
abilities. They are survivors who affirm their own value and worth in the
face of those who would obliterate them.

2. BREW AND ALAYCE: SHAKIN' UP PAZ

I paraphrase these stories at length to show that they have
a resistant *force*. In their own time, they were not read as "talking back."
Distance allows us to see that they shake up categories that seemed self-
evident then. The stories expose the stereotypes, beyond the overly sexed
black man and wild black woman. They represent the force of personal

accounts told by two resilient individuals; they carry the authority of testimonies based on the physicality of pain actually experienced by the material body.

Brew's and Alayce's stories repudiate the Christian narrative of "turn the other cheek," of "the meek shall inherit the earth," and of "Jesus will deliver me." As they see it, the Christian model has been manipulated by white Christian society to limit blacks. That model asks them to comply with and passively accept their oppressed condition. It has brought them mainly hurt, humiliation, passivity, and rape. On the day of his assault, Brew consciously rejects his mother's Jesus-like moral and religious teachings: "Ah ate and lived with that ABC bullshit Momma put down, an' one day I couldn't no more" (173). Brew's mother has adapted to the structures of domination ("So we gotta care. . . . / So we gotta share" [144]) and inhibits Brew from waging a struggle for his freedom. Understandably, she is afraid of the risks freedom entails. Resistance would only bring more intense repression on her sons. She knows this, judging by how quickly she and the uncle get Brew out of town.

Brew and Alayce, on the other hand, understand that oppression turns them into objects.[16] The last thing they want is to be "host" to the oppressor. "We shared awright—white man got the sun and we got a black night," Brew tells Piri (144). For Brew and Alayce, Christianity came along to justify colonization and conquest, putting European whites at the top, blacks and other people of color at the bottom. Their statements foreshadow what Muhammad, leader of the Black Muslim inmates, tells Piri in prison (and what Father Ford, a Coptic priest, tells the black protagonist of *Manchild in the Promised Land*):[17]

> When the black man ate the poison of Christianity, he finally
> was where the white man wanted him. First he took away
> the black man's freedom, then his dignity and pride, then
> his identity. In return, he gave him a secondhand sense of
> values—a concept of nonexisting dignity by putting him in
> a certain place, like low man in anything, then taught him all
> about Christianity and how, as a Christian, he could bravely
> stand the pain of his slavery, all the time softly purring into
> his eyes, "No matter how much you lose here on earth, Jesus
> loves you and you'll get it all back in heaven." . . . The white
> devil has kept chanting "All men are brothers," while all the
> time he meant "if they're white!" (312)[18]

Alayce and Brew are not followers of Islam, but they are critical of the belief that blacks are expected to find salvation through their conquerors.

Brew and Alayce do not represent themselves as helpless victims, yet they run the same risk La Malinche did in Paz's discourse. Like La Malinche, they can be turned into a *chingado* and a *chingada* (in English, someone who is feminized). Paz turned La Malinche, the woman who dared to act like a man, into La Chingada, embodiment of pure passivity, an "inert heap of bones" (85). But such a gutting and laying out does not happen here. Brew keeps his anatomical manhood. His heroic narrative ironizes (or is "signifyin'" on) Paz's category *chingado* because Brew neither is anally penetrated nor does he retaliate by sexually assaulting the "crackers" in their private body parts.[19] Paz's script is based primarily on the penetration of certain body parts classified as male and female.[20] Instead, Brew transfers the oppressed/oppressor power play to the terrain of words because he makes the "cracker" repeat nearly everything he, Brew, speaks (with the exception of "A black man's better than a white man").[21] The rock-in-mouth episode is a surrogate sexual act. Brew "penetrates" on his own terms, not those offered by Paz. Brew describes his act in more active terms than Piri. Piri says, "Brew stood there and his hands *slowly let go* of an imaginary rock" (my emphasis). Brew says, "Ah dropped that fuckin' rock dead on his mouth" (174). Piri's "slowly let go" is less active than Brew's "Ah dropped that."

Whereas the force of Brew's story is that he was able to *retaliate* through physical strength and language, the force of Alayce's story lies in its power to reshape the nonnormativity of black women. Here I look at Alayce against the template of Paz's *chingada* ("pure passivity"), which she is not. For one thing, we hear her story from her lips, as opposed to hearing it, for example, in Piri's indirect discourse. She, like Brew, appropriates the word—a sign of reason taken to constitute humanity and the very thing denied slaves and their descendants as proof of their alleged inhumanity. This unschooled young black woman is articulate; she makes the word her own and fills it with her own intention. This gang rape survivor recognizes that the rapists would reduce her not only to unchaste flesh but also to sexual property for them to use as they choose. The constitutive element of La Chingada in Mexican and Chicano culture is woman "always open," always sexually available, like a fish gutted and laid out. White ideology projected this same element to the "lascivious black woman": the "Hottentot Venus" or the amoral black Jezebel who is supposed to be in a constant state of "presenting."[22]

Alayce reshapes Paz's categories that script women into La Chingada—"like Ah was one big free-for-all pussy" (175). The qualifier "like" provides the dissonant and resistant note. The simile is crucially important because it is the key to her resistance and resolve: it indicates she knowingly refuses the destructive and reductive coding. Alayce positions her subjectivity against the rapists' will. She has agency in spite of what the rapists did to her. She knows they attempted to reduce her to a mere body part. Finally, she could not be clearer that she did not lure the rapists to arousal, as Paz claimed La Malinche did (and hence he punished her), and as he implied all women did. Alayce did not desire to be "fucked"; she did not "want it": "Ah fought them as hard as Ah could" (175).

I stress Alayce's resistance because in a masculine world a woman's resistance to rape makes no difference to how she is judged. Piri himself confirms this when he separates his girlfriend Trina from Alayce—"I ain't gonna *chinga* her [Trina] till we're married" (176), implying that Alayce has been "fucked" and is therefore "damaged goods." Penetration, in Piri's view, whether rape or consensual sex, is what men do to women.

But Alayce is no pushover. The text grants her a material core, a strength that escapes Piri and Brew. Alayce's story is considerably shorter than Brew's, but it has power because it comes after Brew's; it frames Brew's "warrior" narrative. Brew's story takes more narrative space, suggesting that the risk of male feminization deserves more attention than a woman's rape. Alayce's story is not just shorter; it is cruder, more raw. It contains no dramatic embellishment, although arguably more violent and tragic than Brew's. Brew's story has melodramatic narrative elements: an ominous beginning, a dramatic complication leading to an imminent "rape," a struggle in which the hero overcomes his adversaries against their considerable advantage, a sense of time and place, supporting characters (Brew's mother and uncle) who aid the hero in his dramatic getaway; props (the rock), dialogue, and visuals of blood and gore (the spitting of blood and teeth, the "squeezing" action, "limper'n a motherfucker"). We have to read his victory, however, in the context of her rape. Alayce had wanted to tell her story first ("Ah ever tell you what happened—"), but Brew had abruptly halted her: "Goddammit! . . . it don't make no fuckin' difference what happened" (172). That is, what happened to Alayce doesn't matter to Brew. Yet had Alayce been able to tell her story first, the effect of the stories would have been different. The testimonies would have ended not with Alayce's anguished cry—"they hurt me an' hurt me an'—" but with David towering over Goliath. Brew's victory would have been even more victorious and mitigated the horrific effect of her rape. But as the stories stand, Alayce's story puts Brew's triumph in a broader context of the horror and cruelty of a black woman's rape.

But does her rape diminish his victory? No. She does not pull him back into the space of rape and feminization. She does not move; it is Brew who chooses to walk over to her. Even though his words to her sound awkward at this point, would his action suggest that he acknowledges how close he himself came to being raped? Is race what makes *both* Alayce and Brew vulnerable to sexual abuse, not gender? Does race level them, tie them together, put them in the danger zone of feminization and rape? At the end of this moment, the two cling together in the same space. Not black man *or* black woman, the point at which they began, but black man *and* black woman. Although the language at the moment of the publication of *Down These Mean Streets* had not yet been fully articulated in which black women a few years later would speak to and be heard by black men, the text does not buttress the binary of gender difference, as Paz's discourse does. The point is that penetration is tied to race.

3. PIRI AND CHRIST

Brew's and Alayce's commentary on gender is important because it creates a permeable partition (something like an imaginary gauzy veil or curtain) between Brew and Alayce on one side and Piri on the other, interrupting momentarily the racial bond between the two men that is based on skin color. However, this text necessitates that a Puerto Rican be a witness, albeit a slightly reluctant one, to an intraethnic quarrel between a black man and a black woman—a brown man's peek into "blackness." I say this because in terms of plot, Piri is already sitting comfortably and enjoying his cigarette on Alayce's "beat-up sofa" when Brew's anger threatens to splinter the alliance between black man and black woman. Piri neither chooses to leave, nor do Brew and Alayce ask him to. He is their invited guest. Yet he is edgy when they begin to quarrel. To attenuate his unease about his voyeuristic presence, Piri deflects his attention to the picture of Christ on the apartment wall right at the moment when Brew goes into his black pride speech. It is Piri who establishes an emotive relationship with the Christ, not Brew or Alayce. The entrance of Christ at this point emphasizes the permeable divide. Piri is able to hear everything Brew and Alayce say without encroaching on their space. He is both a personally involved insider (he stays, hears, reacts) and an objective outsider (he reports to us on Brew's movements and Alayce's facial expressions). From the angle of the text's margins, Piri makes Christ his focal point, while Brew and Alayce take center stage.

At the point of escalating tension between Brew and Alayce, Piri does a rapid visual assessment of the long-haired, kneeling Jesus. Here is the core part of Piri's reading:

> I took a long drag and stared at a picture on the wall . . . a picture of Christ kneeling with his hands clasped together and looking up at the sky with a hangdog look. The picture was covered with dust and a pair of Alayce's stockings were draped over one side, making it hang lopsided. The Christ in the picture was paddy. I blew smoke toward the picture and watched the blue smoke form clouds around the kneeling figure. I half expected the Christ to cough. He didn't. (172)

The hangdog look Piri sees on the Christ's face is a contrast to the details of revenge, vindication, and self-reliance of Brew's anti-Christian story. Each "text"—Brew's story and Piri's reading—offers a suggestive map for interpreting the other. Christ's hangdog look suggests that Piri is taking note of what appears to him to be a powerless Christ, a not very happy one about his upcoming crucifixion. Piri's hangdog-looking Christ foreshadows Brew's description of his persecutor's actions, when the latter puts his hand on Brew's head and rubs it, "jus' like he musta done a thousand times to one of his dogs" (173). Brew refers to "dogs" three times in his story in the context of a master imposing his dominance over a slave. The "cracker" unfairly imposes his power on Brew, attempting to feminize him, to establish Brew's place under him. Brew says of himself, "Ah almost tore my ass off, I wagged it so hard" (173), emphasizing his own doglike image; he had no choice but to comply in his own feminization. As the object of Piri's gaze, the stationary Christ too, ironically, has little choice but to accept Piri's stares. When the tables are turned in Brew's story, it is the "cracker" John's turn to "whine like . . . his dawgs" (174). Brew also describes his tormentor as "limper'n a motherfucker." The "motherfucker," the agent aiming to penetrate, ironically goes flaccid. Brew's language deflates the agency of the "penetrator" ("motherfucker"). The point is that in all instances—the "cracker" imposing power over Brew, Brew subduing his attacker, and Piri rendering a listless Christ—the dog effect is linked to the powerless or unmanned party, the one forced to occupy the presumed inferior place of the female or penetrated male.

Is Piri seeing in Christ a realization of what the crackers actually wanted to do to Brew? Does he see an emasculated, victimized Christ? Brew's expression "limper'n a motherfucker" may also apply to Christ in that Piri renders flaccid the power of the Christ, God the Almighty.[23] However, at the moment when Brew smacks Alayce, Piri ironically beseeches (in his internal voice) the stationary wilted Christ to save her: *"Pray for her, Christ, she's gonna get wasted"* (172; original emphasis). I assume Piri considers prayer more appropriate to women since it is a *passive activity*, not action-oriented hero material. Nonetheless, he attributes power to this "female" activity that he assigns to the Christ. The female Christ has, it seems, a pulse-beating heart. Is Piri intimating that Christ's nonnormative power is unaccounted for in his own normative definition of *hombre*? Is this the rebellion of the nonnormative making clear that normative cannot be normative without the nonnormative? The female Christ is given the responsibility of saving Alayce, she who, earlier in the scene, ironically had flung her stockings on the Christ, as if to say, "Take that!" Piri is tapping a power here, a kind of masculinity, say, different from the kind acknowledged, practiced, and validated by himself and Brew. It is a masculinity that does not play by their rules. Piri is upsetting fixed oppositions, finding the gray area that will not be pinned down.

The stockings Piri tells us Alayce flung over one side of the picture also point toward a nonnormative masculinity. Alayce's automatic gesture emptied the Christ image of religious iconic power, flattening it to a piece of furniture—a clothes hanger. She reduces a meaningful figure in Christian religious iconography to room decor. It is a different matter with Piri. Unlike Alayce, who forgets all about the stockings on the Christ, Piri notices them. One might imagine, therefore, Piri's Christ "wearing" women's underwear—a Christ in drag. Piri notes that the weight of the draped stockings tilts the picture to one side. That is, it does not hang "straight." The picture is veiled ("covered") with dust. In addition, Piri puffs cigarette smoke in the Christ's face that in turn forms clouds around the picture. The stockings, dust, smoke, and clouds intensify the veil effect, recalling the veil in Christianity and Islam that from a Western perspective appears to signify women's subordination, though arguably the veil is more complex in these contexts. Based on the idea of women as temptresses and seductresses, the veil hides bodily aspects that might arouse male desire. The stockings assign female characteristics to the Christ, giving him a supposedly "weaker" and more precarious female sexuality instead of a "stronger," more stable male sexuality. Christ is linked to Alayce and to femininity, in that their power is uncredited. Both are violated, both have rocklike strength. Alayce and Christ are signaling toward another way to be "active," another definition of agency.

When Piri puffs smoke in the Christ's face, he mocks him with this traditionally manly gesture. This may be a knee-jerk reaction on Piri's part; he is making a gesture from a man "who wears pants" to a man who wears female garb. Piri expects the Christ to cough. But the Christ defies his expectations. Piri's expectations are ironic because he attributes a life-like quality to the picture, as if the image could answer his dare. If Piri's gesture of blowing smoke in the Christ's face is a test of strength (or weakness), a challenge, and the cough is a sign of weakness, or femininity, then the Christ's response, or lack thereof, may stand as *active resistance* to that attempted feminization, just as Alayce's telling of the rape stands as an act of resistance. These responses of Alayce and the Christ are not absences, not signs of paralysis, but rather another way to be active. Christ is not a wimpy, sweet, Milquetoast figure. Christ, like Alayce, has a power that does not fit the binaries victor/victim or active/passive. Survivors of persecutions they are but not victims. Though Alayce has only the language of victimization available to her, she takes the word and makes it work for her. The content is tragic, but her act of telling it, of testify'n, is liberating. Christ too is hardly remembered or thought of as a victim, even by people in the non-Christian world. He is a liberator. The resistance put up by Christ and Alayce may not be a valid form according to the definition of masculinity subscribed to by Piri and Brew. Brew's way of resisting is the way Piri knows, but my reading of Piri's vision of the Christ undermines any claim to absolute certainty. Brew, for example, is certain that Christ and Christianity are instruments of the oppressor, but Piri is not. He asks, "You think he [Christ] was prejudiced against something?" (176). To paraphrase, Piri is asking Brew, "Did Christ have any of the racist attitudes that are eating us up?" Brew answers, after keeping his eyes on the picture for a long time, "He was white, wasn't he?" (176). For Piri, the answer may not be so pat. There may be something to the Christ and his message of a different kind of active resistance after all.

Brew, Alayce, and Piri come to the experience of oppression from a different starting point. Piri, a *boricua malinche* figure, mediates these different perspectives, orchestrating ironies, glimpsing in-between places, offering a space for dialogue. Brew's and Alayce's stories do not reinforce gender difference and hierarchy. That is, they do not resolidify what Brew is, namely, a man who can overcome rape, and what Alayce is not, namely, a woman who *is* raped. They do not reinforce this binary opposition. This is so because Alayce's story frames Brew's, not Brew's hers. Furthermore,

Alayce does not pull Brew back into a space of rape and feminization, undermining his victory. When all is said and done, it is Brew who walks over to Alayce, bends down, and picks her up gently. There is a shared solidarity between them.

Names and name-calling are what people are fighting about in *Down These Mean Streets*. What better way, then, to initiate a discussion about *Down These Mean Streets* than with the trope of La Malinche, the mother of all tropes about naming and name-calling. Whereas Paz and others played God, bestowing names on people, giving them once-and-for-all meaning, *Down These Mean Streets* suggests that names cannot extract from people their "meaning." People cannot be easily labeled.

　　OF NUTSHELLS, FROGS, AND MEN
IN *MANCHILD IN THE PROMISED
LAND*

"Run!" is the first word of Claude Brown's *Manchild in the
Promised Land*. Claude "Sonny" Brown,[1] the protagonist, is running on
the streets of Harlem, at 7th Avenue and 146th Street. He is not far from
his home, which is in the same area the 1943 Harlem riots occurred. It is
1950 now, and a woman with a double-barreled shotgun is in hot pursuit.
Sonny has stolen sheets off her clothesline. She homes in on her thirteen-
year-old target, who is running for dear life through an alley, and lodges a
bullet in his stomach, bringing him to a dead halt on the floor in a "fish-
and-chips joint" (9). Sonny's hospitalization is a blip on a very large curve
of a young life that has drifted toward crime. Soon after his confinement,
Sonny is back on his feet resuming a circuit of petty theft.

Even before he was old enough to attend school, he had imitated his
friends who were playing hooky. When he goes to school, he hits his "little
Jew-lady teacher" (42). At age nine, he sets fire to and almost burns down
his house. Living in the slums, the other side of middle-class achievement,
he knows no one with a high school degree. When he is older, he joins
the pack that gang rapes his black buddy's red-headed, chalk-white girlfriend, only to discover that no matter a woman's color or how fine her
body, "[b]itches were bitches" (115). Schools expel him for truancy, and
judges consign him to correctional institutions that have no observable
rehabilitative benefits. All efforts to rehabilitate him, in fact, only sharpen
the skills and habits—stealing, fighting, lying, and bebopping (gang
fighting)—for which he was sent to the correctional facility in the first
place. As Sonny claims, "We all came out of Warwick better criminals"
(146). Nothing keeps him from cutting loose on the streets of Harlem,
not even his mother's desperate act of hiding his clothes and shoes. Sonny
says, "Harlem [was] home, but I never thought of Harlem as being in the
house. To me, home was the streets" (428). The tough, wily, and willful
Sonny, capable of facing off the devil, "got a head on him like rock" (42),

David Avalos 9/04

his mother says. But Sonny likes to think of himself, and be thought of, as a "bad nigger," a "cat like Paul Robeson," Joe Lewis, Jackie Robinson, and Sugar Ray Robinson, the black sports and entertainment idols of his time (292). Like Piri Thomas, a tough guy with heart, *muy hombre*, Sonny adopts a cool posture, and he expresses his manly sensibility by playing— bluntly—on "the word": a "real bad nigger" (97), a "bad-doin' nigger" (292).[2] Sonny had thought his father was a "real bad nigger" until he saw him fall on his face before some law officials (see interlude 3).

But even Mr. Brown Sr., a weak father figure, steps forward to claim his day in the sun. In a rare father-son moment, Mr. Brown, no longer able to "ass whip" his teenage son (19), takes a different approach to discipline. He steps into the role of a consultant: he converts an incident he knows Sonny has witnessed into a lesson. Sonny used to admire a particular "slick cat" for the way he would pull off tricks on Eighth Avenue in a scam called the shell game. This "slick cat" is Mr. Jimmy of Harlem, a hustling whiz who swirls a pea under nutshells and takes people's money by convincing them that the pea is only seconds away from their grasp. Always, he plants a buddy in the crowd who after one or two guesses finds the pea. When the unwary customers, the real "dopes to be troped,"[3] step up to play the shell game, they never find the pea, no matter how many attempts they make or how much money they bet. The reason? There is no pea.

Mr. Brown re-creates this game, though he does not bedazzle Sonny like Mr. Jimmy. Nonetheless, he manages to slide the "black-eyed pea" (73) under nutshells rapidly enough to confuse his son. After numerous tries, Sonny gives up. Mr. Brown's message? "That's jis what you been doin' all your life, lookin' for a pea that ain't there. And I'm mighty 'fraid that's how you gon end your whole life, lookin' for that pea" (73).

Only one generation from the sharecropping South of his parents, Sonny spends his childhood and teenage years looking for a "pea that ain't there." He mule-headedly aims for a dead-end life. Throughout his adolescent years, he plays shell games, all rigged because they offer only two possibilities, "Topdog/Underdog," to borrow the title of Suzan-Lori Parks's celebrated play.[4] Con before you're conned, cheat before you're cheated, screw before you're screwed is the point. There are poignant shimmerings of the limitations of this two-position, winner-loser, outlook on life throughout *Manchild in the Promised Land*.[5] Sonny must learn to widen his vision beyond dualities: he must learn that participating in scams might give him a high and quick profit turnaround, but these trompe l'oeil are deceptively elusive, like the nutshell game of the Harlem streets. Sonny must learn to assess, to think, to absorb important lessons from his experiences in intercultural contact zones.

In this chapter I concentrate on two male figures that I call "forefathers." Toni Morrison refers to such figures (male and female) as "ancestors"—"timeless people, whose relationships to the characters are benevolent, instructive, and protective, and they provide a certain kind of wisdom."[6] Each forefather tells Sonny a story, a parable, that contradicts the Moynihan report's assessment of weak, emasculated black men. Both these forefather-storytellers propose examples of positive masculinity, and they do it in an intercultural context. However, they fail to escape Moynihan's rhetorical model of the black family, because they, like Moynihan, slight the role that black women play in the formation of Sonny's and, in a wider context, working-class black manhood.

Each forefather takes Sonny into a different ethnoreligious heritage: a Jewish European American heritage and an Egyptian, Ethiopian, Christian heritage transplanted to an African American setting. The first forefather-storyteller belongs to an ethnic group that since World War II at least is commonly glossed into white and dominant America, though Jews, like the Irish, were not quite "white" or "dominant" enough to have escaped racial and religious discrimination.[7] The second forefather-storyteller belongs to a marginalized religious ethnic group, whose origins are in northeastern Africa. This community has less time in the United States than the first and, consequently, is less well known. Sonny's masculinity is an intercultural product, all the more powerful because he draws from these two disparate traditions that resist Moynihan's and Paz's slighting of minoritarian men. The forefathers put Sonny into a wider cultural context, away from the black/white binary that caged in Moynihan. Moynihan's report flattened out the complexity of the calibrated differences of whiteness and blackness, patriarchy and matriarchy, male and female (white and black). He made the first term of these dyads the superior one and took these constructs to be capable of relation only to each other. Puerto Ricans and white Appalachians, for example, were off Moynihan's radar screen.[8]

The groups these forefathers belong to have not been the focus of any serious examination of *Manchild in the Promised Land*.[9] Much has been lost by restricting this book to the material and rhetorical categories of African American literary and cultural studies, although it has been consigned to disregard even in this area. Sonny's sense of his masculine blackness neither totally fuses with nor completely separates from the cultures with which he comes into contact. He learns about his own oppression from people who come from other—albeit differently—oppressed global cultures. Sonny's black consciousness, or more precisely Claude Brown's, takes shape through his participation in a material network of intercultural processes and exchanges. By exploring parallels and crossings between Jewish Euro-American and African and African American modes of thinking about masculinity, I put "blackness" in relation to other ethnic cultures[10]—in this case, both inside and outside the United States—rather than conceive of "blackness" and other cultural units as disconnected, without attachment to a shared history. In the interlude that follows, I take up the question of Moynihan's "matriarch" and read it against iconic images of femininity from white-black and Mexican-Chicano cultural imaginaries to make visible what the Moynihan report and the responses to it kept hidden.

1. ENEMY MEMORIES AND THE FOREFATHERS

Although not the sole groups worldwide with a collective consciousness of catastrophes inflicted on them as a people, Jews and blacks have "enemy memories,"[11] a remembrance of suffering lasting not one or two generations but a very long time. But few groups who claim a history of oppression in the United States can also claim a history of strong collaboration with another oppressed group. Black and Jewish histories of oppression and persecution have linking themes—slavery and exile are two—often invoked to explain the two groups' strong identification and their historical record of cooperation.[12] But the linking themes have different weights and gravities. The historical realities and conditions of the enslavement of the Jews, for example, are not the same as those of African Americans. Slavery for the Jews not only occurred elsewhere; it occurred more than four thousand years ago. For African Americans, it occurred on U.S. soil, as well as in other areas of the Américas, and is a comparatively recent phenomenon. James Baldwin, who wrote extensively about the relations between blacks and Jews in the United States, says that the Jews' history of suffering is not a U.S. tragedy. Although I think it important to recognize that the historical record shows that Jews have been hated and ostracized in the United States, Baldwin's point—that the Holocaust happened elsewhere—holds. He writes, "For it is not here, and not now, that the Jew is being slaughtered, and he is never despised, here, as the Negro is, *because* he is an American. . . . What happens to the Negro here happens to him *because* he is an American."[13] In addition, the interaction of blacks and Jews has registered a conflictive partnership in the United States, especially since the end of the Civil Rights movement. Though neither African Americans nor Jewish Americans unanimously support, respectively, affirmative action and the U.S. position on Israel, the differing perspectives expressed by certain members of these groups on these issues have been breaking points in the dialogue that has characterized their historical relationship, referred to by some as the "peculiar entanglement" of blacks and Jews.[14]

Even so, African American history and culture records a strong identification with narratives of Jewish struggles and liberation. One such Jewish narrative is the Zionist movement institutionalized in 1897 to secure a Jewish state in Israel. The charismatic Marcus Garvey, the "Black Moses" of the early twentieth century, envisioned a similar program of an African Zion when he stirred Harlem inhabitants with his call for the mass return of all black people to Africa.[15] A second narrative goes back even farther in time. The biblical Exodus narrative runs throughout African American sermons and spirituals since at least the early nineteenth century,[16] and it is also embedded in modern writings such as *Manchild in the Promised Land*. The reference to "the Promised Land" in Brown's title points to an implied connection with the Exodus narrative of the Israelites' escape from Egypt. It suggests a parallel between, on the one hand, the flight, struggle, and deliverance of the ancient Hebrews from their captivity in Egypt to their new home in the Promised Holy Land, and, on the other, the deliverance of African Americans from slavery, their struggle under Jim Crow, and the massive migrations to northern cities (mainly) after World War II.[17] What Canaan was for Abraham, the North was for blacks.

Against the Exodus narrative, Brown's use of "the Promised Land" in his title is ironic, especially in the context of what Brown writes in the foreword. African Americans, he says, came from "all parts of the South, like all the black chillun o' God following the sound of Gabriel's horn on that long-overdue Judgment Day"; and having taken the gigantic forward move out of slavery, they thought they were saying "good-bye to the cotton fields[,] . . . to 'Massa Charlie[,]' . . . to those sunup-to-sundown working hours" (vii). Rather, they found "too many people . . . crowded into a dirty, stinky, uncared-for closet-size section of a great city" (viii). At the end of their journey, their flight from the feudal economies of the South,[18] African Americans found that the secular and moral "promise" guaranteed to them by this country's legal and constitutional laws was no good, unlike the ancient promise that Exodus records God kept to the Israelites. Though they did not see it until after numerous punishments by God for their transgressions and rebellion against Moses, the "chosen people" did reach a promised land. The glorious culmination of this biblical story is inscribed in Jewish collective memory. But African Americans knew they had not seen "de Judgment Day." Instead, they had found "slum ghetto[s]" (viii) on the hard pavements of the industrial North, not the milk and honey that "Mammy had been singing about in the cotton fields for many years" (vii), not the touted unlimited opportunities for prosperity and equality, with no "color problem," of the North. Brown asked rhetorically, where do those who have seen the "promised land" and found it spectacularly insufficient go? "[W]here does one run to when [one is] already in the promised land?" (viii).

For this reason, perhaps, Brown also evoked the Pan-African narrative of Ethiopianism, the notion of a return to an ancient homeland—not Palestine or Israel, but Ethiopia. Later I explain Brown's representation of a return to Ethiopia via a detour to Egypt, a pivotal area of the historical meeting among Christians, Muslims, and Jews. I want only to highlight here that the evocation of a homeland in Ethiopia offers a recontextualized, non-Western setting for La Malinche as a point of creolized and hybrid origins. Just as blackness is mobile, so too is the trope of La Malinche.

2. ERNST PAPANEK AND A JEWISH TRADITION

The first forefather is Ernst Papanek, a Jewish émigré from Austria and survivor of the Holocaust. An educated professional, Papanek is headmaster at Wiltwyck,[19] a rehabilitation center where Sonny is sent by the court to live for two and a half years. Papanek's personal history is a metaphor of the Grand Alliance between Jews and blacks: the Jew, Papanek, lived the scourge of Nazi racism; his black youthful counselee, Sonny, is feeling (on top of the pressures of adolescence) the boot of racism on his neck. Papanek's name and Father Ford's religious title stress these men's roles as paternal figures, one "white" and Jewish, the other "black" and African Christian. Father Ford's story speaks of a black Afrocentric philosophy of black Third Worldism. By Third Worldism, I mean the political and social struggles of Third World peoples against European imperial aggression after World War II that had an impact on African Americans as well as on Chicanos and Puerto Ricans. Though Sonny chooses his own path, his decision arises from an intercultural articulation with Papanek and Father Ford.

In a conversation with Papanek, Sonny says that he wants to return to

Wiltwyck because he doesn't think he will survive in the streets: "I don't think I'm gonna stay on the street, Papanek, not for much longer. I don't think I'll see Christmas on the streets" (128). But Papanek, a bald man with a kindly face, speaking an accented English, a marker of a hybrid citizen, forbids Sonny the opportunity to escape personal responsibility. He believes Sonny can resist the temptations the street constantly puts before him and survive outside Wiltwyck. He tells Sonny a seemingly innocuous story about two frogs that fall into a very deep vat of milk. It is a story Sonny says he never forgot:

> They [the two frogs] kept swimming and swimming around, and they couldn't get out. They couldn't climb out because they were too far down. One frog said, "Oh, I can't make it, and I'm going to give up." And the other frog kept swimming and swimming. His arms became more and more tired, and it was harder and harder and harder for him to swim. Then he couldn't do another stroke. He couldn't throw one more arm into the milk. . . . *[I]t seemed as if the milk was getting hard and heavy.* . . . [H]e knows that he's going to die, but as long as he's got this little bit of life in him, he's going to keep on swimming. On his last stroke, it seemed as though he had to pull a whole ocean back, but he did it and found himself sitting on top of a vat of butter. (128; my emphasis)

This little fable, in which one might hear echoes of "Little Black Sambo," is about the power of will and struggle to change a medium that threatens engulfment.[20] It has the structure of an exodus: presence in a hostile environment, the threat of submergence, and a journey forward to freedom. That it is told by a survivor of one of the worst genocides in recent world history renders the fable meaningful and powerful. The fable speaks of deception and betrayal, if one assumes the vat and milk ought to be a medium of guardianship and nourishment. Instead of nourishment, these forces aim to drown, to wipe out, the individual (the frogs). The contract between the individual and the moral order of Western European Christian civilization (the vat and milk) becomes a nightmare. Through sheer persistence and discipline, the individual (the tenacious frog) escapes by using strength and wits and turns the atrocious environment into a foundation for salvation in the present and future.

The milk is a multivalent image, potentially functioning as code for many things, poverty among them. In light of my focus on black manhood, however, it can stand for both female and male pressures. On the one hand, the milk might stand for a maternal pressure that should nourish and support but works against the amphibian creature. To survive, the frog/individual must create a masculine order: he must struggle to transform the liquid milk (can one resist the maternal imagery?) into a hard, heavy substance (or the male imagery?). The transformation, the desired objective, suggests that feminine agency is less valuable than masculine potency and generative power. If read this way, Papanek's parable suggests the core premise of Moynihan's and Paz's narratives—the feminine ground that threatens masculinity—must be mastered. But the white liquid might also stand for milk-colored semen.[21] In this book, there are warnings against those primal sexual urges that overpower and dissipate men. Men must use reason to regulate their sexual energy: mind over matter, in other words, or, "You gon lose your brains through your dick?"[22] (117). In this light, we can read Papanek tapping an intellectual Jewish tradition in which the main "text" of masculinity is the "book"—education, intellectual development—not the cultivation of the warrior's body in military and sports ventures.[23]

This is where Papanek's narrative deviates from Moynihan's, because Papanek's mini-narrative ascribes mental and physical power and potential to a black man. In brief, his framework grants him/them agency. I noted already in chapter 1 that the Moynihan report was a logical outgrowth of a long U.S. tradition of racial liberal philosophy, which had negative implications for black men, and that the term "liberal" in this context refers to a consensus of attitudes and programs about civil rights and equal economic opportunity embraced by American intellectuals and socially progressive politicians from the 1940s through the 1960s.[24] One key premise in the mental furniture of this liberal racial philosophy with respect to African Americans was that the trauma of slavery went so deep and so long that modern-day African Americans (working-class men primarily) were bereft of agency; they could only be recipients of "white" action, of top-down help from the federal government, if they were ever to attain social and economic parity with white men. Thinking in this tradition, Moynihan, a high-ranking officer in President Johnson's War on Poverty administration, sought ways to rectify the "deteriorating" (because it was matriarchal) structure of "the black family," where men could not develop agency to "strut," as he put it (62). And if Robert McNamara, President Johnson's secretary of defense, had made the "deadly connection between 'curing poverty' and supplying additional men for the military," as George Mariscal argues in his introduction to *Aztlán and*

Viet Nam,[25] Moynihan in his report made the gender connection between salvaging black manhood and the military:

> There is . . . [a] special quality about military service for Negro men: it is an utterly masculine world. Given the strains of the disorganized and matrifocal family life in which so many Negro youth come of age, the Armed Forces are a dramatic and desperately needed change: a world away from women, a world run by strong men of unquestioned authority, where discipline, if harsh, is nonetheless orderly and predictable, and where rewards, if limited, are granted on the basis of performance. (88)

Since all this was said in the wake of the country's massive escalation of military troops to Viet Nam and since Moynihan was well connected to state power, his plan of action was a self-interested one with dire consequences primarily for young men of color as well as low-income white men.

But let us return to Papanek's narrative. Whichever symbolism one chooses for the threatening force of the milk, Papanek's story is about a kind of struggle that is not contingent on *if* you try; rather, you *must* try, you *must* make it out, *or* you will die, for sure. That Papanek tells this story to Sonny speaks to an intercultural legacy of struggle on the part of Jews and blacks as a response to oppression. It says that freedom—the butter and the frog's trophy—is not instantly given or achieved but requires arduous work and self-discipline and that established structures can be changed; they are not immutable—liquid, milk, can be turned to solid, the butter. With every stroke, the frog keeps hope alive, generating a sense of possibility for change and liberation.

3. FATHER FORD AND PAN AFRICANISM

Father Ford, the second forefather, is a black priest in Harlem who preaches the Coptic religion, which dates back to the first years of the Christian church in Egypt. In the book's foreword, Brown calls the migrating African Americans "descendants of Ham."[26] These pseudo-"Hamites" arrived in what they thought was "the Promised Land" (the North), "twice as happy as the Pilgrims, because they had been catching twice the hell" (vii). Brown's allusion to Ham is important in light

of the gesture in the text to Pan-Africanism. There is a tradition linking Ham's descendants to slavery (Noah's curse) and to "blackness."[27]
Ham is thought to be the ancestor of the nations of North Africa, and
his descendants are said to have migrated to Egypt and Ethiopia.[28] This
tradition played a role in the U.S. South and in South Africa when some
rabbis and Christian clergymen would invoke Ham's curse in the Old
Testament as evidence to justify the inferiority and savageness of dark-
skinned and "heathen" peoples and their enslavement. In the nineteenth
century, black nationalist clergymen (for instance, Henry McNeal Turner,
an African Methodist Episcopal church bishop; Henry Sylvester Williams,
the Trinidadian architect of the first Pan African Conference; and Edward
Blyden,[29] a Presbyterian missionary born in St. Thomas who emigrated to
Liberia in 1850 and lived there for fifty-five years) transcoded this tradition of Ham's curse when they attributed an uplifting meaning to Ham
and his lineage, seeing in him and his descendants an inspirational basis
for the restoration of blacks to Africa.[30] They too found biblical evidence
to support their vision of a pledge from God to liberate African Americans
and Africans, but they looked to Psalms 68:31: "Princes shall come out of
Egypt; Ethiopia shall soon stretch forth her hands unto God. Sing unto
God, ye Kingdoms of the Earth."[31] This was the prophecy to the Ethiopians, an often-cited passage in the sermons of black nationalist ministers
in the nineteenth century. In this interpretation of the Old Testament,
black-identified and identifying groups are not a cursed race but chosen
peoples.

In Brown's narrative, Father Ford comes out of a contact zone of religious and political action in Harlem, a vibrant area of religious and ethnic
cultural activity—Islamic, Coptic, Western Christian residents, and Jewish shopkeepers, absentee landlords, and professionals like Papanek. By
chapter 9, Sonny has achieved a mature seriousness, no longer involved in
criminal activity, though still imbibing—with restraint. Several of Sonny's
friends are now squeaky clean—no drugs, no raiding of stores, and no
alcohol—as a result of Father Ford's inspirational teachings, which have
put them on a route to self-respect and dignity. Father Ford's purpose in
Harlem is to build up men. Like Papanek's frog rising to the surface of the
engulfing milk, Sonny's companions rise above their previous indulgence
in crime, drugs, and sex but using different tools than those provided by
white Western European thought systems. Father Ford offers Sonny and
his friends an ideology that blends different religious and ethnonationalist strains in order not to drown—as the resilient little frog almost did
in the milky-white liquid of the giant vat—in an environment of matter

over mind assigned to black men by white European civilization since the Enlightenment.

Not the *simpático* Papanek, Father Ford has "one eye that he couldn't see out of, and it was turned around; you couldn't be sure whether the back of the eyeball was facing you or not. . . . [It was] ugly and frightening at the same time." Once this "skinny and spooky looking" (238) priest begins to speak about the Coptic faith, however, he rouses Sonny's interest; Sonny finds his story engrossing to the point of producing a "hypnotic effect" (240). Brown's detail of Father Ford's vision is important. Does Father Ford look backward or forward? Is he a "forefather," an ancestor in Toni Morrison's sense of the word? Or is he a "faux-father," or even a "foe-father,"[32] like the nutshell scam artists in Harlem? The ambiguous description is an apt commentary on the contradictory pulls of the mythohistorical lesson Father Ford gives to Sonny.[33]

What is "Coptic"? Put simply, it is equivalent to the word "Egyptian."[34] Edward Wakin tells us that "Copts" means "people of Egypt,"[35] certain native residents of ancient Egypt who played an important role in the development of early Eastern Christendom.[36] I structure Father Ford's rapid, miniaturized lesson to Sonny about this ancient religion and ethnic community in three parts: Eden, Fall, and Redemption. It goes like this. In the beginning there was Egypt (Eden) whose singularity and stature, says Father Ford, ensued not only from being the very first ancient civilization (predating China, he says) but also from being a *black* civilization. When the Egyptians fought with "their brothers" the Ethiopians, the original Egyptian unity collapsed (the Fall). The Egyptians won the war and enslaved the conquered Ethiopians. At this point in the story, Father Ford shifts his focus away from Egypt—the oppressing territory to flee in a Judaic narrative and a crossing point for both Jews and blacks—to an identification with Ethiopia.[37] The Redemption is the millennial triumph of a black, African Christian Messiah who will come forth from Ethiopia to free its captive peoples. If this Messiah is not the modern Christian Emperor Haile Selassie (1892–1975),[38] descendant of the mixed union of the ancient Hebrew King Solomon and the Ethiopian Queen of Sheba whose journey to Jerusalem united Jews and Christian Ethiopians, then he will come, says Father Ford, from the Selassie dynasty. The Messiah, or mestizo son, will reinstate the black man as ruler of the world and will return people of African heritage, the "chosen people," to Ethiopia, "the True Holy Land."[39] If Israel is a Zion for Jews, Ethiopia functions as an African Zion for diasporic peoples of black African heritage, in Africa and elsewhere.[40]

For Father Ford, Ethiopia is also home to a piece of the Ark of the Covenant given by God to Moses and transported to Ethiopia by the mestizo son of King Solomon and the Queen of Sheba (241).[41] Here, Ethiopia serves as a feminine idiom (locations of "origins" usually are) for a Pan-African and transatlantic black liberation.[42] Encrypted in Father Ford's vision of a creolized civilization[43] is the Star of David, a central Judaic graphic symbol since the Middle Ages, in his repertoire of Coptic logos. He transforms it into the ancient Egyptian pyramid and genders it: "the pyramid straight up symbolizes woman, the inverted pyramid symbolizes man, and the two of them together are a six-pointed star, or the Star of David" (241). Herein is a strong intercultural icon marking Exodus as an intersectional point for Jews and blacks in Africa and the Américas.

In the midst of this "messy" hybridity—Egypt and Ethiopia, the Star of David, the miscegenational marriage of Solomon and Sheba, Jews and Christian Coptics, Jews and blacks—and after allowing for the indispensability of woman in his story of "origins" (the upper triangle of the Star of David; Queen of Sheba as the generatrix of a hybrid people),[44] Father Ford's visionary order of things, we will see, is as empty as the nutshell. He rewrites the story of origins in the Book of Genesis, transmuting the symbol of the snake and making murky the issue of who tempted whom?[45] Stating that the "snake . . . symbolized in the Garden of Eden was merely a sperm" (242), Father Ford asserts that Judeo-Christianity naively misread sperm for the snake because sperm under a microscope look as if they have tails. Here is his version of what really happened:

> The sperm starts down the brain, it goes into what he called
> the genital sac, and then it starts tempting. It makes you
> tempt women, because you get riled up when the sperm cell
> starts moving down. That's how Christian mythology took
> it as the snake tempting woman. The snake was man getting
> excited, the beast in man. (242)

The sperm's activity begins in the brain and invades man's physiological system of sexual potency. The moral is that men must exercise self-control, mind over matter: letting go, giving into sexual pleasure, is the Achilles' heel of black manhood. In Father Ford's little story, man is a self-enclosed, onanistic system that can control his own fate. As for women, they have no power whatsoever, not even as temptresses or traitors, as they do in Genesis, in Paz's poetic myth of the conquest of Mexico, and in Moynihan's synopsis of the black woman and black man since slavery—except as a placeholder for man's "sin" or as the container in which he "performs." In Genesis, in Paz and Moynihan, and in Papanek's anecdote—if we read the latter with the maternal imagery in mind—women have agency to emasculate men, to be "matriarchs" and La Malinches. In Father Ford's Eastern African vision, men do not forfeit manhood because women are effaced, turned into La Chingada. Either way, women come off badly. In Genesis, Paz, and Moynihan, it is madonna or traitor; in Father Ford's story, women have no agency to be either. Con or be conned, trick or be tricked: we circle back to the promise simulated in the nutshell game, with no there there. Father Ford's global vision simulates the heterogeneity of a *mestizaje,* but it delivers "purity." He has his cake of transnational blackness and eats it too as a misogynistic politics against women. Women are allowed to *represent* ethnonationalist identity, to *represent* nation building, whether Ethiopian or Mexican, but they are not to *participate* in its making.

Manchild in the Promised Land is a modern urban story of pilgrimage, migration, and failed expectations and realities; in part, it is an ironic commentary on and a transculturation of the Judaic and Pan-African formative experiences of exile and return. Papanek and Father Ford are communal patriarchs, and their formulations are competing permutations of two "ancestral" legacies of the 1960s that formed African American struggles to achieve self-determination. Such articulations resisted the currents of Moynihan's and Paz's modes of thinking that suppressed the masculinity of minoritarian men. But as influential as Papanek is in Sonny's life, it is to a woman—Eleanor Roosevelt—that Brown dedicates his book.[46] While they may "talk back" to Moynihan and Paz, these forefathers offer incomplete visions to Sonny because, like Moynihan and Paz, they mute the power and influence of women, who are equally important in Sonny's life. Sonny's nickname is apt—a "son," a biological and social product of two parents and an "adoptive" son of both male and female social influences that go beyond "family" in the restrictive sense of bloodlines and lineage. In the interlude that follows, I show that women are forces that prepare Sonny for his eventual encounter with his two forefathers. Only with the support and guidance of women is Sonny able to evaluate Papanek's and Father Ford's messages.

Interlude 3 GRANDMA KNOWS BEST:
THE WOMEN IN *MANCHILD*
IN THE PROMISED LAND

> *I used to wonder how cats who came up in Harlem*
> *with mothers like these could be anything but strong men,*
> *because they came from such strong women.*
> —CLAUDE BROWN, *Manchild in the Promised Land*

There is an incident in *Manchild in the Promised Land* that illustrates the pivotal role of black women in shaping black masculinity. At the time of this incident, Sonny's mother has sent her seemingly incorrigible ten-year-old son down South in the hope that his grandparents will banish the "too much devil in him" (42). She has taken the boy out of the city, but will she be able to pull the city out of the boy once it's in him?

Our hero's paternal grandparents are sharecroppers, traditional country folk whose family roots date back to slavery in South Carolina. They are part of the large, mostly black labor force that sustained the region's staple corn-crop economy. On this day, the rambunctious Sonny is outside on the plantation where his grandparents harvest crops. He is competing with another boy to lift a weighty sack of corn. Seeing Sonny straining to lift the heavy sack, his grandmother comes unhinged. She starts screaming, jumping up and down, striking him and stinging him on the neck with her switch, finally forcing him to drop the bundle. She threatens to kill him if she ever again catches him lifting a load too heavy for him. Dumbfounded and scared, Sonny is convinced that his grandmother is "going crazy" (50). He starts for the highway, determined to walk all the way back home to Harlem from South Carolina. His grandmother catches up with him on the highway. Even angrier now, she hits him again, this time with an even bigger switch for running away from her. She finally quiets down and explains to him that she hit him the first time to spare him his grandfather's sorrowful fate. She refers to the way Sonny's grandfather "swing[s] his left leg way out every time he take[s] a step" (50). It seems Sonny's grandfather suffers from a herniated testicle. Never having been treated medically, it has permanently affected his ability to walk and function in a "manly" way. Grandpa is unable to "strut." Moynihan wrote in his influential government document of 1965: "The very essence of the male animal, from the bantam rooster to the four-star general, is to strut. Indeed, in 19th century America, a particular type of exaggerated male boastfulness became almost a national style. Not for the Negro male. The 'sassy nigger' was lynched" (62).

This grandmother is an odd parental authority, if one assumes the middle-class child-rearing practices that Moynihan probably had in mind in his presentation of white nuclear households. First she attacks Sonny, and then she explains why. With emotional and moral authority, she teaches him a lesson. Using the grandfather as a negative role model ("do not do as he did"), she explains how he became physically and sexually dysfunctional. But first, to prepare Sonny for the point she wants to make, she reminds Sonny, with some urgency, about "the things" he has seen black men on the plantation cut out of the pigs they have just slain with an ax. Then she moves in for her own metaphorical "kill" with her earthy story about the grandfather's unhappy accident. She explains that right above the "things" in pigs—their guts—are the "chitterlings"[1] that "press against a thin window in pigs and boys and men." Sonny recounts:

> Grandma said if somebody lifted something too heavy for him, the chitterlings would press right through that window and the man would have a hard time walking and *doing a lot of other things* for the rest of his life. She said one time Grandpa was in the woods making liquor, and his dog started barking. Grandpa picked up his still and started running with it. The still was too heavy—the window broke, and now Grandpa had to walk real slow. She was saying that she didn't mean to hit me. She just didn't want me to break my window. (50–51; my emphasis)

An elderly country woman, this grandmother gives us an explanation outside the purview of Western rationalism. She speaks in a code of visceral organic images about something momentous. She takes advantage of a central graphic image she knows Sonny has seen in the raw countryside—the anatomy of a killed, gutted, and castrated pig—to present to him a parable about the precariousness of black manhood. Pigs have a terrible time in this book; they represent the "classic" victim, the one with absolutely no agency to control its own fate. In a Pazian schema of female and male sexuality, the pig is the *chingado*.[2] Grandma's use of the plural ("pigs, boys, and men") suggests a larger masculine context beyond a single male individual. The moral is that to survive, black men have to know their limits, both physical limits and the strictures that white racist society imposes on them. She aims to strike fear into Sonny to teach him a lesson in self-preservation because she knows that black masculinity is fragile, and it has to be protected. Her story resonates with the parent's fear for the black child who strays beyond the social boundaries of racial apartheid.[3] This resonance includes the corporeal punishments of lynching and mutilation of black male bodies, a sight that in the South of the 1930s was not uncommon.[4]

The savvy, mischievous Sonny dismisses his grandmother's story because he thinks the South is full of "dumb country people": they don't know any "boogie songs," not even "good blues songs," have no records or record players, and keep singing the same spiritual songs year after year (49). He jokes he had no inkling, until that day, that he had "chitterlings" inside him. Yet, as I explain below, he takes back with him to Harlem the image of the slaughtered pig and relates it to the way white society racializes his father, symbolically the gutted pig/*chingado*. He resists his grandmother's provincial thinking, but he gets her point: "She was saying that she didn't mean to hit me. She just didn't want me to break my window" (51).

1. GRANDMA AND THE PIG

My objective here is to bring to the surface the power of women that the forefather-storytellers, Papanek and Father Ford, suppress in their stories to Sonny. I present three "maternal" influences—one rural and two urban—that lay the foundation for Sonny to be able to engage with his masculine models later in life. These masculine formulations are modifications and not substantive revisions of the infamous representations of "matriarch" and La Malinche as slightings of the feminine. Papanek's and Father Ford's accounts pump up manhood, but they have the same drawback as those of Paz and Moynihan: the belittling, even the implied desire to evacuate womanhood.[5] If not for his maternal influences, however, Sonny would be in no position to absorb and transculturate the messages of the paternal ancestors. In my analysis, the women represent sites of resistance to Moynihan's and Paz's stereotypical images of "matriarch" and La Malinche. Who and what injures Sonny? Who emasculates a black male? The answers to these questions depend on where one stands, how one sees.

I relate the grandmother's metaphor of the "thin window" to the Moynihan report in this sense: Moynihan saw black women as pressing too hard against the "thin window" of manhood, breaking through it and emasculating black men. Let us remember that the report not only assumed an aberrational imbalance between the patriarchal white middle-class family and the matriarchal, state- and government-assisted black family but also proposed to correct the irregularity of power in relations between black men and black women. The black family, to Moynihan, looked upside down, since he held it up against the image reflected in the mirror of the patriarchal white nuclear family, by no means an immutable social entity.[6] He argues that a "fundamental fact of Negro American family life is the often reversed roles of husband and wife" (76). It was not right, not natural, he implied, that black men be powerless and black women powerful. To this imbalance, black men "may react with withdrawal, bitterness toward society, aggression both within the family and racial group, self-hatred, or crime" (80). In Whitney Young's compensatory model of manhood that dominant society attributed to men of color, which Moynihan agreed with, men of color compensate for their insufficiency by overreacting (see chap. 1). This is the official U.S. and Mexican take on *machismo*.[7]

Moynihan assumed a generic masculinity and a generic femininity, and the boundary between them was "natural"—so natural, in fact, that their separation went without saying. Moynihan assumed that his notions of masculinity and femininity were "dominant," in the sense that Richard Terdiman has described it: "the discourse . . . [that is] grant[ed] the structural privilege of appearing to be unaware of the very question of its own legitimacy."[8] The "dominant" is the discourse whose privileged status exempts it from justifying its claims at all. In short, for Moynihan, black women had to step down and let black men be breadwinners and heads of family, earning and controlling the "paycheck," and women were to be subservient, in the home, raising children, dependent on their mates, just as the white woman was doing in her middle-class family.[9] Black women must let the black man "strut."

Moynihan's boundaries mark the point after which the family loses the synchronicity he thought it should have. According to him, black women had done what Paz said La Malinche had done: they had violated the boundaries that separated men from women. They had broken through the thin window. In Moynihan's reductive reasoning, men are men and women are women, two different and separate packages, and each must respect the boundaries that keep their roles and functions separate and unequal in patriarchal society.

2. THE PIG IN THE CITY

Does Sonny's grandmother fit Moynihan's profile of the "matriarch," the female castrator of black men? Is she, in other words, an example of the conventional La Malinche? It might seem so at first, if we judge by the surface lines provided us in Moynihan's report. Sonny's grandmother is the disciplinarian in this family, not his grandfather. She is the supervising agent who interrupts Sonny while he is trying to prove his manly strength—lifting the heavy sack—in front of his competitor. Thus she apparently upsets the pose of the warrior and epic hero, predicated on the equation might equals masculinity. She is the authoritative presence looming over Sonny, forceful, powerful, and she refuses to give in, even when Sonny starts heading for the highway. She is cold-blooded enough to chop the heads off rattlesnakes and leave their bodies twitching in the yard until dark (51), an action that foreshadows a powerful, castrating grandmother. If we are looking from afar, if we are outside evaluators, as Moynihan was, we might well think this grandmother injures young Sonny's manhood. But let's take a closer look.

Assuredly, this grandmother is strong; she has enough force to shape a young black man, but her objective is not to unman him. To the contrary. She makes a Herculean effort to preserve and protect Sonny's potency—a far cry from Moynihan's invention of the matriarch who neither knows how nor ought to mentor her son(s) into manhood. I pointed out in chapter 3 that to solve the problem of black male weakness, Moynihan proposed to take young black men far from maternal influence and thus his recommendation to conscript them into the military, free of women, with all its deadly implications.[10] But Grandma, contrary to Moynihan, mentors Sonny successfully. This is evident not only because Sonny grasps her message but also because he does not easily forget the pig. The pig goes urban. Sonny imaginatively transports a few years later the pitiful pig from the Carolinas to a New York City courtroom when he realizes that the image he holds of his father—"bad-ass nigger"—is more specter than reality (*Manchild*, chap. 3).

Sonny and his father are in a city courtroom where reason and law rule. For Sonny, his father has always been a "bad nigger" who "'didn't take no shit from nobody.' . . . [E]ven the 'crackers' didn't mess with him" (48). A big scar on his neck incurred in a fight is Mr. Brown's totem of bravery in Sonny's eyes; he both admires and fears his father. But in this court scene, Sonny witnesses his father's diminution. Mr. Brown, "yessir[s]" the law-yer and "nod[s] his head up and down. He didn't know he had been hit in the head with an ax" (97). He is the Pazian *chingado,* the put-upon. Sonny knows the lawyers are "patting" them, in a word, emasculating them. It is the grandmother who has given Sonny the tools to analyze this experi-ence. Here Sonny redrafts the meaning of the pig:

> I kept thinking about the time I saw a big black man take a little pig out of his pen at hog-killing time down South. He took the pig and tied him to a post, *patted him on the back* a couple of times, then picked up his ax and hit the pig in the head and killed him. The pig died without giving anybody any trouble, and the big black pig killer was happy. In fact, everybody was happy. . . . The only one there who didn't have a friend was the pig. (97; my emphasis)

This sense of being stroked before being clobbered and disemboweled is an echo of the story told to him by his grandmother. In these circum-stances, Sonny longs for the "matriarchy" Moynihan considered so det-rimental to black men, and he cannot wait to exit this space and get back into the streets where he knows black men can be men, "niggers" on their terms.

Both this backwoods grandmother and the intellectual Moynihan have an investment in a common goal—the protection of black man-hood. Both are sounding alarms about black masculinity. Both perceive manhood at risk, but they have different assessments of what endangers it. It seems not unreasonable to assume that this traditional God-fearing southern woman—who has lived in the South all her life, who must have grown up during Reconstruction, whose own parents probably were slaves—has probably seen one, two, three, or more Negro men hanging from trees, "with blood on [their] pants" (292). It makes sense to think that she would want to do everything in her power to control Sonny, to ensure that he knows his physiological and, by extension, social limits. Literally, the "thin window" in her story is her folkway of signaling the membrane in "pigs and men and boys" that separates the intestines and the scrotum. Figuratively, it is the threshold that makes the difference between male sexual health and impotency, or in social terms, emasculation.

Both Grandmother's folkloric and Moynihan's scientific explanations posit "excess" that lead to "lack." For grandmother, press too much, and the thin window ruptures. The perforation marks the point beyond which masculinity is lost. Her metaphor recalls a mode of thinking about the fragility of the female hymen that, once ruptured, signifies in many cultures the loss of anatomical female virginity. In a broad sense, the thin window is a measure of the fragile quality of black manhood, just as the hymen is the measure of the fragile status of womanhood, the line between virginity and whoredom, purity and "damaged goods." Of interest here is the origin of the word "hymen," derived from the Greek word for "membrane."[11] Just as young girls might break their hymens by engaging in physical activity, young black men might break their thin window by overexerting themselves.

Moynihan considered the black mother to have "excess"; she, not he—the father—was marked with presence: economic, parental, and authoritative. The black woman seemed an excrescence, an abnormal outgrowth, because Moynihan assumed a Freudian geometry of the human body, with social implications, "in which the penis is the figure, or positive space, and the vagina the ground, or negative space."[12] The message is that the black woman owns *surplus* power, the consequence of which is black male deficiency. Hence black families in crisis.

Each in her and his own way, Sonny's grandmother and Moynihan feminize the black man, but the important point is that the grandmother's feminine projection is about preserving Sonny's value, not about emasculating him. The objective of her feminizing metaphor—press too hard and the thin window/hymen breaks—is to safeguard Sonny's manhood, his virility. Her feminizing metaphor defies the polarity of either male or female in Moynihan's report because what applies to women also applies to men. Sonny's grandmother implies that the division between male and female is permeable.

Moynihan saw the black family as an abstraction, an academic issue, grist for the mill of research. He had a fairly rigid view of how things *should be*. Whereas from where Sonny's grandmother stands, the question of Sonny's manhood is a felt issue, tangible and concrete. She is responding to the lived material conditions she knows black men face every day: how things *are*. She puts male sexuality at the center of her story, but she does not take away agency from Sonny. She lays the responsibility to know the physical and social limits squarely on Sonny's shoulders, and thus she avoids Moynihan's error of denying African American men agency. Sonny's grandmother is a rebuttal to the Moynihan report and its representation of the black "matriarch"—black mothers and wives—who, according to Moynihan, jeopardized and compromised black men's masculinity.

3. JUDGE BOLIN: AN ANTI-MALINCHE FIGURE

But one might argue that Sonny's grandmother is living in a rural area and Moynihan is talking about urban neighborhoods and that therefore these are two different worlds. My answer is that there is no neat division between rural and urban because many African American city dwellers had come from the rural South. Sonny's parents, for example, weathered migration to New York, along with hundreds of other African Americans "set flow'n," to borrow an expression from Farah Jasmine Griffin, from the agricultural South to the urban North after World War I.[13] The entrance of the United States into World War II and the need for cheap unskilled labor started the geographic displacements of "thousands of Negroes scrambling North," to quote Amiri Baraka.[14] *Manchild in the Promised Land* is about the effects of migration on families coming from a feudal South to the big cities, about how migration intensifies the pressure on families and the generational conflicts between parents and children. That Sonny transplants the pig into a city environment suggests that the frontier between rural and urban is porous.

The two women at the center of the two scenes that follow live and deal with the impact of migration. They are strong "mother" figures in urban settings. Under his grandmother and these two women, Sonny receives important tutelage that prepares him to absorb the lessons of the forefathers.

In this scene, Sonny and his mother are in a Harlem courtroom for juveniles, a public space where legal power and authority are officiated. My focus is the presiding judge, Bolin, a black woman whose picture Sonny has seen next to those of Joe Lewis and Jackie Robinson on the cover of a black magazine. Bolin is a professional, intelligent, assertive woman: a black female judge executing the white man's law in a courtroom for the black citizenry in the 1940s. Bolin speaks in a low voice, yet she is sovereign in her courtroom: "the softer she talked, the quieter everybody was and the harder they listened" (60). Defensively, Sonny dubs her the "mean queen" (61), a rhyming phrase that has ironic bittersweet overtones.

The rhyming phrase plays like a comic refrain, creating a slightly flippant tone, as though Sonny were at a loss about what to do with this woman who explodes the gender binaries that structure his experience.

For example, he is accustomed to thinking of strength in physical bodily terms. In his neighborhood, reputation is established by a boy's or man's ability to defend himself in a fight. His father disciplines him by whacking him—"Nigger, you got a ass whippin' comin'" (19)—because it is more difficult to talk through a problem than to use the lash. But Bolin's weapon is verbal language. She has everyone in court doing her bidding without having to lift a finger. To her credit, she is a woman who is not where 1940s society dictates she should be. She is, instead, a woman in a man's place, donning men's robes. Is she a woman? A man? A drag queen? This "mean queen" defies long-standing antinomies of white mind/black body in the history of a white imagination's coding of African Americans because she is an intelligent and brave black woman who crosses boundaries constructed as absolute divisions.

For his part, Sonny compliments her because "mean" is his idiom for "terrific," "physically strong," someone who "didn't take no shit from nobody" (48). But the conventional meanings—"nasty," "inspiring fear"—also apply. "She was bullying everybody in that courtroom with a low voice, even the men, who seemed like a bunch of turkeys, scared of a woman" (60). Like the evil queens of fairy tales, she has power to command—"off with his head!" And this time in court, Sonny's fate is in her hands.

Moynihan cast "the black woman" as supported financially by the white welfare state. Some African American women understood his characterization as implying that her need and ability to work and/or obtain funds for family support through public relief was an obstacle to the black man's social, moral, psychic, and economic betterment.[15] In Moynihan's value system Bolin's power would belong really to the "king," implying that the female had usurped the "throne," or patriarchal power. Sonny too probably shares this attitude. His rhyme serves partially to ridicule and delegitimize her "reign."[16]

The same surface elements in Moynihan's portrait of the allegedly "privileged" matriarch—standing in the way of the black man's advancement—are also characteristics of the compressed, elemental trope of La Malinche. Like La Malinche, Bolin seems "out of line" because she is an agent of the white state (the oppressor). She "betrays," apparently responsible for the ruin of her community because it may appear to some in her black community that she willingly aligns herself with the dominant culture. But Judge Bolin looms large as a "maternal" influence, reducible neither to Moynihan's matriarch nor to Paz's La Malinche. If we widen our gaze beyond Moynihan's and Paz's approaches and see through a Chicano

feminist woman's lens, we can locate resistant characteristics to "the matriarch" and La Malinche.

Judge Bolin, I think, qualifies as an anti-Malinche. For one thing, she
is not a matriarch on welfare but a professional woman earning a salary. She is also a maternal force but not literally a mother. Her arena is
the patriarchal space of the courtroom, where she exercises legal authority—deftly; here she negotiates between the black community and state
institutions for juveniles. Bolin allows Sonny's mother to approach her
bench, and the two women confer about Sonny's future. On the verge
of sending Sonny back to a correctional youth institution, Bolin decides,
after speaking with his mother, to release him temporarily in her custody
(66–67). Above all, Sonny knows that he and his mother are "real people
to [Judge Bolin]" (97). After the experience with his father in court, he
longs to be back in Bolin's courtroom where he knows he is not a "pig," a
white person's "nigger."

4. SONNY'S MOTHER AND
THE LIBERAL WHITE MALE

My third and last example takes place outside the courtroom, and it involves Sonny's mother (a matriarch?); Sonny, a young
(emasculated?) black man; and an unknown white man. I take this latter character as a stand-in for Moynihan, not only because the shoe fits,
but also because *Manchild in the Promised Land* and the Moynihan report
were published in the same year. This scene replicates the same triad of
relationships that is of central significance in the Moynihan report.

Out in the street, Sonny's mother, at her wit's end, chides her son: "You
little dumb nigger, didn' you hear that lady judge say she gonna send you
away someplace to a school?" (67). A white man standing at a counter
drinking coffee overhears her. A stunned Mrs. Brown realizes she has been
overheard. The white man, I speculate, is shocked that a black mother
would call her son "nigger." Indeed, how else could he react? For him,
the word will most likely have singular meaning—the worst racial put-
down one can call a black person—and he, the liberal white man, abhors
it. It taps within him centuries of the accumulated weight of pernicious
insults, intended to remind blacks they were once property and chattel.
In contrast, when Mrs. Brown uses it to address Sonny at home, she turns
the historic slur on its head, taking the racial sting out of it. When angry
with Sonny, as in this public incident, she uses it, out of habit, with hard-

edged affection. But because of the marked inequity of power here, the feisty perlocutionary effect the word would normally have for her is lost because a white man overhears, and the racial slur neutralizes the black mother's in-group meaning. Mrs. Brown, like the classically vulnerable La Malinche, is dumbfounded, speechless for having spoken too much.[17]

Sonny says, "[My mother] was ashamed that the white man had heard her call me a nigger" (67). Sonny's mother understands how her action will be interpreted and that the white man's meaning will supplant all its other meanings in her black world. She has reprimanded her son in front of a white person with *the* racial epithet that is "their" (whites') word for "us" (blacks), the word that strips black people of their humanity and black men of their masculinity. The word has this latter connotation of feminizing—diminishing men by implying they are femalelike—since it is intended to dilute their masculine pride and vitality. Even though mother and son are walking in their own Harlem neighborhood, where blacks are the majority and are serviced in public spaces, the effect of the word's meaning in a white world comes down on Mrs. Brown.

Who is this white bystander, drinking his coffee? We are told nothing about who he is or what he thinks. An anthropologist doing fieldwork in Harlem? Maybe. A lawyer doing pro bono work for black customers? Possibly. A social worker making the required visits to his clients? Perhaps. Regardless of who he is (or is not), he stands for the omnipresent white symbol in front of whom Mrs. Brown plays out the drama of Moynihan's black family, just as La Malinche enacted the drama of the Mexican family for Paz, just as Puerto Rican women determined the dynamics of the Puerto Rican family for Lewis. Let's imagine him a surrogate for Moynihan. Let's imagine he shares the same liberal values about race assumed by the long tradition of liberalism out of which Moynihan wrote. Let's imagine further that he is middle class; he means well; he wants to do good; he has lofty egalitarian goals. He is probably a social moderate, a liberal, an integrationist. He is certainly not a segregationist (else he probably would not be here in black Harlem), or a Klan grand wizard.

In my reading, the white man (to the extent that he serves as proxy for Moynihan) and Mrs. Brown have an investment in safeguarding black manhood. Moynihan perceived manhood at risk. So too did Mrs. Brown. However, each assesses what threatens it differently. The white man, as did Moynihan, thinks the mother's behavior injures her son, just as Paz judged that La Malinche debilitates her mestizo son. Mothers, in other words, should inculcate positive values of manhood in their sons—self-respect, honor, dignity—not humiliate them. He sees Mrs. Brown slighting Sonny because he assumes that his definition of "nigger" is operative in this situation. We can easily assume other options. One is that Mrs. Brown is protecting Sonny, not belittling him. Far from emasculating her son, as Paz argued La Malinche did and as Lewis interpreted Puerto Rican women did to Puerto Rican men and as Moynihan implied black mothers did to their sons and husbands, Mrs. Brown believes strongly in black manly manhood (heterosexual, of course); she knows its vulnerability, however, because she lives in a context of the demasculinization of black men by whites. Any erosion of masculinity signals danger for her. The reason she does not want Sonny "to strut," as Moynihan phrased it, is that she understands all too well the power of the oppressive social order and Sonny's willingness to challenge it. She attempts to rein him in, to keep him "in his place," as she would say, but not to purposefully damage or ruin black masculinity, nor because she believes the white world's beliefs about black people are right. She does it, rather, because she does not want her son to be a "bad nigger," in her sense of the phrase: "To mama [a "bad nigger"] was a nigger who was crazy, who would go out and marry some white woman. Mama and Dad would associate a nigger like this with the ones they saw hanging from a pine tree down in the Carolina woods with blood on his pants" (292).

It is impossible to contain the semantic orbit of "nigger," as is true of charged words in any language.[18] Sonny's mother has entered a dangerous crossroads in this scene, where at least three semantic meanings intersect. First, there is white society's hurtful racial epithet, the lowest point of nothingness, the *chingado*. Second, there is the intimate, sometimes jocular term used breezily by some blacks, as the mother does here. Third, there is Sonny's appropriation of the taboo term to signify his positive self-perception, the "bad-assed nigger." He does not forfeit or surrender the word to dominant culture. He transculturates it to fill his self with presence and affirmation.

What collides here is the white man's and Sonny's working-class definitions of "nigger," with Mrs. Brown standing right smack in the middle: between the white man and Sonny. Whereas Mrs. Brown knows that the white man's interpretation of her language is a serious matter, Sonny, in contrast, minimizes its effect: "Mama, that's nothing, 'cause I don' care, and it ain't none-a his business anyway" (67). Mrs. Brown is caught between a rock and a hard place. She knows that in the white man's world, "nigger" represents ultimate lack. Sonny, albeit motivated in part to protect his mother, tells her that the white man's opinion signifies "nothing" to him. Sonny emerges out of this with his own street definition of "nigger" intact, against the white man's value of middle-class respectability. Not without some measure of pride, he demonstrates "cool pose," unscathed, untouched by the infamy the white man's word would bestow on him.[19]

If we think in the way I suggest the white man thinks, if we are unfamiliar with "insider" linguistic codes for "nigger," we will think that Mrs. Brown, like La Malinche, "betrays" her son. She is a dysfunctional mother, "emasculating" her son in the eyes of dominant culture. She gives potentially dangerous information to someone who could use it against herself and her son. After all, if blacks can say "nigger" to one another, why can't whites to blacks? From this vantage point, Mrs. Brown would seem to be a willing accomplice in the service of the white supremacist "master" (from whom this generic white liberal man would dissociate himself). The white man's attitude, whether conscious or not, implies that Mrs. Brown makes her son femalelike (a "fairy") because it conflates power, as Moynihan did, with a warrior mode of masculinity. Women and homosexuals are presumably powerless and inferior.[20] This black mother would then be the treacherous La Malinche who has contempt for her own son (and people).

But if we at least know that this powder-keg word has strategic meaning for blacks in certain situations, we can tap this scene for conditions that characterize Mrs. Brown as an anti-Malinche figure. First, she is protecting black manhood, trying to steer her son away from self-destructive behavior. Second, this illiterate southern sharecropper mother, whom the clichéd hyperbole "mammy" might seem to fit since she cleans and does laundry in Jewish New York homes, has agency; she is neither villain nor victim. Like La Malinche, reinterpreted by Chicana scholars as an enabling force, she has knowledge about how her action will be perceived. She knows how "the eyes of others" assess her soul by the "tape of a world that looks on in amused contempt and pity."[21] Although she speaks nary a word, she "[looks] down at the floor real fast" (67), a gesture that implies consciousness and feelings. How could she not feel badly? Third, she did not do this deliberately, a condition that resists the it-goes-without-saying destructive impulses of Moynihan's matriarch and Paz's La Malinche.

In Paz, the mestizo son of La Malinche is marked with the stigma of shame of his mother's rape by the father and of her abandonment of him. This shame wounds the son, or so the story goes. Moynihan told the same story: the mother is the causal agent who jeopardizes black male masculinity. This was Moynihan's "tangle of pathology" (76). But here a fourth condition moves Mrs. Brown toward an anti-Malinche figure: Sonny feels no shame. The incident washes off him like water on a duck's back. Mrs. Brown's shame ("she was ashamed that the white man had heard her call me a nigger") stays contained in her space without passing to the son. Sonny's relationship to the white world is not mediated or dependent on his mother's ideas or actions. He states, "Mama, that's nothing, 'cause I don' care" (67). The urban, combative Sonny with no firsthand connection to the legacy of violence, injustice, and forced segregation of the Deep South and Jim Crow that characterized his parent's sharecropping experiences before coming North steps back for nobody. Sonny's mother does not produce the effect official society (Moynihan) attributed to her. This is important because Sonny (or Brown) does not subscribe to the role assigned the black man by Moynihan in his script: victim to be rescued.

Like the first and second scenes involving Sonny's grandmother and Judge Bolin, this scene contains debilitating conditions that would link a black woman to Paz's La Malinche and to Lewis's Puerto Rican mothers—dangerous and castrating. But there are also features that suggest none of them fit this reductive stereotype. These features are important because they show how misleading pat assumptions can be, how much depth and complexity shallow stereotypes hide. If we do not strategically link Judge Bolin and Mrs. Brown to the Pazian La Malinche, we do not bring to intercultural prominence a black mother's resistance to the official line of "black matriarch." By anticipating the interpretive frame of La Malinche in an African American context, we are able to see the crevices that reveal that these women do not align with Moynihan's "matriarch" and Paz's La Malinche. We also establish intercultural linkage between African American and Chicano cultural icons. Just as "nigger" has multiple meanings, so do La Malinche and "black mother."

5. THE EPITHET "NIGGER"

The polysemous epithet "nigger" appears numerous times in the pages of *Manchild in the Promised Land*. Since the book received so little attention at its first publication in the black community and since no reviews called attention to the term, it is difficult to assess how Claude Brown's free use of it was interpreted, but it may have contributed to *Manchild*'s reception as an unwelcome intrusion by the few black journals that ran reviews of it. Brown himself characterized the word as "perhaps the most soulful word in the world."[22] Today his book challenges us to reflect on a word of censure that remains a controversial flashpoint in our society. Its denotative and connotative spectrum is wide: from a conveyor of bigotry to an assertion of free expression, from a centuries-old scar of racial subordination to defiant opposition against it.

In the dominant cultural imaginary of the United States, "nigger" marks the intersection of race and gender, and La Malinche marks the same kind of crossing in Mexican and Chicano imaginaries. While "nigger" is primarily a racial term, connoting a black person forcibly emptied of humanity, its emotive inflection in white supremacist usage also connotes a black man forcibly emptied of his manhood. La Malinche primarily signals gender. In its official use, it genders a woman in terms of her sexual functions. Albeit less so than "nigger," La Malinche also has a racial base, since the cipher stands for a native indigenous woman of the Américas, and it always contains a residue of femaleness. I imagine the relation between the two icons "nigger" and "La Malinche" this way:

> "nigger" = race / gender (race is primary, gender secondary)
> "La Malinche" = gender / race (gender is primary, race secondary)

We might think of "nigger" as La Malinche turned inside out and vice versa. The important point is that in either configuration race does not replace gender or gender, race. Race and gender are simultaneously present whenever any one of these terms is enunciated. The terms differ only in degree: how much race? how much gender?

If the denominations of "nigger" and "La Malinche"—huge iconic images—are not mutually exclusive, neither are the denominations of Moynihan's matriarch and Paz's La Malinche.[23] These icons matriarch and La Malinche are predicated on assumptions both cultures make about men and women and that Moynihan and Paz understood and conveyed to their readers. In both narratives—Moynihan's report and Paz's *Labyrinth*—these denominations mark the "mother" as illegitimate origin and ruin of men, community, and/or nation. The "matriarch" is situated in the context of slavery; the Mexican and Chicano mother, La Malinche, in the context of conquest and colonization. These formulaic approaches thematize, explicitly or implicitly, mothers as "traitors," allies of the oppressor/colonizer responsible for the spoiling and deterioration of the subjugated community. They are the intermediaries who allegedly make it possible for the colonizing culture to impose its rules on the subordinated culture. Although not a perfect match, we might say that Moynihan's "matriarch" is a U.S. version of Paz's La Malinche.[24]

The two ciphers "black matriarch" and "La Malinche," with their reverse sides, respectively, "female castrator" and "La Chingada," have remained isolated in their own specific ethnic contexts. Black women conducted their own struggle parallel to that of Chicano women who took on Paz's stereotypical La Malinche and its appropriation by an ethnonationalist Chicano movement. Like Chicano women, they brought female gender to the fore; they did so by critically putting into relief Moynihan's demeaning image of the black matriarch. The report's troubled legacy and Paz's *Labyrinth* continued to lurk in the shadows in the 1970s when tensions between black men and women, Chicano men and women, catapulted to the spotlight at the height of the Black and Chicano Power movements. Maleness, encoded in the idea of "family," had been the unidentified elephant in the room when the initial responses to the report and to Paz appeared, between 1965 and 1970. In the 1970s black and Chicano women exposed and interrogated the taken-for-granted primacy of male gender.

My point is that these ciphers are intercultural. They have a lot in common, though the first two are English words and the last two Spanish (according to Octavio Paz, they come from Nahuatl). None of these designations is anybody's name.[25] Each cruelly misnames. Chicano and black women highlighted these icons in their respective ethnic terrains and in different registers, but this move common to both groups of women invited me to explore the crossing points between African American and Chicano contexts.

Four

OVERCOMING SELF-LOATHING,
LEARNING TO LOVE BROWNNESS:
OSCAR ZETA ACOSTA AND *THE
AUTOBIOGRAPHY OF A BROWN
BUFFALO*

> *What I see now, on this rainy day in January, 1968, what
> is clear to me after this sojourn is that I am neither a
> Mexican nor an American. . . . I am a Chicano by
> ancestry and a Brown Buffalo by choice.*
> — OSCAR ZETA ACOSTA

So speaks author and protagonist Oscar Zeta Acosta[1] in the coda to *The Autobiography of a Brown Buffalo.* What is refreshing about Acosta's phrasing is that he does not oppose Chicano to Mexican or Chicano to American, as was the usual practice of ethnic political action in the 1960s and 1970s.[2] Rather, he allows Chicano to stand in relation to both Mexican and American. He makes Chicano, the name chosen by the Chicano movement of the 1960s and 1970s for building political and ethnic identities, an intercultural term. His word "ancestry" suggests history, parentage, and heritage, not "race." This is Acosta's way of making his liminality "a place to be in and of itself, and for itself—an authentic age-old location that is not western-dominated."[3] Contrary to popular conceptions about Mexican Americans as "neither here—neither there," suggesting chaos and confusion, a no-man's land in other words, Acosta places "Chicano" on firm ground and in a space of substance and power. At the end of his "sojourn" (199), Oscar realizes that he is neither a Mexican nor an Anglo-American but a Chicano. A trickster writer, Acosta inventively twists words and their meanings and shows again and again that to be "Chicano" goes against notions of racial and ethnic purity.

I stand naked before the mirror, preocupación con el cuerpo adornado—Adelante del espejo me veo imagen...hace simpático hacía mente. Every morning of my life I have seen that brown belly. From every angle. I always a fat kid. I suck it in and expand and then brown it. Possibly a loss of a pound here, a pound there? I put my hands to the hips, sand baked el-bows out like wings, and suck that air and recall that Charles Atlas turn profiled to the floor-length reflection. It tighten's...that I can remember that I has notchanged. I wa

Body Builder was a ninety-nine-pound weakling when the beach bully kicked sand in his girlfriend's pretty face. Perha ps my old mother was right. I should lay o ff those Snicker bars, those liverwurst s and wiches with gobs of mayonnaise an d those Goddamn ed caramel sundaes. B ut look, if I suck it in just a wee bit m ore, push that b elly butt on up against the back i can ...you see ill hat w ly come sure pass to

David Avalos 9/04
Apologies to
Covarrubias

1. ARC OF *THE AUTOBIOGRAPHY OF A BROWN BUFFALO*

Published in 1972, seven years after *Down These Mean Streets* and five years after *Manchild in the Promised Land*, *The Autobiography of a Brown Buffalo* recoded the process of Americanization presented by Piri Thomas and Claude Brown. While Thomas and Brown described forward-looking life journeys of adolescent boys in the direction of assimilation, uneven though this assimilation was, Acosta deliberately subverted this familiar Ellis Island model of white ethnicity and "progress." Beginning where Brown and Thomas—quasi-assimilated men of color—closed theirs, Acosta's book opens with the protagonist, Oscar, already an assimilated Mexican American of thirty-three. Piri and Sonny entered the legal system at the wrong end, but Oscar comes into it legitimately. He is a lawyer, a disgruntled and dysfunctional lawyer but a man of the law nonetheless. Leading a largely unsatisfactory life, in flight from himself and his lawyerly responsibilities, on the verge of an emotional and physical breakdown, Oscar turns his back on middle-class life and all it stands for. He jettisons his law license—a talisman of middle-class respectability—and on August 1, 1967, he hits the state highways, in search of "a giant Rolaid, a mysterious Pepto Bismol for [his] hurts" (189). With "no maps" or "plans of any kind whatsoever" (103), he "plunge[s] headlong over the mountains and into the desert in search of [his] past" (71). He knows not what he moves *toward* or flees *from*.

The Autobiography of a Brown Buffalo and its protagonist represent sites where different cultural histories cross; they are signs of an intercultural crossroads. Both in the context of its publishing history and its antiassimilationist perspective, Acosta's book is about liminality, about "betwixt and between," to borrow Victor Turner's well-known phrase.[4] The book and Oscar are in the space of transition itself, rather than in the particular end poles "between which [liminality] is taking place" (Turner 96). Acosta's place, or *sitio* (Oscar/Acosta uses this Spanish word in the *Autobiography* [15]) is *on* the edge, *on* the threshold of "Mexican" and "American"—neither purely center nor purely margin. As I move through this chapter and the interlude that follows, I explore various terrains of liminality to show how Oscar moves from a not-anymore quasi-assimilated Mexican American into a yet-to-be "Chicano by ancestry and a Brown Buffalo by choice" (Acosta, *Autobiography* 199).[5] I want to show that although Acosta wrote his book during the ethnonationalist identity-building politics of the Chicano movement, he cannot invent himself without engaging in conversation with others.

2. PUBLISHING HISTORY

Acosta entered counterculture folklore when the famed journalist-writer Hunter S. Thompson breathed literary life into him in *Fear and Loathing in Las Vegas* (1971), Thompson's best-selling account of how he and Acosta turned a journalistic assignment to cover the National District Attorney's Convention on Narcotics and Dangerous Drugs in Las Vegas into an excuse to overindulge, ironically, in booze and drugs. In *Fear and Loathing in Las Vegas,* Thompson portrayed Acosta as an exotic "300-pound Samoan attorney" and transformed him into the uninhibited, Rabelaisian "Dr. Gonzo,"[6] with a gargantuan appetite for food, drugs, and dangerous living. Thompson's audience, then, first encountered Acosta as a fictional image, an invention rather than a factual person. When *The Autobiography of a Brown Buffalo* appeared in 1972, one year after *Fear and Loathing,* white audiences filtered it through Thompson's fictional creation and Acosta's connection to Thompson. Acosta, a reliably enjoyable companion, was Thompson's sidekick in both fiction and fact. Together, in *The Autobiography of a Brown Buffalo,* they seemed like a parody of the Lone Ranger and Tonto, a classic white man/man of color arrangement.

Unlike *Down These Mean Streets* and *Manchild in the Promised Land,* which were published initially by mainstream presses, *The Autobiography of a Brown Buffalo* was originally published by Straight Arrow Books, a small San Francisco press. Not until seventeen years later, in 1989, did a major publishing house, Random House's Vintage Books, republish it. What explains this delayed move from a small to a mainstream press? A handful of male Chicano scholars wrote brief reviews in Chicano journals in the early 1970s, but for the time, it was a relatively neglected book.[7] One likely reason was that it appeared "out of bounds" to its potentially "ideal" audience—Chicano men and women[8]—for the same reason that it was noted almost immediately by a white counterculture and mainstream audience.

Acosta's tie with a member of dominant society proved momentarily disadvantageous for him with Chicano audiences. The times were such that a Chicano readership would have seen Acosta as a "token boy" of the white man. Acosta's personal (albeit complex) friendship with Thompson was bittersweet. On the one hand, it gave him entry to counterculture and mainstream audiences and to the publishing world. Thompson's contacts were instrumental in Acosta obtaining a contract for the publication of *The Autobiography of a Brown Buffalo*.[9] On the other hand, Acosta too helped his white mentor: he gave Thompson entry into the barrios of East Los Angeles, but this linkage with Thompson also made Acosta's Chicano cohorts wary of an association with someone they perceived as an intruder, a *gabacho*.[10]

In the introduction to the 1989 edition of *The Autobiography of a Brown Buffalo*, Thompson referred to Acosta as a "dangerous thug" (5), a "rotten fat spic" (6), an "overindulged brown cannonball of a body" (6), and a "high-powered mutant" (7). But long before Thompson wrote these words, Acosta already engaged in the ironic banter that characterized his relationship with Thompson. In the *Autobiography*, Oscar and Karl King (Acosta's fictional proxy for Hunter S. Thompson) cut each other down with racial slurs (139). Chicano men and women, influenced by the strict nationalist agenda of the Chicano movement and tired of seeing themselves continually represented in the commonplace, disparaging stereotypes of 1940s and 1950s print and visual media, kept their distance from Acosta's book.

There is, I think, another reason for this seventeen-year hiatus. Oscar was far from either the heroic protagonist, in a classic epic sense, or the innocent preadolescent boy the Chicano movement prescribed and sanctioned. A sexually semi-impotent hero, with a "limp prick" (184), bleeding ulcers, and a discouraging blank for a future, Oscar hardly qualified for poster child of the Chicano movement. He made use, ironically I believe, of stock responses: his racial slurs about himself and others and his myopic view of women as sexual objects would have offended Chicano and women audiences at a time when "minorities" and women disagreed fiercely that stereotypes were trivial and harmless.[11] Hence Chicano demand for the book during the 1970s proved inconsequential. By 1981, when the first review appeared, the nationalist agenda of the Chicano movement had waned and Chicano readers were in a better position to understand that Mexican Americans confronted their ancestral and historical past in myriad ways. In other words, people adjudicate identities in different ways. By the mid- to late 1980s, there was demand for *The Autobiography of a Brown Buffalo* and *The Revolt of the Cockroach People*, Acosta's sequel about his actual participation in key events of the Chicano movement.

3. A CHICANO ROAD NARRATIVE

Two of the three authors I present in this book re-create literal mini-geographic journeys, taking their protagonists from New York City to the South: Piri to Galveston, Texas, and Sonny to the rural Carolinas. Acosta, however, not only changes the direction of the journey but also makes the road the leitmotiv. *The Autobiography of a Brown Buffalo* is a road narrative.[12] Oscar's time on the road represents his break with his middle-class, assimilated self, the formation of a link to his *mexicano* past, and the preparation for his high-end purpose as leader of the brown buffalo people. The road is the space of liminality.

In choosing this antidomestic genre that eschews private space, Acosta tied the book to a larger tradition of travel writing initiated by some of the iconic figures of the white counterculture literary movement. Even before Thompson's *Fear and Loathing in Las Vegas,* for example, Jack Kerouac's *On the Road* (1957) established the road novel as a literary rejection of the increasing conformity of the postwar period. However, whereas Kerouac's hero begins his automobile trip on the East Coast and travels to San Francisco and Los Angeles, Acosta, a longtime California resident, begins his trip in San Francisco and goes halfway across the country before venturing into Mexico. After Oscar has driven across the western United States, a trip that takes up most of the six-month temporal span of the novel, he boards a Greyhound bus to El Paso and crosses the international border into Mexico. Although in *On the Road* Kerouac also sent his characters into Mexico toward the end of their road trip and although Acosta seems to share Kerouac's one-dimensional Hollywood view of Mexico and its border towns—the typical bordello scenes, for example—still the crossing of the border for Oscar is different. It means a return to his Mexican-born parents' land and raises culturally specific issues of race and sex that it would not have done for Kerouac and the Beats.

Acosta also ties his book to a heroic U.S. mythology of game hunting by making "Papa" Hemingway's grave in Ketchum, Idaho, in the U.S. heartland, one of Oscar's road stops, "a simple, flat burial ground for the local citizens of Ketchum" (104). However, unlike Hemingway, Oscar's masculine identity is not about killing big animals. In fact, Oscar, by inventing himself as the "brown buffalo," establishes a relationship with the slaughtered indigenous creatures whose heads have been "rack[ed] . . . on . . . living room walls as trophies" (199). He is the hunted, not the hunter: "I'm on the loose, can't you see?" (36); "just a fucking buffalo on the lam"

(99). Acosta makes an intercultural gesture to Native American culture with his invocation of the buffalo in his title and in the text. He links Native American cultural signs to his Mexican-Chicano ancestry in that he is a *brown* buffalo. For some Native American groups, such as the Plains Indians,[13] the buffalo is sacred but also fragile and vulnerable. Acosta appropriates this animal's Native American and Euro-American signification—its raw animality, its flesh,[14] its restlessness and homelessness, its sacred majesty and vulnerability—and links it to his own Mexican-Chicano ancestry. Oscar's physical and cultural body, once his albatross, becomes his "brown buffalo," his collective phoenix, and he makes it his totemic sign. Acosta's attachment to this wild American bison, nonpredatory and connoting pristine land and its original inhabitants, suggests he sees himself connected to the land and people, destroyed and displaced in the name of New Spain's settlement of the Southwest and U.S. westward imperial expansion.

The temporal trajectory structuring this Chicano road narrative falls into present and past. The opening chapters (1 through the beginning of 5) precede Oscar's time on the road. They make up his present, which is continued in the road trip chapters (6, 8, 10, 12, 14–16). The preroad chapters are set in San Francisco[15] during Haight-Ashbury's Summer of Love; the road chapters take place primarily in the ski resorts and expensive tourist towns of the mountain states Nevada, Idaho, and Colorado—odd places to find the warm-blooded Oscar, who was born in El Paso and raised in landlocked Riverbank, California. Riverbank is near Modesto, in the San Joaquin Valley; its sign welcoming strangers reads, ironically, "The City of Action" (72). Instead of initiating Oscar's quest for self-discovery with a trip south to Mexico, in the direction of the geographic area sanctioned by the Chicano movement, Acosta sends Oscar north to Sacramento and east of California to the Nevada side of Lake Tahoe; Ketchum and Sun Valley, Idaho; to Alpine, "a small, western town, high in the Rockies" (136),[16] where he meets Karl King; and then to Vail, Colorado. Acosta's road narrative, then, is aligned with and subverts both a tradition of the white counterculture road novel and the Chicano aesthetic and political tradition that posited Mexico as a point of origin for a nationalist identity. *The Autobiography of a Brown Buffalo* cannot be contained within itself. In form and content, it is created in conversation with other cultural traditions.

Oscar's past—his formative years in rural Riverbank, his experiences in the U.S. Navy and Panama—is told in five flashback chapters (6, 7, 9, 11, 13), which alternately interrupt the forward-moving road chapters. The events of chapter 13 bring us up to Oscar's decision to enter law school, his passing the bar, and his job with Legal Aid in East Oakland; here the plotline intersects the events of the opening chapter in San Francisco and continues forward to Oscar's border crossing and beyond.

Chapters 14 through 16 narrate the final days of Oscar's six-month trek. At Vail, Oscar boards a Greyhound bus to El Paso—warmer, apparently more hospitable, Chicano terrain—and a streetcar to Juárez and back to El Paso. *The Autobiography of a Brown Buffalo* concludes with Oscar's return to California, this time to Los Angeles.[17] He resumes his profession as a lawyer, no longer just an officer of the court as before but a Chicano civil rights, activist lawyer determined to stir things up, using "politics of confrontation" tactics, in the Los Angeles court system. With a renewed sense of self-efficacy and vigor, Oscar anoints himself a leader of the Chicano social activist movement in Los Angeles,[18] a mecca for a Chicano movement generation. He stands ready, an eccentric and vociferous lawyer, to present "the demands for a new nation to both the U.S. Government and the United Nations." At his side, he predicts, will be "one million Brown Buffalos." His sojourn comes to an end on January 1, 1968. By then, having graduated to a solidarity with a political community engaged in collective resistance, Oscar reenters the "real" world. Adopting an ironic grandiose tone, he says, "Once in every century there comes a man who is chosen to speak for his people. Moses, Mao and Martin are examples. Who's to say that I am not such a man?" (198).

4. OSCAR'S BROWN BODY

But before this "Savior" can lead a million "Brown Buffalos" into the "Promised Land" of Aztlán, he must strip off the self he has fashioned and that has been fashioned by social forces in the Americanization process. Acosta's point is that Oscar's problems stem precisely from his having tried, however unsuccessfully, so hard to assimilate—not because he has not tried. Oscar's quasi-incorporation into U.S. society has been a sloppy, irregular business.

Oscar's Latino body (flesh/*carne*) is a physiological measure for the state of his soul. His body tells the tale of a man who has been racialized and sexualized throughout his life by a white world that confronted him with allegations of his Mexican inferiority. When the book opens in medias res on July 1, 1967, Oscar stands nude before a full-length mirror in his Polk Street apartment in San Francisco. His nakedness prefigures the shedding of his assimilated self, the start of self-contemplation. He confronts the sexualized feminine and racialized male brown body of color he has been taught to loathe, a metaphor for "the unclean," "the dirt," rejected in the Americanization process. What Turner says in the context of explaining his influential category "betwixt and between" is apropos here. I paraphrase: those who cannot be unambiguously defined or fixed in clearly defined categories tend to be linked to the "unclean."[19] Oscar's body is a center of cultural energy; it stands for the unassimilable, a spectacular reminder that the social order failed to contain his difference and energy. Its brown color captures the tint of the novel's title.

As he looks into the mirror, Oscar focuses on his body surface: shape, proportion, and color. He sees excess poundage (250 lbs.),[20] a "big, brown ass" (12), "an enormous chest of two large hunks of brown tit" (11), and a "brown belly" (11). Oscar's sexual parts—"ass," "tits," "belly"—register bulge and excess mass: material that official norms of race, gender, and class (he refers to his "peasant hands" [11, 64]) of his time were not able to harness within their bounds. "Always a fat kid" (11), he is prone to self-consciousness about his body image and weight, though women are more likely than men to obsess about these concerns. As to color, he says several times that his arms, hands, and belly are *brown* arms, *brown* hands, and *brown* belly. Oscar paints himself in terms of "brown," the official color of pride and protest of the Chicano movement but which in his youth has been used to make him "other," and others call him "nigger" (88) and "Jigaboo" (85, 88), in the regions he has inhabited, especially his hometown, Riverbank. His brownness collapses into blackness in Riverbank, and the Catch-22 of black or white leads him to identify himself later in life as a Samoan, or as an Indian chief named "Henry Hawk" (10, 124).

Oscar's "brown protrusion" (15) is undeniable proof that he is male, yet this male organ is a hairless "flaccid banana" (51), and, like his belly and breasts, it is pendulous, extending beyond the limits of the torso. It is matter out of place. Oscar's "brown belly," "brown ass," and "brown tits" suggest female fertility and procreative powers, like classic figurines of pre-Columbian goddesses. The "ass" and "tits" are Oscar's constant standard for measuring women's worth; Oscar applies to himself, therefore, the same synecdoche that he uses for women, acknowledging his own effeminacy. What he does to them he does to himself. His negative sense of self pulls in negative visions of others. These elements—a clunky, corpulent, brown body, a "limp prick" (184), and "abandoned lily" (52), feminine markings too glaring to ignore—represent rejected matter in the ordered, "pure," and masculine system of assimilation.

The ordeal of assimilation for this man of color takes its toll. Oscar's physiological functions irrupt to conduct an insurrection against the body's racialized and sexualized status. His gastrointestinal, digestive, and neurological systems are breaking down: "green bile" (25) in his mouth, reflux from a "sour stomach" (21) and burning chest. The "gurgling convulsions [that come] from down under" (12) are the result of his stomach ulcer. His bowels malfunction. He is constipated. Bending over the toilet, the self-proclaimed "champion pukerupper" (12) vomits to rid his "gas-laden belly" (18) of the "refuse in [his] gut" (25). This turmoil in his lower body comes from drinking "booze" (12), eating the "hottest . . . hot sauce[s]" (165), "spicy gravies" (12), salsa, "sawdust hamburgers" (25), and those Asian entries from Wing Lee's food counter that get Oscar through law school: "beancake with the blackbean sauce" (13), "Chinese curry" (25), "Wing Lee's won-ton soup" (37) and "hot rolls of pork and chicken" (13). Oscar finds intercultural foods irresistible to his palate as well as nourishing for his soul, but he cannot digest them comfortably. Acidic, spicy foods aggravate his "jangled nerves" (18): "My huge body is a massive quivering nerve that shakes inside the dark blue Macy's suit my father gave me when I graduated from law school a year ago" (27).

Oscar quibbles with Dr. Serbin, his Jewish psychiatrist of ten years. He grows prickly and defensive when criticized by Serbin about the root of his mental anguish. Oscar believes the cause is physiological—the stomach ulcer he has suffered since eighteen. Serbin, however, thinks Oscar's sagging organ and spirits are the result of unhealed psychological wounds, his inability to confront his own agency and reality. As a Legal Aid attorney, Oscar defends "the poor, the downtrodden and the lonely" (20), the husbandless, low-income, desperate "unkempt women with bloody noses and black eyes from the old man's weekend drunk" (21) who come to his office seeking his aid. These women, with matted hair and "grubby . . . kids," line up outside Oscar's office for Temporary Restraining Orders (TROs) (21).

But Oscar cowers under the strains of the job, pleading that he is a "mere pretender" (30), only posing as a lawyer. Female transsexuals want Oscar to annul their heterosexual marriage contracts; others bring him "tattered contracts with coffee stains" (28), hoping he will reinstate their defaulted loans with Household Finance. His reactions are telling:

And they [the women] want *me* to counsel them!

No, not today. . . . I duck into the toilet. If they even see me, their expectations will increase. Things are bad enough for these poor suckers without having to cry over me. (24–25)

With unsentimental seriousness, Serbin refuses to accept Oscar's defenses. He pokes fun at Oscar for thinking himself a victim: "Oh, of course, you can't give them [the women seeking TROs] any false hope. After all, you're just a little brown Mexican boy" (25). Serbin attributes Oscar's problems to "[s]ex and race. It's one and the same hangup" (19). The plain truth is that Oscar's angst is psychosomatic: his racial and sexual anxieties are inseparable from his gastrointestinal pains.

Let's explore the relationship between mind/body in more detail. Oscar's choice in foods is a metaphor for his need to be out of bounds, his unpinnableness to either *here* or *there*. "What value is a life without booze and Mexican food?" he complains. "Can you just imagine me drinking two quarts of milk every day for the rest of my life?" Six doctors have warned: " 'Nothing hot or cold, nothing spicy and absolutely nothing alcoholic.' Shit, I couldn't be *bland* if my life depended on it" (12). Oscar cannot stay within the parameters of the diet set by medical wisdom. He will not be fenced in. But when he goes "out of bounds," into an "intercultural" savory food realm, to swallow bits of other people's culture, he suffers acute indigestion. Something similar happens when he exercises his sexual cravings for blond, blue-eyed, white girls. Oscar is exogamous, attracted to girls of a culture "forbidden" him; his intercultural sexual appetite is outside the boundaries set by society's norms prohibiting miscegenation.

Take, for example, Jane Addison of Oscar's high school days. Oscar's title for Jane, the "original *Miss It*" (90), denies her the convention of gender. Jane, a shy "pig-tailed American girl" (88) from Bend, Oregon, with "red acne all over her beautiful face" (89), whom Oscar dreams of "every night for two years" (90), shimmers just out of his reach. After earning the manly status of hero among his buddies by finally beating up the school bully, an "Okie"[21] by the name of Junior Ellis, Oscar is confident he has risen in Jane's estimation. But his precipitous rise to "hero" turns into rapid disillusionment when just moments after the fight, shy Jane, back in the classroom, in the seat right behind him (Acosta, Addison), scorns him by yelling to the teacher in front of the class, "Will you please ask Oscar to put on his shirt? . . . He stinks" (94).

Devastated by this shameful embarrassment, Oscar conjures up this image of himself:

> I *am* the nigger, after all. My mother was right. I am nothing but an Indian with sweating body and faltering tits that sag at the sight of a young girl's blue eyes. I shall never be able to undress in front of a woman's stare. I shall refuse to play basketball for fear that some day I might have my jersey ripped from me in front of those thousands of pigtailed, blue-eyed girls from America. (94–95)

Oscar's shirtless, sweaty, and smelly body only excites Jane's derision, which in turn reinstates his self-loathing. Whatever self-confidence Oscar might have gained is gone. Having removed the "nigger" stigma with his victory over Junior Ellis, thus acquiring a new suit of masculine armor—"no Okie sonofabitch ever called me a nigger to my face ever again" (94)—he now loses the suit of armor to Jane Addison, who penetrates it right to his bones, tearing off his thin veil of security.

Oscar misreads the unethnicized blonds of his life.[22] They correspond, for him, to the hot, spicy ethnic foods he craves and the Mexican brunettes correspond to the bland, "two-quarts-of-milk-a-day" foods he finds plain and uninteresting. He thinks the Mexican girls of his school too ethnocentric: "they always stuck to themselves," refusing to mingle with others. They were, he says, "quite simply, a drag." Not "[his] type," they do not arouse "the beast" in him (112–113). The Latinas represent what the young boy who desires to assimilate wants to forget.

Acosta, here, performs one of his trademark tricks: he reshuffles, plays with, our usual stereotypes, using women as a synecdoche for cultures. An ethnic minority perspective of Oscar's time held, a bit too simplistically, that its culture was "hot"; in other words it had feeling, "soul." For Oscar, it is "cold," dry, and dull. The allegedly white, bland, and milky "cold" culture is for Oscar "hot," passion-arousing. The perspective of our national imagination would also stereotypically see Mexican culture as "hot," but here Oscar denaturalizes our stereotypes and opens the door into the intercultural by unlocking this association and making us perceive Mexican culture as "cold." In a similar playful vein, Oscar's passage of self-flagellation also shows the intercultural inventive transliterations Acosta performs. The Okies' "nigger"—they have told Oscar he is "a nigger faking it as a Mexican" (187)—is brought on by Jane Addison's contemptuous remark. This remark then slips into Oscar's English translation of "Indian," which for him means the stereotypical television images of the 1940s and 1950s—the "savage yells and tom-toms," "black and white eagle feathers," the "wild Indians" (86).

But before "nigger" can slide into "Indian" for Oscar—"I *am* the nigger, after all. My mother was right" (94)—it must pass by way of his mother's mediation of *indio*. For Oscar's mother, *indio* does not mean what Negro or "nigger" means in the United States. For her, light-skinned or dark-skinned persons could be *indios*. It has nothing to do with one's genetic makeup or physical appearance and everything to do with social class. It signifies unacceptable (to her) social behavior and comportment. It has to do with how one lives, how one behaves, what one does, and not with skin color. Anyone who behaves in ways Oscar's mother disapproves of is absorbed into *indio*. Yet she gives the word racist overtones because she inculcates in Oscar a desire to be "white" and always applies the term *indio* to "Mexicans":

> My mother, for example always referred to my father as *indio* when he'd get drunk and accuse her of being addicted to aspirin. If our neighbors got drunk at the baptismal parties and danced all night to *norteno* [*sic*] music, they were "acting just like Indians." Once I stuck my tongue in my sister Annie's mouth—I was practicing how to French kiss—and my ma wouldn't let me back in the house until I learned to "quit behaving like an Indian." Naturally when Bob refused to get up and salute the American flag, he was just another one of "those lazy Indians." And when my sisters began to develop their teen-age fat, as their *chi chis* expanded my mother was always after them to lay off the tortillas with hunks of colored margarine if they didn't want to end up marrying "some Indian." (86)

This is the way Oscar and his siblings hear their mother use *indio* at home, and they, being English speakers, translate it into "Indian." The absent presence in Oscar's thinking is the mother's *indio*. Oscar is suggesting that in his Mexican mother's social hierarchy, *indio* functions like "nigger" does for some "whites" in Riverbank, California. The white Jane Addison reconnects Oscar with his Mexican mother's racialized image of *indio* for "Mexican."

If there is one moment to which Acosta traces the origins of Oscar's "secret gnawing at [his] belly" (91) and his emotional current of self-loathing, it is the night Oscar comes face to face with Sheriff Lauren,[23] Riverbank's Texas Ranger. Lauren "plucks" Oscar's "feathers," an emasculating action. Oscar has told us previously that he dreams about helping Texas Rangers "pluck" (86) the feathers of Indians; here again Oscar identifies with the colonizing culture. Traveling in Ketchum, Oscar tells a "fat, pimple-faced cowboy" he meets in a bar that he is a Blackfoot chief from Oklahoma on his way to Wyoming to pick up a few bulls. "So you're a chief? . . . a *real chief?*" asks the cowboy. Recognizing what the cowboy assumes the figure of "Indian chief" means, Oscar aims to disarm the cowboy's incredulity or his expectations of how an Indian chief ought to look. "Well, I ain't got no feathers. But I'm the head man, yeh," replies Oscar (102). This statement on his road trip connects back to his experience with Lauren. In the present of Ketchum, Oscar is punning on his emasculation in his Riverbank past. A plucked "Indian," "no pubic hair," Oscar has no plumage to display.

On this fateful night of his encounter with Sheriff Lauren, Oscar is on a date with the "crippled" Alice Joy Brown (another flaw in feminine beauty?), the second "Miss It" of his last year of high school. Ordered by Alice's Baptist parents to sabotage the date—because Oscar is a "Mexican"—Sheriff Lauren forbids Oscar to see Alice again. He warns Oscar, "But under the law, if I catch you, I'll take you in . . . Savvy?'" (119). Lauren punctuates his order with "Savvy," a popular "cowboy" corruption (in the style of "amigo" and "Hasta la vista, baby") of the Spanish verb *saber.* Lauren assaults Oscar's ancestral tongue by transforming *saber* into the Anglicized "Savvy," striking subliminally a sensitive nerve in Oscar. Forget that Oscar himself speaks limited Spanish. "Perhaps if he hadn't thrown in that 'Savvy' bit," thinks Oscar, "I'd have kept still, but as it stood, I lashed out" (119). Oscar explodes and yells the vulgarism that some Mexicans, for example, Octavio Paz, consider the worst in the Spanish-speaking Américas, "Chinga tu madre, cabron! [*sic*]" (Fuck your mother, you asshole) (119). Thus "Savvy" distorts a word in Spanish that designates a cognitive faculty that ignites a visceral reflex: the mind-body tension. Lauren exceeded Oscar's threshold for how much deracination a man of color can take. Oscar has sought to ally himself with the culture that belittles him, but "Savvy" is too much: "The convulsions down under began on that night. The wretched vomit, the gas laden belly formed within my pit when the chief of police asked me if I understood. Savvy?" (119–120).

5. THE TWO OSCARS

I conclude this chapter by suggesting an intercultural connection between Oscar Zeta Acosta and Oscar Lewis, the two Oscars that
I discuss in this book.[24] Like his contemporaries Moynihan and Paz who
wrote about failed "ethnic families," Lewis wrote about a dysfunctional
Puerto Rican extended family in *La Vida*. As late as the 1960s, *La Vida*
offered to a mainstream U.S. audience one of only two national images
on Puerto Ricans; the notoriously stereotypical Hollywood film, Robert
Wise's *West Side Story* (1961), offered the other.[25] Both cultural products
were extremely pejorative depictions. However, unlike African Americans
and Chicanos, who expressed strong displeasure with Moynihan's and
Paz's unflattering pronouncements about them, comparatively few mainland Puerto Ricans responded in writing to Lewis's book.[26] I use Acosta to
fill this gap in the reception by considering *The Autobiography of a Brown
Buffalo* an intercultural response to *La Vida*. Just as I have placed *Manchild in the Promised Land* and *Down These Mean Streets* in dialogue with
Moynihan and Paz, I now present Acosta's character Oscar talking back to
Lewis about his conceptual "culture of poverty" and the historic War on
Poverty conducted by the Johnson administration.[27]

"Culture of poverty" was Lewis's umbrella term for the life habits
of marginalized people in developing capitalist countries of the Third
World. Economic changes brought about by rapid modernization in
class-stratified societies had relegated "the poor"[28] to the social margins.
The thesis was that the urban lower classes of Mexico and Puerto Rico,
the main areas of Lewis's research, lived, presumably, in a cycle of poverty with no hope of someday breaking out of it. More specifically, the
"culture of poverty" was a corpus of traits, supposedly innate and inbred,
that described the attitudes and behavioral practices of the marginalized
city dwellers of Mexico City and San Juan that kept them in a state of
perpetual poverty.[29] Long before he decided to do research in Puerto Rico
(ca. 1961), Lewis had done extensive fieldwork in rural Indian villages in
Mexico, but in the 1950s he shifted his focus to develop his family-study
approach in Mexico City's poor urban neighborhoods. Crucial for the
codification of his "culture of poverty" was his work among the *vecindades*
in Mexico City. By 1961 he had published several books describing and
developing further his ethnographic research and methods on Mexican
family subjects.[30] One of his most successful ventures in Mexico had been

his tape-recorded interviews, beginning around 1956, with the Sánchez family of Mexico City. His research in Mexico culminated with the best-seller in the United States, *The Children of Sánchez*,[31] an attempt to inte-grate new social subjects into Mexico's paternal order of national identity and modernization. Lewis was a paternal benefactor to the Sánchez fam-ily, a representative to them of the power and success of the United States and a representative of the culture of modernization. He seems to have been an especially important influence on the only member of the fam-ily who achieved literacy, the young girl named Consuelo, who admired Lewis and aspired to be like him (Franco 157–174). Despite Lewis's theory that the culture of poverty kept people locked into poverty—the gen-eration-to-generation component of his model—he credited Consuelo with breaking out of it.[32] In fact, Susan Rigdon in her important book, *The Culture Facade,* tells us that Consuelo Sánchez became one of Lew-is's assistants in Puerto Rico. According to Rigdon, Consuelo made field notes about her household observations of the Ríos family that were never published.[33] Consuelo's behavior and aspirations to upward mobility ex-posed the lie to probably the main characteristic of the culture of poverty, which argued that "[o]nce it comes into existence it tends to perpetuate itself from generation to generation because of its effect on the children" (Lewis, *La Vida* xlv).

Lewis was more enthralled with and felt more at home in Mexico than Puerto Rico. He had developed deep attachments to Mexico's people and was well versed in its history and cultural traditions. Mexico for Lewis had a great pre-Columbian and Hispanic history and culture, as well as great achievements in art and in the intellectual sphere. In contrast, his knowledge and appreciation of Puerto Rican history and culture were more fragmented and hastily acquired. His experience there was not the happy, fulfilling one he had had in Mexico. While working in Puerto Rico, thinking back to his work with the Sánchez family, Lewis remarked, "I suppose Consuelo would be a social worker's dream because she was so aware of the values of the larger society and in effect she was saying—if only I could be like the middle class."[34] Though he saw problems, Lewis respected Mexico and its people, especially the Sánchez family whom he had come to know well and who had proven compatible with his research interests and objectives.

Not so Puerto Ricans. By 1965 Lewis had worked with several Puerto Rican families (one hundred of them, he said [*La Vida* xviii]), but he chose to write only about the Ríos family. As anthropological subjects, the Ríoses seemed not to fit his parameters for the "culture of poverty,"[35] especially when he judged them through the lens of his work and personal relationships in Mexico. In Mexico he could at least idealize his culture of poverty, allow for more flexibility in the relation between the construct and the reality of what he found, and emphasize the more positive, adaptive features of his model. But unlike the Mexican families Lewis studied earlier in his career, the Ríoses presented a difficult puzzle. Indeed, Lewis even wondered if the endemic practice of prostitution put the Ríos women outside the boundaries of his subculture of poverty (Rigdon 78), that is, on an even lower rung of humanity.[36] It was harder to see Puerto Rico's "shanty town" population as gratifying informants for his research. In Puerto Rico Lewis seems to have found "poverty of culture," to reverse his own catchy phrase.

In essence, Puerto Rico for Lewis had no culture or at best an unhealthy one. Its history, he said, was "unusually sad. . . . [It was] a history of isolation and abandonment . . . with few glorious moments." The people he interviewed in San Juan were "more broken" by the Spanish conquest and colonization than those he had known in Mexico,[37] and they had a "higher incidence of hysterical symptoms" (Rigdon 252). Puerto Ricans had a "truncated" and "shallow" knowledge of their national history (Rigdon 247).[38] In Mexico Lewis had found strong men heading families, but in Puerto Rico strong women headed households and dominated weak men.[39] He emphasized the Ríos family's interest and expression in "lower" bodily activities—mothers practicing prostitution; women marrying twenty times, mostly in consensual unions; stepfathers seducing daughters; sisters succumbing to sexual rivalry; and mothers encouraging sons to masturbate to ensure virility. All in all, Lewis thought the Ríos family, and implicitly all Puerto Ricans, "closer to the expression of an unbridled id than any other people [he had] studied" (*La Vida* xxvi). The "uncleanliness," the "dirt," was unassimilable to his culture of poverty.[40]

The phrase "culture of poverty" enjoyed wide currency during Johnson's War on Poverty, when the subject of the poor and poverty and how to solve it rose to the top of the national political agenda. Lewis's culture of poverty was one of the major sources of information for understanding economic deprivation during the declared War on Poverty, and it was available to policy makers interested in lessening the gap between "haves" and "have-nots."[41] The social anthropologist Charles Valentine, a leading commentator on scientific approaches to culture and poverty and probably the principal detractor of Lewis's culture of poverty, states that it influenced Michael Harrington's *The Other America*, a pivotal study of economic disenfranchisement, published in 1963. Harrington's book, in turn, helped to popularize Lewis's phrase.[42] Harrington echoed Lewis when he argued that, notwithstanding the economic prosperity of the 1950s, "[p]overty in the United States is a culture, an institution, a way of life" (172). What is important about Lewis's reputed influence on Harrington's book is that *The Other America,* written in accessible English, reached a mass audience. Its objective was to awaken the public to the fact that poverty existed in the richest country of the world. It was a book that reached the top levels of government. President John F. Kennedy read it.[43] Moved and shocked that poverty was a fact in a country that John Kenneth Galbraith had called only five years earlier the "affluent society," Kennedy initiated legislative steps to address poverty. In his State of the Union address on January 8, 1964, President Johnson declared, "This administration today, here and now, declares unconditional war on poverty in America."[44]

The "culture of poverty," then, was an important piece of the War on Poverty and of the national discussion dedicated to the making of knowledge about the causes of poverty and the shaping of public antipoverty policies. Acosta's Oscar speaks back to both Lewis's construct and the War on Poverty. Like the Puerto Ricans who defied clear definitions and who in their liminality could stand for "the unclean"—the degraded—Acosta's Oscar represented a contravention of an ordered system. I discussed above Oscar's body as a metaphor for resistance to the order and classification of assimilation. Oscar represented the unclean, the entire cluster of deleterious effects of a culture of poverty, what society could not assimilate to its norms, thereby assigning him to the realm of the "inferior." He was matter out of place. Society did to Oscar much the same thing that Lewis did to the Puerto Ricans of *La Vida.* Lewis saw the Ríos family and their activities as pathological or unclean. Acosta, through Oscar of course, engages the stereotype of the unclean that dominant society had judged him by and that Lewis attributed to Puerto Ricans. Oscar's ironic and comic flaunting of his unclean body is an irreverent but creative violation of the norms of health (white, middle-class, heterosexual, forward-moving) implicit in Lewis's culture of poverty. *The Autobiography of a Brown Buffalo* ironically and dramatically flaunts the "dirt" that social science models such as Lewis's attributed to marginalized peoples.

Oscar's pathological behavior has a strong performative dimension and speaks to his id as a Chicano subject. His gestures are not the typically defensive ones of blaming the social order for one's shortcomings, because in writing the novel, Acosta has had to reassess his individual choices and take responsibility for them. He transforms the traumatic after-effects of assimilation into a novel that offers the perspective and cultural knowledge he achieved about his long-dormant ethnic self. The examples I have given in the previous section of Oscar's vulgarities fit into Bakhtin's grotesque carnivalesque,[45] or the Chicano dramatist Luis Valdez's mode of *rascuache,* meaning bawdy, ribald, of low taste.[46] Both carnivalesque and *rascuachismo* are strategies that discombobulate ruling hierarchies and superior authority. Acosta turns topsy-turvy the Lewis impulse of seeing the body as a source of the unclean. In emphasizing his ethnic body as the site of the unclean, he exposed the underside of a system of apparent health that rejected any agent it considered "foreign" and "contaminating" to itself. In *The Autobiography of a Brown Buffalo,* Acosta spoofs Lewis's presumably objective, Western-scientific mode of analysis, in which the social scientist is like a traveler who reports to his metropolitan audience the curious practices of the natives.

If the perspectives of *Down These Mean Streets* and *Manchild in the Promised Land* predate the closure of Lyndon B. Johnson's Great Society, then *The Autobiography of a Brown Buffalo* looks back at the Great Society, told from the perspective of one who lived "the glory days" of robust social reforms and the white counterculture and Chicano social activist movements. This means that Acosta enjoyed a good vantage point from which to speak back to the War on Poverty.

The War on Poverty is the novel's specific backdrop, and it calls to mind the social and political setting of the ideas of the "culture of poverty." Beyond the fact that the narrative of *Autobiography of a Brown Buffalo* takes place between July 1, 1967, and January 1, 1968, a span of time that places the novel's linear plot at the height of Johnson's War on Poverty, Oscar is, as was Acosta, a lawyer in East Oakland for Legal Aid, one of several antipoverty agencies of Johnson's Great Society.

Each morning, Oscar enters a "drab grey building" in the "heart of the Oakland Poverty Program's *target area*" (20). Oscar exposes with sarcastic irony and humor the futility and contradictions of the poverty programs, the die-if-you-do, die-if-you-don't of it all: "We have … training programs for the so-called black and brown people who know damn well they'll never get more than the two bucks an hour they get for training in the first place. We even help people with immigration problems. Mexicans who've been here longer than LBJ himself" (20). He also knows that shot-in-the-arm programs will not rehabilitate a citizenry that considers itself to have no stake in the system. "Doesn't LBJ know that Watts burned in '65? That Detroit rioted in '66? That the Panthers started carrying guns in '67? Am I to prevent all this with a carbon copy of a court order that com-

pels a Negro janitor to pay child support for his nine kids?" (28). Oscar
gives us a view of one not only involved firsthand in the morass of solving
poverty but also on the verge of a nervous breakdown because of it.

The two Oscars, then, mediate between economically marginalized
people and governmental agencies mandated by Congress to serve "the
poor." Whereas Lewis unselfconsciously replicated the tradition of color-
ing the sexuality of Third World people as pathological, Acosta uses irony
and humor to show that Oscar's self-loathing and self-abnegation are a
result of his internalized colonialism. Lewis saw himself in the role of a benevolent authority figure who made intelligible to the "developed" world
the behavior of "impoverished" people: in his own words, he mediates
between "'the very poor and . . . middle-class personnel—teachers, social
workers, doctors, priests . . .—who bear the major responsibility for carrying out anti-poverty programs'" (Rigdon 151). Oscar, in contrast, knows
he is not what "the poor" think he is; he is unable to deal with "the enemy
our president so clearly described in his first State of the Union address"
(*Autobiography* 22): "[W]e [lawyers] listen to . . . [the poor's] tales because
we have a mandate from Congress . . . and a pretty good salary to boot"
(20–21). The sequence of this sentence begins lofty enough but tips into
blunt honesty; lofty seriousness collapses into comic irony. Oscar cannot
mediate from the standpoint of a society that has racialized and sexualized
him. His dropping out critiques Lewis's task of paternal mediator, of the
classic ethnographers who make pronouncements about poor communities in "underdeveloped" countries they study and write about. The "king
of rascuachismo" ironically pokes fun at Lewis's seriousness and dignity
with his own avoidance of the challenge and panic about it.[47] Oscar Zeta
Acosta serves notice on the culture and war on poverty. I can imagine him
saying, "See, this is what you've done to me; this is how you've seen me; I
now take it and throw it back at you! *¡que se vayan pal' carajo!* [you can all
go to hell!]."

Interlude 4 THE BROWN BUFFALO PUTS
ON BLACKFACE

I turn once again to the text examined in the previous chapter, *The Autobiography of a Brown Buffalo,* but my focus here is Oscar's exploitation of one of the permutations of the La Malinche trope. This permutation is the Chicano pachuco.[1] The broadest historical meaning of the term "pachuco" refers to Mexican American marginalized male youths of 1940s urban Los Angeles who by way of their stylized dress (the zoot suit), their comportment (gait and stride), and their language (*caló* talk) announced their defiance to Anglo mainstream society and their refusal to conform to its defined normativity. They also refused the norms held by their Mexican and Mexican American families and society.

In official dominant canons of Mexican (and U.S.) masculinity, the icon of the pachuco has been weighed down with negative meanings and associations: violence, gangs, "willing victim." This last descriptor, a somewhat oxymoronic rendition, also has been used to characterize La Malinche: the woman who asks to be raped. This male system of thought grants women will and intelligence but only to consent to be used sexually by men. Likewise the pachuco: he is the hunted who attracts the hunter. The pachuco is a liminal companion figure to La Malinche and belongs to the same family of symbols; that is, La Malinche is the matrix, the prime focal symbol, and the pachuco is one of its extensions. While La Malinche represents the woman who invites her own rape, the pachuco stands for the man who invites his own persecution.[2] He is the invention of the screwed, penetrated male. Another way to phrase this is that he is La Chingada (another extension of La Malinche) in male drag. The intellectual who most vividly described—and constructed—the pachuco as a feminized and racialized man, in which the subtext is a drag queen, is (who else?) the Mexican writer Octavio Paz.

Acosta never spells out the term explicitly in the *The Autobiography of a Brown Buffalo*—perhaps because Oscar's youthful experiences take place in rural Riverbank, the infamous "City of Action" (72), and the pachuco is primarily a large-city phenomenon. I nonetheless make the pachuco my interpretive lens because Oscar assumes the pose of the racialized and feminized male implied by the thought systems articulated by Paz, Moynihan, and Lewis against men of color, such as Piri and Sonny. Hard as he may try to put up the closed aura of the traditional man, Oscar reveals the open, vulnerable man in almost everything he does. What is different about Oscar—different from Sonny and Piri, that is—is that Oscar pushes this stereotype to such fantastic lengths that the lie behind the banal classification becomes ridiculous, hilarious. Oscar assumes this stereotypical pose not to reinforce its power to debilitate and humiliate but to ridicule and neutralize its force, achieving ironic and comic effects.

Oscar is a trickster, a figure of fun and ridicule, and the pachuco lies at the core of his tricksterism. By "tricksterism," I mean a system of contradictory choices and moves, or performances, that energetic Oscar, with his penchant for theater and drama, makes. Oscar turns upside down the masculine systems we so often perceive as "natural" and unchangeable, the same systems that Piri Thomas and Claude Brown subscribed to and that attempted to unman them. The trickster is predominantly a Native American and African American trope,[3] but Acosta defies boundaries that restrict the trickster to a single ethnicity when he incorporates it into his Mexican-Chicano culture. He makes an intercultural gesture to Native American culture with his invocation of the buffalo in his title and in the text; the buffalo is one of several masking devices Oscar uses to create a liminal space, linking himself to Native American and Chicano cultural terrains. The pachuco trickster is at once linked to and separate from tricksters in these two other traditions. In *The Autobiography of a Brown Buffalo,* the pachuco is an intercultural trickster figure.

1. OSCAR, CHICANOS, PAZ

As is true of trickster figures in Native American and African American oral and literary traditions, the pachuco trickster expresses the contradictions and ambivalences that result from a history of colonization. To be both comic and tragic, active and passive, victimized but not a victim, to avow and disavow, turn high into low, low into high, to be "a coincidence of opposite processes and notions in a single representation" is Oscar's enduring trademark (Turner 99). Watching Oscar topple and play tricks on the hierarchical system of warrior masculinity, readers learn to tolerate paradox, to do what Maxine Hong Kingston's narrator in *Woman Warrior* learns to do: "make [the] mind large, as the universe is large, so that there's room for paradoxes" (Kingston 29). In his role as a trickster, Oscar enacts the seemingly irreconcilable views about the pachuco expressed by Paz and Chicanos in the political and rhetorical discourse of the 1960s.

Let me explain. As Moynihan assumed about African Americans and Lewis about Puerto Ricans, Paz assumed that Mexican Americans ought to assimilate. Paz found fault with the pachuco—his shorthand term for Mexican Americans—because the pachuco refused, so Paz claimed, to integrate himself into mainstream U.S. society. As Paz would have it, the pachuco neither desired to return to his Mexican roots nor to accultur- ate into conventional U.S. society. The pachuco was thus a liminal figure for Paz, but for Paz and others, liminality, at least as far as the pachuco was concerned, was a negative, nihilistic state of being.[4] Paz's ideas on the pachuco thus were compatible with the dominant script on hybrid identities, a script that represented mestizo identities as symptoms of in- ferior cultures. The pachuco chose to marginalize himself, to be outside the "normal," at the extreme end of the social order,[5] tantamount to "no- where," similar to the Ríos family in *La Vida,* according to Lewis. In Paz's words: "The *pachuco* is the prey of society, but instead of hiding he adorns himself to attract the hunter's attention. Persecution redeems him" (17). With such statements, Paz gave Chicano men and women the decided impression that the pachuco isolated and inflicted pain on himself and enjoyed pain—a willing victim, in other words. Chicanos, in contrast, argued that the larger U.S. society ostracized the pachuco, considered him a burden and a sign of danger, casting blame on him and his culture for occurrences in public life over which he/it had no control.

Chicano men and women, understandably, took issue with Paz's un- flattering portrayal of the pachuco. For a generation of politically active and militant Chicanos, historical heirs of the actual scapegoated youths of the 1940s, Paz misrepresented a character that they regarded as prefigur- ing symbolically the collective assertion and political-social resistance of the Chicano movement. For Chicanos, the pachuco was iconic, a cultural hero. He no more had a self-destructive mentality for Chicanos/as than the Harlem zoot-suiter[6] had a frustrated and menacing mentality for Af- rican American men and women.[7] Chicanos sought to "[peel] back the layers of falsehood and fantasy that obscure[d] his [the pachuco's] true history" (Madrid 31), to situate the pachuco in that history as a powerful symbol of cultural recoding, of transculturation: someone who turned society's stigma of self-marginalization into a gesture of self-definition and resistance to racial oppression (Madrid 31). What society ascribed to him as failure, he, like youthful zoot-suiters from other ethnic groups, turned into virtue.

Chicanos agreed with Paz that the pachuco chose to display his differences. But it was not to act out victimhood, as Paz implied. Rather, his masking—his ample zoot-suit dress (baggy or ballooning trousers with cuffs tapered at the ankles, long, fingertip coat, broad-brimmed hat sometimes capped with a feather, chain, ducktailed hair), his street argot, or *caló,* and his cocky "strut"—was a visual, concrete emblem of racial and ethnic group identity. What Ralph Ellison says about African American zoot-suiters is also true of the pachuco: "His masking is motivated not so much by fear as by a profound rejection of the image created [by dominant institutions] to usurp his identity."[8] The pachuco took apart the dress codes of white male "outsiders" and reassembled them into his own subversive code.[9] As Trace Hedrick suggests, the zoot-suited pachuco is a kind of visual pun. For just as a verbal pun plays upon a double meaning of a word, so the image of the pachuco plays upon the image of the conventional gray-flannel-suit-wearing man by exaggerating it, as well as the movie image of the white ethnic cultural outlaw (the gangster images cultivated by James Cagney and Humphrey Bogart). This visual pun works because it defamiliarizes conventional and alternative images of male dress and makes them strange and frivolous by exaggeration and decontextualization (Hedrick 150).

Oscar is Acosta's transculturation of the pachuco representations offered by both Paz and a core group of Chicanos.[10] Oscar shares the hallmark characteristics of both the Pazian and Chicano portraits: his love of role-playing, his "outsiderness," his "between and betwixtness."[11] The difference is that Paz produced the image of a victim lost in a state of limbo and Chicanos created the image of a cultural hero. Acosta, however, loosens up the deadlocked dyad of "victim" or "hero" and accommodates a third term. He locates the subtle modulations the binary refuses to recognize. Acosta's Oscar spoofs simultaneously Paz's image of the pachuco as a tragic village idiot, who "asks for it," and the Chicano movement's image of him as a warrior hero, a definite heterosexual, active man. Oscar challenges these two opposable possibilities: pushed down, he bounces back up again, like a jack-in-the-box; he rebounds transformed from defeat, reinvigorated to repeat the challenge once again. His expressive maneuvers interconnect with both Paz's and Chicano commentaries, but Oscar as trickster is neither Paz's lost soul (his menacing clown) nor the Chicano culture hero represented as being outside dominant culture. Again, I turn to Victor Turner, who sees a positive productivity to the liminal character's position of being "neither this nor that and yet . . . both" (Turner 99). Oscar deviates from the pachuco's traits registered by Paz and Chicanos, but the deviation only heightens the comedy.[12]

Oscar appropriates a trickster mask and by so doing, opens up the two tragic scenarios of the pachuco embedded in our bank of images (negative victim image, positive heroic image) about him. He escapes the binarized frame of dominant and subdominant officialdom, breaking out of, though momentarily, these two manifestations of patriarchal order. He explodes patriarchy into farce.

2. OSCAR—THE BLACK PACHUCO

All this is by way of setting the stage for Oscar's series of confrontations that play upon the pachuco image as an intercultural figure. It is 1946 and twelve-year-old Oscar is gallantly walking the "black-haired Mexican babe" Senaida home from a Halloween party (Acosta, *Autobiography* 87–88). On this night of disguises, Oscar casts himself in the racial mold fashioned by his "Okie" tormentors. In essence, he does what Piri did in the Texas brothel scene, when Piri adopted the "black-face" society assigned to him.[13] Oscar too crosses racial contexts; he too plays with the signs of blackness and whiteness, except that he puts them in comic relief. Furthermore, he is seemingly the butt of the joke. He "dresses up": he takes his father's white navy gloves, his mother's rouge to paint on himself stylized huge red lips, and the black dye of burnt wood to spread on his face. He literally acts out the national scapegoat, as though speaking through the voice of white supremacist power. He plays out in black and white the stereotype of the "darky" entertainer who provides white fun. Had Oscar used grease paint, he might have represented himself as a "greaser," another stereotypical name Acosta plays upon ironically in the novel (93). Out of nowhere comes his rival and nemesis. The "Okie" Junior Ellis, supported by his brothers, ambush Oscar and Senaida. One brother, five years Oscar's senior, grabs Oscar by the hair, knocks him to the ground, kicks his "balls," puts his foot on his crotch, and pulls his pants off—in this ascending order of harassment. This older brother yells, "Whooee! Look at that. This nigger ain't even a man." Junior adds, "This pussy Jigaboo ain't even got hair on his prick" (88). The attack is reminiscent of the supremacist "cracker" who ambushed Brew as well as of those photographs showing pachucos of the 1940s stripped to their underpants.[14]

Oscar is forcibly stripped, feminized, laughed at. In his self-deprecating style, Oscar makes himself the object of ridicule, a symbolic and ironic self-maiming. Oscar may be foolishly jumping straight into the frying pan by choosing this stereotyped mask, but he also achieves a comic reversal of Paz's view of the pachuco. Paz argued that the pachuco was "the prey of society"—"exhibiting a wound . . . that . . . decks itself out for the hunt" (*Labyrinth* 17)—because *he did not assimilate* into the mainstream. The point of Acosta's hyperbole here is that it is precisely because Oscar is trying so hard to adjust to the contours of white society that he adopts the "darkie" mask and attracts the "Okie" hunters. Acosta deliberately presents Oscar in the image imposed on him by his tormentors. Oscar could not have chosen to wear a more emphatic sign of assimilation than the grotesque mask of the "darkie" minstrel who acted out the role of "slave" for his "master" audience. This is Oscar's intercultural gesture as a cunning trickster figure.

This tragicomic situation stands Paz on his head. The ambushers scream "blood and rape." They grab Senaida's "gorgeous cans" (*Autobiography* 87–88), but Oscar's "mask" diverts the attacker's attention from Senaida and focuses it all on himself. Unlike the Texas brothel scene in which Piri focuses on "fucking" the white prostitute, expending his anger on her, Oscar succeeds in pulling "the girl" out of the equation of male rivalry. He shows that the girl/woman is the man's pretext, his accessory, because Senaida's standing as Oscar's date means nothing when it comes to man-to-man competition. Oscar creates the opportunity for Senaida to escape the ambushers: "Run, Sena, run!" (88). But Senaida freezes with fear. The good news is that neither she nor Oscar is raped. Oscar thwarts the attacker's expectations, takes the wind out of their sails. The absence of hair on Oscar's "prick" creates an emperor-has-no-clothes effect. Oscar, let us say, fails to deliver the goods. The tension fizzles because Oscar has nothing to offer; yet he has shown that the girl, like the traditional La Malinche, is only an excuse to justify male-on-male combat. It is as if his tormentors opened an elaborately wrapped package and found nothing in it.

3. OSCAR—TALKING BACK, INTERCULTURALLY

While in his transitional stage, during the intervening period of his detachment from assimilated society, Oscar imagines himself "talking back"/"returning the gaze" to Dr. Serbin, his "Ivy League," Freudian-trained psychiatrist of ten years, and representative of white middle-class rational authority. Serbin functions as a symbolic surrogate for Paz—the one who occupies the role of the researcher in the observation tower and who hardly sees himself in the act of looking. In therapy with Dr. Serbin of his own volition, Oscar, revealing an unwillingness to be accountable for his decision, protests:

> I refuse to continue the conversation with that Ivy League,
> black-haired bastard. He is unfair, that Jewish shrink of mine.
> He takes advantage of my condition. He wouldn't dare talk
> that way to me on the street. If we were on my turf, you can
> bet your ass he wouldn't hound me the way he does in his
> hot-shit office with me flat on my back. . . . There's no court
> of last resort when you lay plastered to his black leather couch
> telling him all your dirty stories which you know damned
> well he repeats to rouged Pacific Heights matrons over cock-
> tails and chicken-shit crackers with dry salami from North
> Beach. (13–14)

In this, Oscar's caricaturesque rendition of what Dr. Serbin does to him, we have an intercultural metaphor of what Chicanos thought Paz did to the pachuco, of what African Americans thought Moynihan did to black men and black women, and what mainland Puerto Ricans thought Lewis did to Puerto Ricans.[15] Paz, the critic-analyst; Moynihan, the ivory-tower sociologist; and Lewis, the field ethnographer: all verbally stripped the subjects they wrote about. All three intellectuals had the advantage of outside spectators, "looking," in Sartre's sense of the word, at their subjects without the subjects able to look or speak back. They wrote in the anthropological tradition that the learned anthropologist Clifford Geertz humorously rendered into "they [the studied others] have a culture out there and [my] job is to come back to tell you [the metropolitan audience] what it is" (Geertz, *After the Fact* 43). Paz verbally penetrated, opened up, the pachuco. The "object penetrated," whether sexually or linguistically, is always, in Paz's view, the "inferior" woman or the male "passive" homo-sexual. The role of sexual and social penetrator belongs to the active male, the only one of Paz's "types" with a viable identity.

Dr. Serbin, for Acosta, represents the symbolically active mind, the in-tellectual who probes ("hounds") the depths of Oscar's psyche. Oscar is closer than Serbin to the representation of the penetrated "body" or flesh ("flat on my back"), the pachuco, the one feminized, the person on the hot seat. Penetrate is exactly what Oscar feels Dr. Serbin does to him. Then too this more or less middle-class lawyer implies that the street is his turf, connecting himself to the pachuco, whose turf really was the street, and separating himself from Serbin's intellectual middle-class terrain ("hot-shit office").

Oscar, a man of color, feels this white analyst takes advantage of him (Oscar is his prey), putting him in a feminized position ("lay plastered on his black leather couch"). If the tables were reversed, if on the street, Oscar is certain he would be calling the shots on Dr. Serbin. Nonetheless, Oscar practices the above words to himself, creating a scenario that evokes the sentiments of Chicanos who responded to Paz, of black men and women who answered Moynihan, and of Puerto Ricans who, in later years, con-tested Lewis's images of themselves. Oscar's rebellion climaxes when he breaks into another client's private sessions with Dr. Serbin. Invading the space of the rational, he announces to Dr. Serbin he is quitting therapy. He will undertake healing on his own and do just fine, thank you.

4. MISTAKEN IDENTITY: OSCAR AND THE BORDER

Since his departure from San Francisco that initiated his quest, Oscar has crossed several geo- and psychospatial borders: state borders and mental borders brought on by hallucinogenic drugs. Now at the end of his quest, Oscar crosses the geopolitical international bor-der at El Paso to Juárez. The Mexico-U.S. border is, of course, one of the major tropes of Chicano literature. Oscar is desperate because his "so-journ" is just about over and he is "still want[ing] to find out just who in the hell [he] really was" (*Autobiography* 184). Almost a total washout on the Mexican culture front at thirty-three—he still thinks "Mexican music . . . corny" (73) and Mexican girls boring—Oscar decides to travel from Vail, Colorado, to El Paso, the place of his birth, and then to Juárez, a decision that reverses the direction of the two midpoints of his parents' (im)migration. Originating in Durango and ending their migration in

Riverbank, California, they went from Juárez to El Paso; Oscar now goes from El Paso to Juárez.

The setup of this scene makes for a rollicking parody of the Chicano identity quest narrative of the 1960s and 1970s, and Oscar is the spark of the humor. In crossing to Mexico, Oscar returns to a point of origin made sacred by Chicano writing and thinking, Mexico as a kind of homeland. He hopes to find unity and resolution to the "hurts" of his life, and he does find a "cure for [his] ailing stomach, . . . ulcers and the blood in the toilet" (189), but he also finds disruption, confusion, and physical and emotional torture. Oscar is a trickster figure who falls into the apparently dark pit of liminality, fenced in—this time—between two cultures, two countries; but by falling here he reveals the sham of essential identities. The trickster is tricked, but like all tricksters worth their mettle he bounces back from the "black hole of Calcutta" (192)[16] and makes his border experience a productive "failure." In this sense, he gives new meaning to the return to origins, because by going to Mexico, he comprehends that he belongs here in a U.S. context, working to right the world for the millions of "brown buffalos."

On boarding the trolley to the border, Oscar remembers he lost his wallet in Taos and realizes that he carries no passport and speaks no Spanish. No money, no papers, no Spanish: a deadly combination that puts him nowhere in Mexico. He can no more prove he is a bona fide U.S. citizen than he can prove he is a Mexican citizen. Feeling his precarious situation, he fears the Mexican guard on the trolley will charge him with "[i]mpersonating a *mexicano*" (187). Is Oscar a *norteamericano* masking as a *mexicano*? Or a U.S. resident *mexicano* masking as a Mexican national?[17] If so, this is a switch for U.S. readers. Accustomed to envisioning Mexican nationals crossing U.S. borders with no papers, we think it odd that Oscar, a U.S. citizen, is an "illegal alien" in Mexico.

Acosta's view of Juárez is the stereotypical Hollywoodish dingy town: corruption, sex, prostitutes. The first thing Acosta has Oscar do is visit a bordello, the "Cantina de la Revolucion" [*sic*] (190), where two prostitutes, Sylvia and Teresa, mistake him for a *mexicano* because he has brown skin, even though they, being Mexican, do not. Locked into the same faulty perceptions of phenotype and skin color as they, Oscar assumes they are from the States because Sylvia is a red-haired beauty with peach skin and Teresa is a tall blonde. He thinks they are North Americans "faking" Spanish. "What kind of jackshit is this? . . . They get American girls to fake Spanish so well they speak it better than I do" (189). Sylvia and Teresa (mis)perceive him to be a *mexicano* impersonating a *norteamericano:* "Y *este, no me digas que no es Mexicano? [sic]"* (189). They mistakenly surmise that Oscar deliberately refuses to speak Spanish to them. Thus they think he is in denial of his "Mexicanness," judging him according to standards they would not use for white-looking North American tourists. The prostitutes and Oscar are miscommunicating and living the misunderstandings that commonly occur in contact zones. Neither hits the bull's-eye with the other. They think he is *mexicano;* he thinks they are *norteamericanas.* This scene shows that though racial, ethnic, and national categories may be inevitable, they are also arbitrary and artificial.

The Mexican prostitutes nurture him into his full-blown sexual performance and relieve his "ulcers and blood-in-the-toilet" ailments—they give him the "mysterious Pepto-Bismol and giant Rolaid" he has sought since leaving San Francisco. But he gets into trouble with some Mexican hotel clerks who turn him over to Mexican police for insulting them in English, the way he did Sheriff Lauren in Spanish (119). Oscar, once with the *putas,* becomes a *puto* in prison because the guards forcibly sodomize him. When he shows up for his arraignment, long-haired, not "exactly *look*[ing] like an attorney" (192), before a woman magistrate in Juárez, the much-represented Oscar, he who has taken on so many roles, including a Samoan, a "nigger," and an *indio,* cannot represent himself, especially in Spanish. He fears that this *mexicana* judge, like the prostitutes and guards, will think he is a *mexicano* deliberately refusing to speak Spanish, trying to pass as a *norteamericano.* The assumption here is that all U.S.-born *mexicanos* ought to be able to speak Spanish. She, on the other hand, is bilingual and chastises him in perfect English for behaving like an "ugly American": "Cut your hair or leave this city. We get enough of your kind around here. You spend your money on the *putas* and then don't even have enough to pay for your fines when you're caught with your pants down" (193–194). On top of exposing him—"courtmartialed by a woman! In Spanish, at that!" (192)—she tells him to go home "and learn to speak your father's language" (194).

But what is the language of Oscar's father? Spanish? English? "Spanglish"? The cruel irony here is that Oscar is supposed to return to the United States, where the official language is English, to learn Spanish, the language of his *indio* father from the hills of the Mexican state of Durango, who (im)migrated to the United States, fought in the U.S. military in World War II, and rigidly enforced the English language at home. When Oscar returns to El Paso, his national identity is again questioned, this time by the U.S. border agents who suspect he is a *mexicano* impersonating a *norteamericano:* "You *americano?* . . . You don't *look* like an American, you know?" (195). With no "legitimate" firm identity, Oscar, like a ping-pong ball, bounces back and forth. The lesson he learns is summed up in the quotation that opened chapter 4: "What I see now, on this rainy day in January, 1968, what is clear to me after this sojourn is that I am neither a Mexican nor an American. . . . I am a Chicano by ancestry and a Brown Buffalo by choice."

Oscar's choice of a "Brown Buffalo" takes us to a preborder time, before 1848, to the moment in U.S. and Mexican history when there was no international border between the two countries. He is neither a "Mexican" nor an "American." The Mexican guards sexually violate him in prison, actually doing to the adult Oscar what his Riverbank "Okie" friends tried to do to him when he was a pubescent adolescent on that Halloween night. Using irony as a kind of radar that searches for a dark side, Oscar spoofs the notion of warrior masculinity that Piri and Sonny struggled to preserve for themselves as well as the scourge of feminized masculinity they fought to be free of as men of color. Racism put all these men into this bind. What Oscar tells us is that in the long run no identity can be imposed by force. Both cultures have tried to force their identity on him, and both rejected him because he has "something" of the "other" culture. Both cultures want him "pure"; want him to contain elements of their culture only. With his insistence on liminality, Acosta's Oscar brings La Malinche home because he shows us just how permeable and artificial national and gender borders are.

Epilogue   LA MALINCHE COMES HOME

In an article titled "Life among the Anthros," Clifford Geertz tells the following anecdote that paraphrases a story told by André Gide:

> During the German occupation of France, André Gide published, and was allowed to publish because he was Gide, a series of "*interviews imaginaires*" in the public press commenting, in an oblique, Aesopian way, on various aspects of literature, politics, and the cultural scene. In one, he takes up the question, then current, of the supposed responsibility of the "intellectuals" for the fall of France, and he ends it with a striking parable.
>
> A rowboat, moored at a riverbank, sits low in the water. Into it step in turn (as I remember it), a fat politician, a large general draped in medals, an enormous madam, and a bloated capitalist, the boat sinking deeper and deeper, water to the gunwales, as they board. Finally, a clergyman, thin as a rail, steps in and the boat finally sinks. The others all point at him: "It is he who is the culprit! It is he who has caused the disaster!" (21)

This opinion—evidently stubbornly held by some French citizens, who presumably are unidentified by Geertz because Gide, I assume, did not identify them either—was, according to Gide, of widespread currency during the occupation of France. Gide wanted to make the point that the accusation that certain intellectuals were to blame for the "fall" of France was, to say the least, an exaggeration without merit. I recite Geertz's citation because it pointedly, as well as humorously, captures a familiar easy gesture. The gesture is the one that purports to easily explain, simplify, or do away with complicated social problems, issues, and legacies of history with quick and easy approaches and solutions. After all, the obese politician, the imposing military general, an ever-consuming society (gendered female), and the overfed capitalist have weighted down the boat sufficiently enough for it to capsize long before the rail-thin clergyman ever boarded it. The clergyman is simply the feather that sinks the boat.

Gide's metaphor enacts the ridiculousness of a gesture that relies on an available scapegoat for explaining away long and deep social and political problems. It suggests that the timing of the last and most vulnerable actor to come on the scene, that the intricate nexus of social and economic conditions brewing under the surface, and that the negation of a history influencing and determining the present are all causes of substance that contribute to the "disaster" that leads to fingerpointing at the easy target. The moment and circumstances produce the opportunity of an available "victim" that is too good to pass up by those searching for the immediate gratification of a seeming remedy to systemic social problems.

The gesture that tops off Gide's story is not without relevance to dominant and subdominant traditions of thinking that I have worked against in this book. The La Malinche trope and its variations have been misused in this same way. In other words, just as Gide's unidentified and culpable passengers blamed the fragile clergyman for their ruin, the one who happened to board the boat (a microcosm of society) at the very moment it was ready to capsize, so likewise, in the context of this book, La Malinche—the native woman implied in the stereotypical trope—became a timely scapegoat. Strains in dominant and subdominant traditions I have examined in this book pointed to her and blamed her—the native woman—for the "fall" of the Mexican population and the "fall" of the southwestern states to the Anglo-American. In the seemingly parallel contexts of the other two dominant liberalist discourses (Moynihan and Lewis) and African American subdominant ethnic nationalist discourses, the black mother and the Puerto Rican mother were blamed for the alleged failure of the black family and of the Puerto Rican people. Whether it stands for women, gays and lesbians, subdominant racial groups, the disabled, low-wage workers, the undocumented—the socially and politically vulnerable, in other words—La Malinche has been a unifying rubric that has served as a smoke screen for the deeper causes and complicated histories that irrevocably define a society's present and future. "*Shakin' Up*" *Race and Gender* has been concerned with broadening the historical and literary context of the trope of La Malinche. I have shown that it is too reductive to accuse the stereotypical mother of color, the whore of color, the family of color as "origins" of social failure. The equation for obtaining social progress is far more complicated.

In interlude 4, I brought the trope "home" to its Chicano and Chicana surroundings. It came home with a difference—the difference being that we are able to see it in its intercultural dimensions. Just as the trope of La Malinche offered new intercultural perspectives on *Down These Mean Streets* and *Manchild in the Promised Land*, it was a viable vehicle for showing that a Chicano text is intercultural. What we learn is that this trope has been intercultural all along, even in its Mexican and Chicano home cultures, where it has been naturalized since its first application to Chicano literature during the Chicano nationalist movement.[1] The tropes—La Malinche, La Chingada, and the pachuco—are already inside and outside Chicano cultural bounds from the start, even if we are focused only on a Chicano text—in this case *The Autobiography of a Brown Buffalo*. These tropes are integrated in a network of different ethnic and cultural strains and thus give a more expansive vision of relations among and between different ethnically identifiable segments of the U.S. population.

The metaphor that encapsulates the La Malinche trope is the border. If the trope of La Malinche, the mantra of this book, represents anything, it is border crossings, on literal and symbolical levels, whether these are geographic, linguistic, gendered, or ethnic. How disconcerting it is, then, that the trope that stands for border crossings has been confined for so long to only Mexican-Chicano locations. This book has been about releasing the trope from its consignment only to Mexican and Chicano contexts. I have imported the trope from Mexican and Chicano social places into "foreign" contexts where readers, especially those who know the trope, would not be disposed to see it; indeed, they might resist seeing it. Such an unexpected placement of the trope in Puerto Rican and African American situations allowed me to reveal details about the trope and its contexts that would otherwise have lain concealed, below the surface.

I believe that Chicanos and Chicanas, especially those in the academy, cannot afford to stay glued to the limits of the parochial readings given the trope in an ethnic nationalist context. Since the Chicano ethnic nationalist movement in the 1960s and 1970s, it has been frozen in a Pazian amber of time, space, and context and to the particular meanings assigned to it. Chicanos and Chicanas have consistently seen La Malinche as frozen in a Pazian context and in a dominant-subdominant relationship. The generation of the Chicano movement has loved to hate Paz, or hated to love Paz, and a Pazian mode of thinking has influenced us to keep La Malinche "in her place." Though I am indebted to a Chicana feminist tradition, I recognize that even feminist readings that recuperate La Malinche in positive ways still keep the trope anchored in a Mexican-Chicano context. In this book I have shown how the exportation of the La Malinche trope leads to evidence of a rich intercultural history, a history that dominant intellectuals and policy makers of the 1960s and 1970s discouraged us from seeing. Their visions of isolated dominant-subdominant histories made it difficult to see the applicability of this trope to other cultural contexts. The trope is far more versatile and diverse than we have given it credit for. I have "shaken' up" the usual contours of the trope—subdominant to dominant—to include interethnic relationships between subdominant groups.

Rather than dismiss Paz, Moynihan, and Lewis as passé intellectuals, no longer relevant to our projects of study, and La Malinche as a trope that we, especially the generation of the Chicano movement, have outgrown and transcended, I have engaged with the dominant intellectuals and the history of the trope itself. I have not attempted to redeem these intellectuals or a Pazian mode of thinking about La Malinche, and all it implied to us in the 1960s and 1970s, but rather to revisit them from the perspective of our own time in order to arrive at an intercultural history through and in literary texts.

What we have learned from my readings is that La Malinche is "home," since the concept of home for me is varying and changing. In summary, I can say that home is in the middle, the interstices, always in the process of being made. The trope can work in familiar and unfamiliar places. Cross-cultural transactions, migrations, mediations, and appropriations have been constant metaphors in this book for those actual and real negotiations that take place in history. The point is that the application of this trope in "alien" contexts made visible what remains invisible as long as the trope is restricted to its familiar settings. The point is also that what became visible merited being seen.

NOTES

PRELUDE

1. See Hughes, *The Big Sea* 54. See also Edward J. Mullen, ed., *Langston Hughes in the Hispanic World and Haiti* 39 n. 11.

2. I use "intercultural" to designate the complex historical, cultural, and literary relationships among these three cultures. For a fuller definition, see the introduction.

3. Since there is no definitive resolution on the capitalization of "black" and "white" when these terms refer to racial and ethnic identifiers, I have chosen to follow the common language practice of newspapers and magazines and use lowercase for both. However, I capitalize "black" when I use it to refer to a specific group of the African American community, such as Black Muslims, or to a specific location, such as Black Harlem.

4. The term "contact zone" was first used to refer to Latin American narrative by Angel Rama, *Transculturación narrativa en América Latina*. Mary Louise Pratt moved the term onto the English-speaking stage of literary and cultural studies; see "Arts of the Contact Zone." The term refers to geographic spaces where "native" cultural systems or epistemologies intersect with those of the conquerors. These spaces are shared and demand that their inhabitants continually negotiate resources, geographic areas, and vying interests.

5. Piri Thomas lived many of the same experiences he attributes to his protagonist, also named Piri Thomas. To distinguish between the author and the character, who both share the same name, I refer to the author by his surname, Thomas, and to the character by his first name, Piri. I deliberately alternate between "Thomas" and "Piri" in order to accommodate the context I am describing at the time.

6. Aztlán is an indigenous term that refers to the region north of what today is Mexico, or loosely speaking, the southwestern borderlands. To some, during the Chicano movement of the 1960s, the term meant the homeland stolen by the United States in the 1846–1848 war, and the objective was to retake the land as a

Chicano nation. To others, it was a rallying cry on which to build a Chicano identity with a sense of a people and a land of origins.

INTRODUCTION

1. Following Spanish and English usage in Chicano communities, I use "Chicano" in its broadest sense to refer to the culture of women and men of Mexican origin living in the United States, as well as to designate Mexican American men alone. I use "Chicana" to refer to individual Chicano women and to an academic discourse that challenges the patriarchal structure of Chicano culture. However, at times I prefer to use "Chicano woman" instead of "Chicana" to stress the importance of gender that might be overlooked with the small vowel change from Chicano to Chicana. At other times I use "Chicana" to stress ethnicity first and gender second. I alternate between "Chicano woman" and "Chicana" when appropriate.

2. I follow Louis Menand's periodization; the years 1945 to 1975, dubbed "the Golden Age," saw dramatic growth in the size of the system of higher education. Its composition (who went to college, who taught, and the nature of the subject matter) remained much the same as before World War II. The period from 1975 to the present, says Menand, "is a period not of expansion but of diversification. Since 1975 the size of the system has grown at a much more modest pace, but the composition—who is taught, who does the teaching, and what they teach—changed dramatically." Menand, "College" 44.

3. I realize that "minority" is a highly contested term with respect to "Latino" groups because these groups are no longer "minorities" in terms of their numbers. However, there is still much to be done to overcome the status of these groups with respect to economic, educational, and political equality and representative power. It is in this sense that I use "minority." I use quotation marks around the term to show that I recognize its contested usage.

4. Whiteness as a category often reduces ethnic differences among western European, British, and Scandinavian immigrants for the sake of assimilation. For recent work on white ethnicity, see Noel Ignatiev, *How the Irish Became White;* George Lipsitz, *The Possessive Investment in Whiteness;* Tomás Almaguer, *Racial Fault Lines;* David Roediger, *The Wages of Whiteness;* Eric Lott, "White Like Me"; and Neil Foley, *The White Scourge.*

5. The title in Spanish is *El laberinto de la soledad.* Originally published in 1950 by Cuadernos Americanos in Mexico, it was revised and expanded in 1959 for the second edition published by the Fondo de Cultura Económica. The English translation by Lysander Kemp, published by Grove Press, appeared in 1961. In my discussion, I refer to Kemp's translation. The translation, rather than the original, is coincident with the writings of Moynihan and Lewis and therefore the important text in my book.

6. There were fewer written responses by Puerto Ricans on the mainland to Lewis's *La Vida* than to Paz's *Labyrinth* by Chicanos/as and to Moynihan's report by African Americans. See note 8 below.

7. I take the phrase "interpretive power" from Jean Franco's *Plotting Women*, xii. "Citizen" and "citizenship" refer not only to the legal definition of status acquired by birth or parentage in a country, or even that imposed by decree, as in the case of Puerto Ricans, but also to cultural and social status, especially for marginalized communities. William V. Flores and Rina Benmayor develop the concept of "cultural citizenship" in *Latino Cultural Citizenship*. In their sense, "cultural citizenship" recognizes that communities shape and influence the geographic and political spaces they inhabit and that they affirm their human, social, and cultural rights through community building, or rebuilding.

8. For responses from Chicanas, especially the implications of Paz's discussion about family, see chapter 2. For responses by Chicano men to Paz, see chapter 4. Most of these responses revolved around the image of La Malinche. For responses from black women to Moynihan and black men, see the Interlude following chapter 3, notes 15 and 23. The Lewis case breaks up the parallelism among the three groups because far fewer written responses by mainland Puerto Rican women or men appeared to take issue with the portrayals in *La Vida*. One example, however, is the pioneering anthropologist Elena Padilla, who reviewed Lewis's book and raised important critical questions about his study. Manuel Maldonado-Denis, an island Puerto Rican, was one of fourteen expert reviewers invited by *Current Anthropology* to respond to Lewis's précis of his works, including *La Vida*. See Maldonado-Denis, "Book Review of *The Children of Sánchez, Pedro Martínez*, and *La Vida* by Oscar Lewis." Maldonado-Denis makes reference to "those in government circles in Puerto Rico and New York" (496) who felt their image as Puerto Ricans was tarnished by Lewis. Maldonado-Denis's review is supportive of Lewis: *La Vida*, he says, "offers to both the social scientist and the layman valuable insights as to the world view, the attitudes, and the orientations of those who live on the lowest rung of the social ladder" (496). Among others, reviewers were Robert Cole and Eric Wolf.

9. This word is pronounced "ma lean che," with "che" as in "Che Guevara."

10. Some feminist scholars choose to employ the term "transcultural" to refer to a similar, yet different approach. Though I share the ideas that values, customs, beliefs, and other social practices can and do cross back and forth between cultures, I want to stress the space in the middle, the moment and zone of contact. For work on transcultural studies, see Paul Gilroy, *The Black Atlantic;* Mary Louise Pratt, *Imperial Eyes;* Joseph R. Roach, *Cities of the Dead*.

11. In my usage of this term it encompasses the dynamics of power not only between dominant and subaltern subjects but also between subdominant groups, especially various Latino and African American ethnic groups. See Pratt, "Arts of the Contact Zone"; *Imperial Eyes*.

12. Two contemporary examples of intercultural work in the field of history

and border studies are Patricia Nelson Limerick, *The Legacy of Conquest;* and Edward H. Spicer, *Cycles of Conquest.*

13. Benmayor writes: "Thus, analogies of a 'salad bowl' picture minorities as condiments or additives to the basic ingredient of lettuce, but fail to consider a whole new salad (perhaps bean or teriyaki chicken)." See Flores and Benmayor 9. I would add that the changing nature and dynamics of the demography, inclusive of white ethnic peoples and those of color, also makes possible thinking about a new "pot" or "bowl."

14. Although *Brown v. Board of Education* (1955) is considered the landmark legal case, there were previous challenges to school segregation in the U.S. Southwest that belie the black/white binary. Two cases prior to *Brown v. Board* that involve the children of Mexican American families are *Alvarez v. Lemon Grove School District* (1931) and *Westminster School District of Orange County v. Mendez* (1947). Both cases challenged the "separate but equal" standard created by the 1896 Supreme Court ruling in *Plessy v. Ferguson* (1896). *Alvarez v. Lemon,* the first successful challenge to school segregation, is chronicled in Paul Espinosa's docudrama, *The Lemon Grove Incident* (1985). See Espinosa, *The Lemon Grove Incident.* A case in reference to Asian Americans before *Brown v. Board,* though not involving school-age children, was *United States v. Thind* (1923).

15. Ramón Gutiérrez, a historian, and Juan Bruce-Novoa, a literary critic, both attribute the characteristic of a "monolithic concept of community"—in more contemporary vocabulary, "identity politics"—to Chicano writing of the 1960s and 1970s. Gutiérrez goes further and attributes it to Puerto Ricans and Native Americans too. See Ramón Gutiérrez and Genaro Padilla, eds., *Recovering the U.S. Hispanic Literary Heritage;* and Juan Bruce-Novoa, "Canonical and Non-Canonical Texts." I am primarily interested in finding in writings of these decades historical ground for interculturalism.

16. I thank Paul Espinosa, anthropologist and filmmaker, for bringing these shifts to my attention.

17. Despite a lingering belief that the racial categories on the U.S. Census are rarely changed, they have been altered several times since its inception. Racial categories have been removed and added, ethnicities have been collapsed and expanded. See Frederick G. Bohme, *200 Years of U.S. Census Taking.*

18. Melvin Maddocks, "The Knuckle-Hard Code of the Barrio."

19. Coined by Pratt, the neologism "autoethnography" explicitly signals mixed genres. These three texts, for example, fit this rubric as they contain elements of both "autobiography" (self-reflection by insiders of the "home" cultures) and "ethnography" (reflection by outsiders of different cultures). See Pratt, "Arts of the Contact Zone."

20. See Luis M. Neco, "Review of *Down These Mean Streets.*"

21. I thank Frank Bonilla for this information. Bonilla was one of the intellectual and political founders of Puerto Rican studies in the City University of New York in the 1960s and director of El Centro de Estudios Puertorriqueños from 1973

to 1993. He is also the author of several articles and books, including *The Failure of Elites,* and coeditor of *Borderless Borders.* Bonilla now lives in San Diego, California. Also, Jay Kinsbruner claims that the majority of island Puerto Ricans "did not identify with the civil rights movement either in Puerto Rico or in the United States." See Kinsbruner, *Not of Pure Blood* 5. Whatever the case, racial identification with their African heritage becomes even more complex when Puerto Ricans experience racism on the U.S. mainland.

22. I am grateful to the University of Texas Press reader for pointing out to me the role played by class in the Puerto Rican reception of *Down These Mean Streets.*

23. Juan Flores, "Back Down These Mean Streets" 53.

24. Though violence, drugs, and gangs are not its emotional center, Mohr's narrative is not entirely free of these elements.

25. Edna Acosta-Belén, "Conversations with Nicholasa Mohr" 36–37.

26. Abdul Basit Naeem, "Comment on First Novel by Black Harlem Writer" 10.

27. Loften Mitchell, "Growing Up Ghetto" 511, 535.

28. Daniel Aaron, in "Out of the Closet," cites these words with no attribution. I take it that the reviewer he refers to is probably a black American.

29. For what is still the best summary of the context of the Moynihan report, the controversy, and black and white responses, see Lee Rainwater and William L. Yancey, *The Moynihan Report.*

30. For possible explanations of this time gap, see chapter 4.

31. As these three texts have main characters whose names are the same as the authors', I use first names when referring to the characters and last names when referring to authors.

32. Douglas Massey, "Explaining the Paradox of Puerto Rican Segregation" 306–331.

33. George Lipsitz, *Dangerous Crossroads.*

34. I thank the University of Texas Press reader for bringing this important detail to my attention. This tripartite structure is, of course, true in the abstract, but in concrete situations, as Piri Thomas shows in *Down These Mean Streets,* Puerto Ricans shift their relationship to these identities. For example, the identity "Indian" has served as an escape hatch for Puerto Ricans wishing to distance themselves from African Americans. Massey, in "Explaining the Paradox of Puerto Rican Segregation," says that Puerto Ricans are more likely than other groups to live near African Americans, a situation that suggests economic factors determine the living choices for working-class Puerto Ricans. Therefore, I stress again that racialization is never only dual or binary but always shifting in relation to the subject's position—whether economic, racial, gendered, cultural, historical, or otherwise—to others.

35. See S. M., "In the Arms of Lady Snow" 96.

36. John O. Killens, "On *El Barrio* and Piri Thomas" 96.

37. See chapter 2. These terms are often used derogatorily by Puerto Ricans and Chicanos to refer to black Americans.

38. The term is used and understood by different communities, at different times, as having different meanings. Much depends on the speaker and the audience.

CHAPTER 1

1. "Pachuco" is a colloquial term used by Mexicans to designate the marginal proletariat in Mexico and by Mexicans and Mexican Americans to refer to urban youths of the Mexican American community in Los Angeles who resisted assimilation into both Mexican and U.S. dominant cultures in the '40s and '50s.

2. Paz spoke mostly about Mexicans in Mexico to Mexican nationals, but he also devoted attention to Mexicans on the U.S. side of the border. I take his pachuco as his shorthand for Chicano Americans. In interlude 4, I take up Paz's comments on the pachuco of Los Angeles in the context of Oscar Zeta Acosta's *The Autobiography of a Brown Buffalo*.

3. The representation of the groups by Paz, Moynihan, and Lewis came across as deficient to those who responded to their writings. I do not want to slip into a comfortable indifference regarding the differences that separate these cultural theorists, but I do not want to ignore their common points either. It is the intersection of their ideas that interests me.

4. See my lengthy discussion of La Malinche in the introduction.

5. See Maxine Baca Zinn, "Political Familism"; Miguel Montiel, "The Social Science Myth of the Mexican American Family"; and Octavio Romano-V, "The Historical and Intellectual Presence of Mexican-Americans."

6. See Marta Cotera, *The Chicana Feminist;* Cotera, *Diosa y Hembra;* Alfredo Mirandé and Evangelina Enríquez, *La Chicana;* Rosaura Sánchez and Rosa Martínez Cruz, *Essays on La Mujer.*

7. See Samuel Ramos, *El perfil del hombre y la cultura en México/Profile of Man and Culture in Mexico.*

8. Chicano responses to Paz clustered around the ideas of family and *machismo,* a gloss for Paz's version of Mexican manhood and a term Americans attribute to Latino men. The responses bifurcated along two main lines. On one side were Chicanos and Chicanas who refused to let an English-speaking American audience decide the terms on which machismo was to be interpreted. They knew that this polysemic signifier had a nonpathological cultural specificity that was inassimilable into Paz's or a North American, English-speaking monocultural society's frames of reference. For example, in *The Chicano Manifesto*, Armando B. Rendón says, "The essence of machismo, of being macho, is as much a symbolic principle of the Chicano revolt as it is a guideline for the conduct of family life, male-female relationships, and personal self-esteem"; and "The Chicano revolt is

a manifestation of Mexican Americans exerting their manhood and womanhood against the Anglo society. Macho . . . can no longer relate merely to manhood but must relate to nationhood as well" (104). For this nationalist segment, *macho* became a symbolic strategy for linking male masculinity, already positively empowered in its own "native" context, with the idea of a Chicano ethnic nationalist revolt, just as Paz had coupled Mexican male masculinity with Mexican nationalism. This interpretation has troublesome nationalist implications, but it nonetheless endowed the term with authority.

On another side were those who vehemently refused the epithet as applicable to them—in any way, shape, and form. Romano-V responds to what he called Paz's " 'put down' " of the pachuco, a Chicano figure I take up in the Interlude following chapter 4. See Romano-V, esp. 39–40. Montiel and Baca Zinn worked to dissociate the semantically pathological lineage of machismo from Chicano masculinity by arguing that the white popular imagination had racialized Latino men (usually working-class) into machos, dangerously perpetuating a white American stereotype of them as "aberrant." For this audience, the term was already too contaminated, and they tried to contain its racial implications by rejecting the cipher. But in choosing this route, they surrendered the definition of *machismo* to the dominant group.

9. The language "Negro problem" goes back at least to Gunnar Myrdal's *An American Dilemma* of the 1940s.

10. There was also interest in the report because President Johnson had called for a White House conference in his speech. The conference, scheduled for the fall, was to deal with the "rising walls" and "widening gulf" separating white and black America. In this speech, Johnson sought "not just equality as a right and a theory but equality as a fact and as a result." Referring to the historical scars of racial injustice, Johnson uttered words that in light of the legal and social controversies surrounding affirmative action in the 1980s and 1990s are remarkable: "You do not take a person who, for years, has been hobbled by chains and liberate him, bring him up to the starting line of a race and then say, 'you are free to compete with all the others,' and still justly believe that you have been completely fair." See Rainwater and Yancey 126–127.

11. Of special interest here is Claude Brown's appearance, along with that of his friend Arthur Dunmeyer, before Senator Abraham Ribicoff, chairman of the U.S. Senate Subcommittee on Executive Reorganization in 1966, to testify as the author of *Manchild in the Promised Land* about "ghetto poverty." The charge of Ribicoff's committee was to determine how federal and local governments worked toward "the alleviation of ghetto misery and the elimination of the ghetto itself" (1085). See Brown's lengthy testimony in U.S. Senate, *Hearings before the Subcommittee on Executive Reorganization.* My thanks to Leslie Peterson, my student at UCSD, for locating this information.

12. Much was written during these years on the "underclass." Among the many sources are Michael Harrington's landmark *The Other America*, published

in 1963, which was held by Lewis to have helped to spark the War on Poverty (see chap. 4, n. 42); and Moynihan's anthology, *Understanding Poverty,* in which he includes an article by Oscar Lewis on the "culture of poverty." See also Michael Harrington, "Everyday Hell."

13. Namely the members of the Mexican Society of Geography and Statistics, an organization in Mexico. See *La Gaceta;* Susan Rigdon, *The Culture Facade* 288–294. Rigdon suggests that Lewis believed the scandal had been politically motivated—that "rightist and centrist antiforeign elements in government and industry" wanted to remove the head of Fondo de Cultura Económica, the Argentinean Arnaldo Orfila Reynal, and "replace him with a Mexican." Orfila Reynal had supported the publication of books by other progressive-thinking North Americans (165). See also Jorge Castañeda, *Utopia Unarmed* 176.

14. Lewis and Paz knew of one another and of one another's work, though it is unlikely that the two men ever met. That Lewis was familiar with *The Labyrinth of Solitude* is clear from what he wrote in his correspondence: "Many things that [Paz] has said about the Mexican character in general in *The Labyrnth [sic] of Solitude* [and that were] written from pure intuition and genius, I have written about a small town after many years of research." Lewis thought that though he and Paz were saying similar things about Mexicans and even though his ideas were based on field research, "[o]nly a Mexican like Octavio Paz could [say such things and] escape [the criticism]" that he had to suffer on the publication of *Hijos de Sánchez* (Rigdon 294).

15. Lewis systematized the "culture of poverty" into a matrix of more than seventy social and psychological behavioral attributes that, he thought, explained "the poor's" subcultural status.

16. The daughters are not active players in this drama; Paz never uses the feminine *mestizas.* Although the daughters are implied in *mestizo,* it is very clear that the system is gendered in favor of the male.

17. By "Mexican United States," I mean those areas with substantial populations of Mexican immigrants as well as Mexican Americans, English speaking and Spanish speaking.

18. Only in passing does Paz mention Mexican homosexuality. In a very brief but important passage, he says: "It is likewise significant that masculine homosexuality is regarded with a certain indulgence insofar as the active agent is concerned. The passive agent is an abject, degraded being. . . . Masculine homosexuality is tolerated, then, on condition that it consists in violating a passive agent" (Paz 39–40). Almaguer clarifies that homosexuality in a Mexican/Latin American sexual system is defined according to *sexual aim,* "the act one wants to perform with another person (of either biological sex)"; in a western European– North American sexual system, on the other hand, it is based on *sexual object choice*—"the biological sex of the person" one chooses as partner in sexual activity (Almaguer, "Chicano Men" 77). It may be argued that Paz is simply explaining the way dominant society scripts the recipient in the male homosexual act. However,

his uncritical interpretive portrayal of the active/passive sexual system suggests his acceptance of this view.

19. For further details on La Malinche, see the sections on the trope in the introduction and chapter 2.

20. Paz's linguistic exegesis of the name "La Chingada" is important because it shows how he arrives at this key term in his story. He tells us that the name is derived from the infinitive verb *chingar,* a Nahuatl word that "probably comes from the Aztecs" (75). In its active mode, this socially taboo verb refers to the act of "penetrat[ing] another by force" (76), where "penetrate" carries sexual and extrasexual connotations. The one who commits the act is the "penetrator," the *chingón.* This last variant is the noun form of *chingar.* Paz equates the *chingón* to "the *macho,*" the closed male ("The *chingón* is the *macho*" [77]). The words *macho,* "closed," "penetrator," and "violator" are all synonymous and opposed to "woman," "open," "penetrated," and "violated." It is important to understand that the word *chingada* is the feminine passive participle of the root verb and *chingado* is the masculine passive form of the participle. Paz's attribution of the female grammatical suffix *-ada* to "the Chingada," whom he makes the generative source of a flawed biological and national genealogy, points to his feminization of Mexico's people and history.

21. This love of things foreign is the flaw of *malinchismo.*

22. Paz does not build his narrative on the Spanish verb *castrar,* from which he could have derived *castración, castrado* (the one castrated, always male), *castrador* (the castrator). Instead, he uses *chingado* and *chingada.* That he never uses Spanish-language variants of "castration" suggests the erasure of the generative masculine principle, the colonizer and conqueror, the *chingón.* He insists on a feminine lineage, a feminine genealogical and biological line. Moynihan and Lewis, on the other hand, assume a patriarchal line.

23. In Spanish *hombre* is "man" and *macho* is a particular kind of man. In Paz, the latter term means excess virility. This term occurs frequently in *Labyrinth* and was much circulated in the 1950s and 1960s in mainstream literary and social science studies in the United States, almost always with negative connotations. By 1960 a U.S. audience had been introduced to *machismo,* the English neologism, used by Ernest Hemingway; Beatrice Griffith, *American Me;* and probably coined by Norman Mailer, *Advertisements for Myself.* For more current studies on machismo, see Matthew Gutmann, *The Meanings of Macho;* and Roger Lancaster, *Life Is Hard.*

24. This term is fairly contemporary in literary studies. It refers to a cultural practice of removing masculine vigor and strength from men of color, male homosexuals, and men who do not act typically "masculine," by likening them to females and hence lessening their value as men.

25. My thanks to Cecilia Ubilla for pointing out the implication.

26. The emasculation of the male may be literal, as I describe above, or metaphoric, losing a verbal duel to one's antagonist, for example (Paz 39). I take up

the *chingado* facet of the La Malinche trope in the Interlude following chapter 4. There I discuss Oscar Zeta Acosta's transculturation of Paz's feminized image of the pachuco in relation to *The Autobiography of a Brown Buffalo*. For Paz, the pachuco is a symbolic *chingado*, a male embodiment of the female *chingada* and one of the extremes the Mexican male psyche can take.

27. Historical sources point to Marina and Cortés having one son, but in Paz the male children are the Mexican nation. Marina was the Spanish Christian name given by the Spanish conquerors to the woman known as La Malinche.

28. All page citations from Moynihan are taken from his text as reproduced in Rainwater and Yancey, *The Moynihan Report and the Politics of Controversy*.

29. Castration did not operate only at the symbolic level, but also on the physical level, as documented in cases of actual lynching and mutilation of black men.

30. He compared U.S. slavery to the Spanish and Portuguese system of slavery in Brazil, which he said was more humane (61).

31. The following line was often quoted in commentaries on the report: "[A]t the center of the tangle of pathology is the weakness of the [African American] family structure" (76). Moynihan took the expression "tangle of pathology" from Kenneth Clark, a black social scientist and the author of *The Dark Ghetto*. See also Carl Ginsburg, *Race and Media* 18.

32. There was nothing naturally wrong with matriarchy, Moynihan conceded, but it was not good for a minority population to be operating on a matriarchal model of family while the dominant population lived according to a patriarchal one (29).

33. Moynihan put the black family into a fishbowl to be evaluated and scrutinized according to the terms of patriarchy in which it had not been permitted to participate. Carol B. Stack showed how necessary it was to study families in terms of their internal structures. In *All Our Kin* she explored the functions of black kinship networks as distinctive domestic arrangements that responded to enslavement and oppression. Joyce Ladmer also called for more productive frames to study black families and women. Similarly, Herbert Gutman wrote a critical review of Moynihan's report and the responses to it in his afterword to *The Black Family in Slavery and Freedom*.

34. I follow Walter Jackson, who refers to this consensus and social policies as "liberal orthodoxy," embraced by intellectuals and politicians "in their rhetoric, if not in their actions" (*"Gunnar Myrdal"* 272). The pioneering research of the black sociologist E. Franklin Frazier, author of the classic *The Negro Family in the United States* (1939), had helped to lay the basis for this racial liberal philosophy in the social sciences. Others were Ralph Bunche and St. Claire Drake. In the 1930s they placed the black family in the foreground of U.S. sociology as a legitimate area of study. Myrdal is another social scientist in this tradition.

35. Moynihan simplified the research of previous scholars of "the Negro family," for example, Frazier and Myrdal. In the 1940s the Swedish sociologist Myrdal

was funded by the Carnegie Corporation (private money) to study "the Negro problem." He argued his case for black social equality in *An American Dilemma* (1944). According to Alexander Saxton, Myrdal's book "influenced virtually everything since written on the subject of race in the United States"; see Saxton, *The Rise and Fall of the White Republic* 3. James Berger claims that it became "the major reference for liberal policy makers from the Roosevelt through the early Johnson era." See Berger, "Ghosts of Liberalism" 413. Walter Jackson says, "For twenty years after its publication, *An American Dilemma* remained the leading work of social science concerning Afro-Americans" (273). Frazier insisted that the "Negro family" was both a product of and an adaptation to the trauma inflicted on Negro Americans during three wrenching periods of U.S. history: slavery, emancipation, and Reconstruction. He called the period during and following World War I the "Flight from Feudal America," when Negro migrants from southern plantations went beyond small southern cities and descended on northern industrial centers (New York, Philadelphia, Detroit, Chicago) after World War I. See *The Negro Family* chap. 14.

36. Machismo is usually seen in official studies as pathological male behavior, a compensatory mechanism for psychological insecurity; it functions as a handy gloss to type men, giving the impression that it is an ensemble of personality and cultural traits presumably innate and endemic to Latin American and U.S. Latino men. See note 8 above.

37. This conceptualization is, of course, in direct contrast to and does not negate an equally pervasive stereotype of the hypersexualized, black, male rapist. This latter stereotype was used by whites to justify their illegal and unjust acts against black men.

38. In retrospect, this thinking is highly ironic because Betty Freidan had written *The Feminine Mystique* in 1963. There were already rumblings in the kitchen.

39. Sapphire is the "tough, domineering, emasculating strident, and shrill" black woman. In the sense that the caricature of Sapphire is domineering and emasculating, it fits Moynihan's matriarch. See Regina Austin, "Sapphire Bound" 540.

40. Lewis considered the "culture of poverty" to characterize societies in African countries (except South Africa) but not socialist-oriented countries, such as Cuba.

41. Although Lewis argued that the "culture of poverty" was related to economic causes, his statements also implied the poor were responsible for their own poverty. Valentine discusses the contradictory nature of Lewis's research, especially the disconnection between his theoretical perspective and his concrete data. See Charles Valentine, *Culture and Poverty* 48–77, esp. 68. At times Lewis was very clear on where he stood, especially when defending himself against readers he thought had misunderstood his argument. For example, in 1965, in answer to Joseph Finney, a psychologist who had suggested that people who are unable to move out of the "culture of poverty" have "personality failures," Lewis replied:

"Implicit in your model is the notion of a laissez faire system with free mobility and so the people who don't make it are either sick individuals or don't have the proper personality traits. ... [I]t may ... be that you are not giving sufficient attention to the nature of the social structure, the built-in obstacles to upward mobility, and the inherent limitations in the system which would make it difficult, if not impossible, for more than a small number of the poor to move out of their present situation, irrespective of their personality traits" (Rigdon 252). However, if this was his position, he misstated himself when he established cause-and-effect links between poverty and culture, not between poverty and capitalism (Rigdon 88).

42. That Lewis considered both the father-centered families in Mexico and the mother-centered families in Puerto Rico within his "culture of poverty" framework suggests to me that the feature of father-centered or mother-centered was not an essential ingredient of the culture of poverty, though the applications of the culture of poverty tended to emphasize the "matrifocal" structure of families that came to be labeled "dysfunctional."

43. Lewis's decision to include an introduction to *La Vida* and his title—*La Vida: A Puerto Rican Family in the Culture of Poverty—San Juan and New York*—frame the Ríos family within the "culture of poverty."

44. Though Lewis said that in *La Vida* he did not speak about Puerto Rico as a whole ("I should like to emphasize that this study deals with only one segment of the Puerto Rican population and that the data should not be generalized to Puerto Rican society" [xiii]), he does generalize to all Puerto Ricans. For example, he says, "The Ríos family, their friends and neighbors, reflect many of the characteristics of the subculture of poverty, characteristics which are widespread in Puerto Rico but which are by no means exclusively Puerto Rican" (xxv). Valentine calls attention to this contradiction in his critique of Lewis (Valentine 52).

45. It also did not help that Lewis refrained from overtly stating his questions and questionnaires in the book. He says something about these in the introduction but then allows the characters to run the show, providing no help to readers about how he sees the material. He justifies his decision by saying that he wanted them to speak for themselves. It is obvious that Lewis is in control: editing interviews, devising questionnaires, translating material, and so on.

46. In the expression "una mujer de la vida," "la vida" is popular usage for prostitution. See Maldonado-Denis 496. In this sense, Lewis's title *La Vida* is a pun referring not only to daily life but also to "the night life." Lewis found prostitution the most vexing problem of "slum" life in Puerto Rico.

47. For consideration of *Labyrinth* in this context, see José Manuel Valenzuela-Arce, *Impecable y diamantina* 102. For Lewis, see Clara E. Rodríguez, "Puerto Ricans in Historical and Social Science Research" esp. 15–26; Bonnie Urciuoli, *Exposing Prejudice* 47. For Moynihan, see Valentine. Valentine critiques formulations that blame poverty on the poor and considers both Lewis and Moynihan under this critique (15).

CHAPTER 2

1. As with many novelized autobiographies, similarities in character and author abound. For example, both Piri and Thomas were born in Harlem in 1928 and grew up during the depression; both knew street environments of poverty, racism, and crime; both had gang, drug, and prison experiences; both took trips into the South; and both underwent spiritual awakenings through Islam and Pentecostal faiths. One major difference is that whereas Piri's mother and father are Puerto Ricans, Thomas's mother is Puerto Rican and his father Cuban. See Binder, "An Interview with Piri Thomas" 65.

2. I use "sexuality" to refer to sexual desires and behaviors—what is done with/to the constructed sexed body and with whom—and "gender" to refer to socially constructed differences by which societies define maleness and femaleness.

3. For my explanation of how I use the terms "Chicano" and "Chicana" in this book, please see note 1 in the introduction.

4. See bell hooks, "Race and Sex"; Toni Cade Bambara, ed., *The Black Woman* esp. 101–110; Patricia Hill Collins, *Black Feminist Thought* esp. 8–9; Adelaida del Castillo, "Malintzin Tenepal"; Angie Chabram-Dernersesian, "I Throw Punches for My Race, but I Don't Want to Be a Man"; and Arnaldo Cruz-Malavé, "Toward an Art of Transvestism." For a discussion of nationalisms and sexualities in an international context, see Andrew Parker et al., *Nationalisms and Sexualities*.

5. Different variants have emerged in Chicana feminist critical discourse from the political and academic experiences of Chicana women, primarily of working-class origin, who participated in the Chicano movement. One variant is a Chicana feminist "herstory," which argues that Chicanas, although absented from U.S. and Mexican history books, have been present in history. For pioneering works, see Marta Cotera, *Diosa y Hembra*; Cotera, *The Chicana Feminist*; Alfredo Mirandé and Evangelina Enríquez, *La Chicana*; Rosaura Sánchez and Rosa Martínez Cruz, eds., *Essays on La Mujer*. A second variant is represented by Chicanas who have re-semanticized the historical antecedent of La Malinche. A third perspective might include those who have articulated the sexist biases of Chicanos in the movement: see Ana Nieto-Gómez, "La Feminista"; Guadalupe Valdés-Fallís, "The Liberated Chicana"; Mirta Vidal, "Women: New Voice of La Raza." My point of departure in analyzing *Down These Mean Streets* is rooted primarily in the second and third variants. Gloria Anzaldúa and Cherríe Moraga compiled a cross-cultural anthology that challenged the ethnocentrism of the second-wave feminist movement of educated and economically privileged white women; see Gloria Anzaldúa and Cherríe Moraga, eds., *This Bridge Called My Back*. For a discussion of foundational writings related to Chicana feminism, see Alma M. García, ed., *Chicana Feminist Thought*. Examples of contemporary cultural criticism are Norma Alarcón, "Traddutora, Traditora"; Chabram-Dernersesian, "I Throw Punches"; Rosaura Sánchez, "Reconstructing Chicana Gender Identity." For an application

of the significance of La Malinche to a lesbian context, see Deena González, "*Malinche* as Lesbian."

6. The judgment of betrayal in the myth of La Malinche is based primarily on women's sexual roles of mother, temptress, and whore. Since the 1970s allusions to La Malinche have circulated widely in various branches of Chicana feminist literary discourse. Alarcón, del Castillo, and Candelaria were among the first to revise the stereotyped figure; they stressed La Malinche's skills as a military strategist and a translator between European and Native American worlds. See Norma Alarcón, "Chicana Feminist Literature"; Cordelia Candelaria, "La Malinche"; del Castillo, "Malintzin Tenepal." I discussed La Malinche's role in Lucha Corpi's "Marina Poems"; see Marta Sánchez, *Contemporary Chicana Poetry* 183–195. See also Alicia Gaspar de Alba's poem "Malinchista, A Myth Revised" 212–213. Moraga has reclaimed La Chingada (the "fucked woman") as a symbol of interpretive power for Chicana lesbians. See Moraga, "A Long Line of Vendidas." Alarcón discusses La Malinche in the context of Mexican nationalism and Chicano and Chicana ethnic nationalism; see Alarcón, "Traddutora, Traditora." Pratt explains how Chicanas have reconceptualized the figure in poetry beyond bipolar national models in "'Yo Soy La Malinche.'" Sandra Messinger Cypess argues that "the sign 'La Malinche' functions as a continually enlarging palimpsest of Mexican cultural identity whose layers of meaning have accrued through the years"; see Cypess, *La Malinche in Mexican Literature* 5. Chicanas have generally argued for the separation of La Malinche and La Chingada. They have argued against La Malinche's representations as a traitor to nation and culture but not against the concept of La Chingada as a figure of passive sexuality. Hence my analysis of Piri and the transvestites in the final section of this chapter suggests a revision of the sexual role of La Chingada from a passive into an active one.

7. See chapter 4 of Paz.

8. I am suggesting not that Mexican and Chicano cultures are the same but that history, patterns of migration and immigration, language, religion, and culture attest to strong continuities between them. The La Malinche trope "migrated" from Mexico to the Chicano and Chicana Southwest during the Chicano and Chicana academic and social movement in the 1960s and 1970s, probably through the movement's reception of the writings of Mexican authors and thinkers, for example, Octavio Paz and Carlos Fuentes. The Chicano movement, part of the Civil Rights movement of the 1970s, exposed racism against people of Mexican origin in the United States and insisted that their history and lifeways belonged inside a national collectivity.

9. Bernal Díaz notes that the Mexican Indians referred to Hernán Cortés as Malinche: "Doña Marina was always with him. . . . So they gave Cortés the name of 'Marina's Captain,' which was shortened to Malinche" 172. See Díaz, *The Conquest of New Spain*. Although gender-neutral, the name is more commonly applied to men, since they more frequently populate the world of politics and foreign relations. Pratt asserts that "betrayal is coded in the language as *female*. To be

a traitor is by implication to become female, while to be female is to be inherently a potential traitor." See Pratt, "'Yo Soy La Malinche'" 860.

10. Paz was probably the first to link the two names. In his 1950 collection of essays, *The Labyrinth of Solitude,* he explains that the past participle *chingada* derives from the verb *chingar,* "to act on." Despite the verb's almost invariably aggressive connotations, *chingada,* "acted upon," is "even more passive" than "pure receptivity." La Chingada's passivity, he continues, is "abject: she does not resist violence, but is an inert heap of bones, blood and dust" (85). Paz's book is perhaps cited more often than any other source on these two epithets, both by those who criticize it and by those who encounter it for the first time. Although I reject Paz's views, I recognize how enabling his comments have been for the Chicano and Chicana social activist movement as well as for Chicana feminists who contest Paz's demeaning sexual metaphors and their implications for Mexican women, Chicanas, and women in general.

11. A "Chicana feminist tradition" of the La Malinche trope includes Mexican as well as Chicano and Chicana terrain.

12. The term *nuyorican* or *neo-rican* is used to designate Puerto Ricans born on the U.S. mainland. See Edna Acosta-Belén, "Beyond Island Boundaries" 980; Frances R. Aparicio, "From Ethnicity to Multiculturalism" 19. Like "Chicano" and "black," the term has had shifting connotations over time. Although island Puerto Ricans used it pejoratively before 1970 to refer to mainland Puerto Ricans, as Mexican nationals and some in the United States used "pocho" to refer to English-speaking Mexican Americans, the generation after Thomas reclaimed it as a strategy for signaling a hybridized identity.

13. Thomas also wrote *Savior Savior, Hold My Hand* (1972), his sequel to *Down These Mean Streets,* and *Seven Long Times* (1974). He has also written *Stories from El Barrio* (1978). In 1997 *Down These Mean Streets* was translated into Spanish (*Por estas calles bravas*) to commemorate the thirtieth anniversary of its publication.

14. Thomas called Long Island a "foreign country," where "[he] was the only little coffee grain for miles around in a sea of white milk." He speaks very favorably about some white English teachers who encouraged his interest in writing. See Ilan Stavans, *Race and Mercy.*

15. The book appeared two years after the Watts riots and Malcolm X's assassination and one year before the 1968 Democratic National Convention in Chicago and Martin Luther King's assassination. As I mentioned in the introduction, 1967 also marked the Supreme Court's decision in *Loving v. Virginia* that the prohibition of interracial marriage was unconstitutional.

16. For readings of the novel as a black nationalist text, see John O. Killens, "On *El Barrio* and Piri Thomas"; Lennox Raphael, "What's Happening Here." For readings of it as a novel of rehabilitation, see Melvin Maddocks, "The Knuckle-Hard Code of the Barrio." Also see Elmer Bendiner, "Machismo"; Daniel Stern, "One Who Got Away."

17. Although Puerto Ricans, those in New York for example, knew that this

text was Puerto Rican, they did not intervene in the written reception to complicate the racial binary.

18. See Eugene V. Mohr, *The Nuyorican Experience;* Clara Rodríguez, *Puerto Ricans;* Virginia E. Sánchez-Korrol, *The Puerto Rican Struggle.* The Center for Puerto Rican Studies (Centro de Estudios Puertorriqueños) was established in New York in 1973. The first issue of the *Américas Review* (formerly *Revista Chicano-Riqueña*), a journal devoted to literature by and about U.S. Latinos, also appeared in 1973. Few forums existed in the late 1960s for the discussion of a Puerto Rican identity.

19. This location between two cultures and territories linked by routine flights between San Juan and New York is dramatized in the short story "La guagua aérea" ("The Air Bus") by the island Puerto Rican Luis Rafael Sánchez.

20. While Cruz-Malavé's recent work on this issue covers island and mainland literature, I am more interested in cross-cultural intersections on the mainland. See Cruz-Malavé, "Toward an Art of Transvestism"; and "'What a Tangled Web . . .!'"

21. On the relation of gender and sexuality to ethnicity, for an African American context, see Lee Edelman, "The Part for the (W)hole"; bell hooks, "Race and Sex." Edelman examines gendered metaphors in relation to homosexuality, and hooks examines them in relation to colonization. Cruz-Malavé's "'What a Tangled Web . . .!'" and "Toward an Art" are indispensable sources on the feminization of colonization and on the construction of gay male sexuality in Puerto Rican literature. For discussions of gender and sexuality with respect to race and ethnicity in Chicano culture, see Alarcón, "Chicana Feminist Literature"; Almaguer, "Chicano Men"; del Castillo, "Malintzin Tenepal." For a focus on intracultural contexts, see Gloria Anzaldúa, "La Prieta"; Moraga, "A Long Line of Vendidas." A study on gender and sexuality in relation to island colonial rule is Margarita Ostaloza Bey's *Política sexual en Puerto Rico.*

22. As I state in the introduction, there are no figures of "fucked," violated, or betraying women in the Puerto Rican social imaginary of the Spanish Conquest. In fact, its oral tradition tells of native women who resisted the Spanish conqueror. The Taíno princess, Anacaona La Brava, is one example who paid with her life. See Josefina Oliva de Coll, *La resistencia indígena ante la conquista* 28–30. To be sure, the Puerto Rican "nation" has been codified (by the *independistas* for example) as "female" but not in terms of sexual positionings, as in Paz, in Mexican nationalism, and in the early expressions of Chicano ethnic nationalism. "I am Joaquín," by Corky Gonzales, is one example; see Rodolpho (Corky) Gonzales, *I am Joaquín. Yo soy Joaquín.* The dramatic *actos* and *mitos* of the early Luis Valdez are also examples. Among others, see Luis Valdez, *Pensamiento Serpentino;* Luis Valdez and El Teatro Campesino, *Actos.*

23. Racial differentiation in Chicano and Chicana families and communities is a theme in Richard Rodriguez's *Hunger of Memory,* Anzaldúa's "La Prieta," and Moraga's "La Güera."

24. Used commonly in Puerto Rico and the Caribbean to denote things black, *moyeto* is Piri's intraracial term for designating and denigrating (albeit unconsciously) American blacks. *Moyeto* suggests *mayate,* a racist term used by some Chicanos and Chicanas to refer to African Americans.

25. The English word *Negro* must be differentiated from the Spanish word *negro,* which does not represent a discrete racial category. I explain these terms in section 6 of the introduction. It is my sense that Spanish has no linguistic counterpart to the English pejorative "nigger."

26. Puerto Rico, like other Latin American countries, never had antimiscegenation laws. Though Puerto Rico and other Latin American countries have histories of slavery, they did not fight civil wars to eliminate it. In Puerto Rico, slavery was declared illegal in 1873.

27. The one-drop rule classifies individuals as black if they have one black ancestor. The hypodescent rule, acknowledged historically in the United States by the federal courts, the Census Bureau, and other government agencies, assigns people of mixed racial origin to subordinated racial groups. See F. James Davis, *Who Is Black? One Nation's Definition.*

28. The parallels obfuscate the differences in the two societies' scripting of race relations and conflict. The U.S. ideology of racial purity has historically treated racial categories as dichotomous oppositions and as totalized self-contained spheres rather than as positions on a racial continuum differentiated by degrees, a model that would allow a more positive social recognition of hybridity. A graduated system of "pigmentocracy" has been more characteristic of Spanish America, as notions of *mulatismo* (mixing of Europeans and Africans) and *mestizaje* (mixing of Europeans and indigenous peoples) confirm. To be sure, Spanish American societies have racial hierarchies as well, anchored in biology and genetics—with white at the top, Native American and black at the bottom. But in these societies' coding of race, mestizo or mestiza and mulatto or mulatta, are only two of the numerous categories invented to accommodate a racially diverse population.

29. In Latin America, *mestizaje* is a political ideology that has been deployed to reaffirm whiteness and to disavow both indigenousness and blackness. It sometimes functions as a Latin American melting-pot theory because though it purports to acknowledge racial mixture it winds up upholding it as a kind of purity, as the most socially valued. See Marta E. Sánchez, "Calibán: The New Latin American Protagonist of the Tempest." See also Díaz Quiñones's introduction to Tomás Blanco's *El prejuicio racial en Puerto Rico.* Blanco was one of the first island thinkers to write in the 1930s on Puerto Rican racial prejudice. Díaz Quiñones recontextualizes Blanco's ideas in a modern setting. On free persons of African descent and on nineteenth-century racial prejudice in Puerto Rico, see Kinsbruner. For useful discussions and critiques of *mestizaje* as a political ideology, and the various purposes it has served in different regions, countries, and historical periods in Latin America, see Lourdes Martínez-Echazábal, *Para una semiótica de la mulatez* and "*Mestizaje* and the Discourse of National/Cultural Identity in Latin

America"; and Marisol de la Cadena, *Indigenous Mestizos*. They note its usages as a whitening tool and as a nation-building strategy.

30. Almaguer discusses the active-passive axis as a continuum; see Almaguer, "Chicano Men." Studies of Puerto Rican sexuality also observe this split; see Acosta-Belén, "Beyond Island Boundaries"; Celia Fernández Cintrón and Marcia Rivera Quintero, "Bases de la sociedad sexista en Puerto Rico"; Ostaloza Bey.

31. Fanon's discussion of the white woman's allure for the black man (63–82) is applicable to Poppa's marriage and to Piri's behavior with a white prostitute in a Texas brothel in my third example below. Piri's behavior in the brothel only proves the "value" of the white woman. See Frantz Fanon, "The Man of Color and the White Woman," in *Black Skin, White Masks*. What Fanon writes in *Black Skin, White Masks* is applicable to Piri's father: "An anxious man who cannot escape his body" (65).

32. See prelude, note 6.

33. Almaguer claims that *maricón* (sissy or fairy) is the most benign of the contemptuous Spanish labels for homosexuals; see Almaguer, "Chicano Men" 82.

34. None of the other Spanish-speaking characters including Piri's mother, father, and his girlfriend (a recent arrival from Puerto Rico) has this overtly camp accent.

35. Paz says that Mexicans tolerate male homosexuality "on condition that it consists in violating a passive agent" (40). Almaguer concurs: "a Mexican man's masculine gender and heterosexual identity are not threatened by a homosexual act as long as he plays the inserter role"; see Almaguer, "Chicano Men" 81.

36. These vulgar terms are used in Spanish to erase so-called passive male homosexuals.

37. "Haras" probably derives from "O'Hara," a name that suggests the stereotypical Irish cop.

INTERLUDE 2

1. As Charles E. Silberman wrote in *Fortune* in 1965, "As recently as 1940, more than two-thirds of all Negro Americans lived in the eleven states of the Old Confederacy, most of them in rural areas. As a result of the tremendous migration of Negroes that occurred during the 1940's and 1950's, about half of all Negroes now live in the cities outside the Deep South." See Silberman, "Beware the Day They Change Their Minds!" 153; and "The City and the Negro."

2. Citizenship for Puerto Ricans in 1917 spurred migration, which grew rapidly in the 1920s. Between 1898 and 1940 the number of Puerto Ricans in New York City was substantial, more than 61,000, but nowhere near the number after World War II. See Stephan Thernstrom, Ann Orlov, and Oscar Handlin, eds., *Harvard Encyclopedia of American Ethnic Groups* 860.

3. Oscar Handlin, *The Newcomers* 50–51.

4. Operation Bootstrap (Operación Mano de Obra) was a U.S. endeavor to inject investment capital into Puerto Rico. It brought industrial development to the island and employment for Puerto Ricans in the large cities. The cities could not absorb the influx of people, and a massive migration from the island to metropolitan centers on the mainland resulted. Most of the migration was to New York.

5. Thomas attributes no surname in the book to Alayce.

6. Paz did not talk about La Malinche as La Chingada in the context of Chicano culture, but he did talk about the pachuco and described him as an "open" male, a male feminized as La Chingada. What he said about La Chingada had ramifications for Chicano women and men. I take up the relation between the pachuco and La Malinche in interlude 4.

7. The dangers of Jim Crow values and practices were both real and mythic in their proportions. Not only did African Americans in the U.S. South witness the devastation to black families as well as the corpses resulting from the murderous activities of white supremacists, but they took their stories to the North. See Benjamin Schwarz, Rev. of *Without Sanctuary*. Also see Robin D. G. Kelley, *Hammer and Hoe*.

8. Piri sometimes jokingly pronounces "Porty Rican," which might explain why Alayce says it this way, though an uninformed majority society gives it this pronunciation. For Puerto Rican readers, this spelling and pronunciation creates an ironic sonic effect, given the fact that the island's name was officially distorted for a few years as "Porto Rico." In legislative bills, in Puerto Rico supreme court and U.S. Supreme Court decisions, and in the annual reports of Puerto Rico's governor, the island was referred to as "Porto Rico." Titles of books by white Americans are *Porto Rico and Its Problems* and *Porto Rico: A Broken Pledge*. See José Trías Monge, *Puerto Rico* 83–84 and chap. 7, notes 4, 23, 26, 29.

9. "Mr. Charlie" is black slang for "white man" in the novel.

10. One example taken from a Negro testimonial is, "a voice like thunder seeming to enter my soul, saying, I am your God and am with you; though the world be against you, I am more than the world; though wicked men hunt you, trust in me, for I am the Rock of your Defense." See Charles T. Davis and Henry Louis Gates, Jr., eds., *The Slave's Narrative* 310.

11. I comment on the "dog" image in this quotation later in this chapter.

12. Thomas's use of the Spanish *amigo* links Brew's defense of manhood to Piri's affirmation of the same.

13. What the crackers try to do to Brew—to make him their receptacle—is an example of feminization. I recognize that what divides *emasculation, feminization, demasculinization* and *penetration* is a fine line. *Emasculation* is castration, neutering; *feminization* is imposing feminine characteristics on a male with the intent to belittle him. At a physical level, it involves penetration. Strictly speaking, Paz's discourse is feminization, not castration.

14. Brew does not share W. E. B. Du Bois's outlook when the latter summed up the feelings of many black men: "but one thing I shall never forgive, neither in

this world nor in the world to come; it's [the white South's] wanton and continued and persistent insulting of the black womanhood which it sought and seeks to prostitute to its lust." Quoted in Barbara Omolade, "Hearts of Darkness" 359.

15. I paraphrase what Brew seems to say: "Now, now Alayce; it's not the end of the world, because you are a woman. But I, I am a man, and well ... that's different."

16. A good word in Spanish for objectification is *ningunear:* literally, to "thing-ify," to turn someone into a nobody.

17. See chap. 3, sec. 3.

18. Notably, Thomas's Muhammad says nothing about black women.

19. I borrow the term "signifyin'" from Henry Louis Gates Jr., *The Signifying Monkey.*

20. Paz talks about "penetration" at the linguistic level but the basis of his commentary is male and female biology. The linguistic level in Paz involves verbal dueling, which is not the case here.

21. Brew's transference of the battleground from the body to the mind makes an ironic comment on the theatrical practice of whites who would "black up" to perform racist caricatures of blacks in the tradition of blackface minstrelsy. Brew controls who speaks what. He "violates" the oppressor by feeding him words. He makes "white face" wear "blackface," but with the difference that a black man is in charge of directing the "puppet show."

22. Susan Bordo, *Unbearable Weight* 9. This means that a chaste Negro woman is an impossibility, that assault is never against her will. This is what critics of this racist position mean when they say that white supremacist culture holds that the black woman is "unrapeable."

23. Here it seems Piri's reading agrees with Brew's resistance to a Christian code of conduct; Christ embodies feminization.

CHAPTER 3

1. In an episode in *Manchild in the Promised Land,* the narrative conscious-ness makes explicit that "Sonny" is Claude Brown. When in family court, Sonny says, "The lawyer came over to me and said, 'Hello, Claude; how are you?'" (96). Another explicit relationship between Sonny and Brown occurs on p. 134.

2. Famous examples of "bad niggers" in Sonny's sense are the runaway slave Nat Turner and the boxer Jack Johnson. Of course, rap and hip-hop have given the word a new sound ("nigga") and context. To Claude Brown's generation, a "bad nigger" was someone like Paul Robeson, Sidney Poitier, and the sports fig-ures already noted.

3. Henry Louis Gates attributes "tropes-a-dope" to Kimberly W. Benston, who invents the pun to call attention to verbal tricks in an African American tra-dition. See Henry Louis Gates Jr., "The Blackness of Blackness" 286.

4. Suzan-Lori Parks's Pulitzer Prize–winning *Topdog/Underdog* opened at the Joseph Papp Theatre in New York City in summer 2001. I thank my former colleague Susan Larsen for telling me about this play in which "three-card monte" is an important image-device. See Nancy Franklin, "Double Dealing" 86. For "conning a dope," see Parks, *Topdog/Underdog*.

5. One example is the scam called "the Murphy," an extension of the nutshell game in which women are shuffled around just like the pea. In Times Square, men, "country cats," "out-of towners," and soldiers, are promised "some-a the best pussy in New York," but after paying money to the con man and going to the designated hotel room, the customers find no one. See Brown, *Manchild* 160–162.

6. Toni Morrison, "Rootedness" 339–345.

7. See Ignatiev; Lipsitz, *The Possessive Investment in Whiteness*; Lott, "White Like Me"; Roediger; Rogin; Saxton.

8. Moynihan was aware of a Puerto Rican population in New York during that time. Glazer and Moynihan studied five ethnic groups, with Glazer writing the chapter on Puerto Ricans in the context of the tenets of the "culture of poverty." See Nathan Glazer and Daniel Patrick Moynihan, *Beyond the Melting Pot*. Moynihan would also have been aware of the study by Handlin. Yet Moynihan's document, the most influential in terms of a legislative agenda and public policy, only made two minor passing remarks to Puerto Ricans. He made none to low-income whites.

9. Generally, there were a few early critical essays on Claude Brown's text. See Houston A. Baker, "Environment as Enemy in a Black Autobiography"; Thomas L. Hartshorn, "Horatio Alger in Harlem." A recent study is by Carlos Rotello, "The Box of Groceries and the Omnibus Tour." I suggest the main reason for the omission of a discussion of the intercultural forefathers was probably that the book was received as either mainstream "white" or "black." See section 5 of the introduction for a discussion of *Manchild*'s reception.

10. My discussion of blacks and Jews in interlude 3 should make clear that I do not reference the either/or of whiteness and blackness without acknowledging that "ethnic" categories such as Jewish American and Italian American were quite developed by the 1960s, and Jewish American, at the very least, was a recognized category of "ethnic" literature.

11. The term "enemy memories" comes from a *New Yorker* essay by Berman about blacks and Jews; see Paul Berman, "The Other and the Almost the Same." Berman credits the term to Shelby Steele.

12. For an interesting discussion of the strong identification between the two groups, see Berman. Cooperative work between blacks and Jews dates to before the Holocaust. Murray Friedman locates the origins of black-Jewish relations in the foundation of the National Association for the Advancement of Colored People (NAACP) in 1909; see Murray Friedman, *What Went Wrong?* Berman calls the founding of the NAACP the first important moment in the black-Jewish Alliance

(64). Hasis Diner documents Jewish support of African American struggles for social justice and political equity between 1880 and 1935, the decades when blacks, moving north into major cities, and eastern European Jews, fleeing pogroms in Europe, settled in urban areas in the United States. See Diner, *Almost Promised Land*. Thulani Davis, a black woman, writer, and cultural critic, writes that the intimate bonding between Jews and blacks spans roughly the era of "the life of W. E. B. Du Bois from the days of [Jewish] immigration from Europe to the days leading up to the March in Washington 1963." See Davis, "We Need to Do Some Work" 30.

13. "[W]hen [the Negro] rose," says Baldwin, "he was not hailed as a hero fighting for his land, but condemned as a savage, hungry for white flesh." See James Baldwin, "Negroes Are Anti-Semitic Because They're Anti-White" 744–745.

14. This expression, an ironic play on "peculiar institution" for the system of slavery, refers to the connections and tensions in black-Jewish relations, particularly since the end of the Civil Rights movement. See Jack Salzman and Cornel West, eds., *Struggles in the Promised Land* 2. For more on the tensions between blacks and Jews on affirmative action, see Berman, esp. 67–68.

15. See Marcus Garvey, *Philosophy and Opinions of Marcus Garvey*. Robert A. Hill states: "It was in Harlem that the program for Africa's redemption was nurtured under the banner of the Garvey movement." See Hill, "Black Zionism" 52.

16. Some examples are the biblical themes in slave spirituals (e.g., "Let my people go"), the journey out of Egypt as a backdrop image for an African American struggle against white domination in the works of James Baldwin, and the sermons of the nineteenth and twentieth centuries, including those of the Reverends Martin Luther King Jr. and Jesse L. Jackson Sr. See Lawrence W. Levine, *Black Culture and Black Consciousness*. This is not the place to examine whether this process of emulation has also worked in the inverse direction, but there are claims that U.S. Jewish writers and artists have embraced black motifs as a way of expressing their own Jewish identities and culture: Al Jolson, Irving Berlin, and George Gershwin are a few examples. See David Brion Davis, "Jews and Blacks in America" 57.

17. I see this identification as primarily symbolic, for rhetorical effect, though I do not mean by this that it is unmeaningful. Sometimes the symbolic has more power than what might be argued is historically accurate. But I would say that the exodus of the Israelites in the Bible has as much to do with the migration of blacks into northern cities on historical terms as the vision of Aztlán has to do with Chicanos and Mexicans living in the Southwest. Salzman offers a quote from a slave by the name of Charles Davenport that makes my point: "De preachers would exhort us dat us was de chillen o' Israel in de wilderness an' de Lord done sent us to take dis land o' milk and honey. But how us gwine-a take land what's already been took?" See Salzman and West 6. For the passage in the context of Davenport's oral testimony, see Norman R. Yetman, *Life Under the "Peculiar Institution"* 75.

18. Negro migrants from southern plantations went beyond small south-

ern cities and descended on northern industrial centers after World War I. For E. Franklin Frazier, there were three wrenching periods of U.S. history: slavery, emancipation, and Reconstruction. It was during Reconstruction and after that the great migrations of African Americans to the North took place. See Frazier.

19. Wiltwyck was an actual correctional school, mainly for African American boys in its early years, founded in upstate New York in 1936 by Judge Justine Wise Polier, a Jewish American, the first female justice of New York, and a crusading reformer of the family court system. Polier founded Wiltwyck for nonwhite children excluded from the more humane rehabilitation programs of the time by juvenile justice laws. She enlisted and received help from First Lady Eleanor Roosevelt in 1942 when Wiltwyck was in danger of closing. Wiltwyck kept its doors open to children like Claude Brown until 1983. Its most famous student was probably Floyd Patterson, the heavyweight champion of the world. See www.sitesofconscience. org/eng/roosevelt_wiltwyck.htm. See also the "Justine Wise Polier" entry on the "Jewish Women's Archive" Internet source, www.jwa.org/exhibits/wise/jp7.htm. As I point out at the end of this chapter, Brown, who graduated from Howard University in 1965, dedicates *Manchild in the Promised Land* to Roosevelt. James Traub's review of Nina Bernstein's *The Lost Children of Wilder* in the *New York Review of Books* discusses the work of Judge Wise Polier. See Traub, "Bleak House."

20. The tale is of a little black boy who loses his beautiful garments to several menacing tigers. The tigers vie for superiority. They whirl round and round so much that they melt away and leave nothing but a big pool of melted butter. The little black boy takes the butter home to his mother, who makes him pancakes for supper. It is the energy created in the tale by the tiger's whirling movements and the resulting product and prize of the butter that stimulates listeners to think of this well-known tale by Helen Bannerman (1862–1946) and its later twentieth-century spin-offs.

21. My UCSD colleague Stephanie Jed brought the Italian expression, *latte alle ginocchia,* to my attention. It means literally "milk on the knee" but depending on the context may symbolically allude to semen.

22. Sonny's older black street-friend Johnny teaches Sonny that to win street fights he needs to exercise self-control, not let passion overwhelm him. He says, "When you git excited, you can't do a goddamn thing, man" (116–117). Two opponents fighting, Johnny says, is like a man who desires "a bitch. If you gon pull a bitch, you can't git excited and let her know that you want that pussy so bad you about to go crazy" because "you gon lose your brains through your dick?" (117). I paraphrase what Johnny is saying to Sonny: "focus, be impervious, or at least appear that way" because "a horny cat was lost" (111).

23. There is an interesting discussion about body versus mind stereotypes in African American and Jewish traditions in chapter 3 of *Jews and Blacks: Let the Healing Begin* by Rabbi Michael Lerner and the African American scholar Cornel West. West writes, "When we look at some of the uglier stereotypes of black people, one of their more telling features is the absolute denial of the capacity

for critical intelligence. When we look at the stereotypes of Jewish people, some might be concerned with aesthetics, but rarely is it a denial of access to critical intelligence" (62). Lerner writes, "So where does a Jewish man become a man, if he can't compete on the same grounds as the dominant culture? The answer is, he does it by becoming a scholar, a reader of texts, or a scribe, someone who can act out his prowess in the realm of written words" (64).

24. See chap. 1, sec. 5; and chap. 1 n. 34. The leading work in this racial liberal tradition, of course, was by Myrdal. For discussion on the relation between "liberal orthodoxy" and the topic of the black family, see Berger 412.

25. George Mariscal explains how McNamara and Moynihan created Project 100,000, a recruitment policy that resulted in what some have called an "alternative army." Project 100,000 aimed to educate men previously rejected by the armed forces for failing performances on the mental aptitude Selective Service education tests. Under the auspices of contributing to the domestic objectives of Johnson's War on Poverty, the military also set out to remedially educate low-income, uneducated youth. Thus the policy would "kill two birds with one stone": poverty and the preparation of additional men to augment the numbers of combat troops for Vietnam. See Mariscal, *Aztlán and Viet Nam* 20. The "New Standards" men recruited under this alternative method were popularly dubbed inside and outside the armed forces "McNamara's Moron Corps." See Lawrence M. Baskir and William A. Strauss, *Change and Circumstance* 127; Myra MacPherson, *Long Time Passing* 560. Mariscal notes that once military escalation in Vietnam became a reality, "the draft pool would have to be expanded, either upwards (to include middle-class college students) or downwards" into the lower-income groups (20). Among these were low-income whites and recruits of color, African Americans, Native Americans, Chicanos, and Puerto Ricans.

26. In Genesis 9:24, Ham is one of Noah's sons. After the Flood, he sees his drunken father naked. As punishment, Noah lays the curse of slavery on Ham's descendants (or Canaan's) who now must serve as slaves to Noah's other two sons. Noah blesses his other two sons, Japheth and Shem, and in the same prayer he utters his curse on Ham (Canaan). Brown, however, links him to his own vision of a "promised land," the North. Brown's second book was titled *The Children of Ham* (1976).

27. Where and when this link between Ham's curse and blackness is made is beyond the scope of this book. In his chapter "The Spell of Africa," Sundquist suggests Ham's blackness is part of Noah's curse: "the curse, said to be marked by his [Ham's] black skin, purportedly placed upon Ham by his father, Noah, which proslavery theologians had used to justify the enslavement of Africans." See Sundquist, *To Wake the Nations* 556. George M. Fredrickson acknowledges the use of Ham's curse, his black skin that is, to support white supremacy in the U.S. South and South Africa, although he points out that even more powerful than religious teachings in the consolidation of this belief were secular defenders of white supremacist institutions. See Fredrickson, *White Supremacy* 172–173.

28. According to *The New Interpreter's Bible,* "Ham was the progenitor of the nations of the Egyptian orbit." See entry "Ham," vol. 1.

29. For Turner and Williams, see D. Davis 60. For Blyden, see Sundquist 556. Fredrickson discusses all three men (he calls them "pioneer black nationalists") in the context of Ethiopianism and Pan-Africanism in *Black Liberation* (61); for Turner, see 76–80; for Williams, 149; and for Blyden, 67–71. Paul Gilroy provides a summary of Blyden's life and his importance as a "Black Atlantic" intellectual in "clarifying the connections—and the differences—between blacks and Jews." See Gilroy 208.

30. See D. Davis 60.

31. See Sundquist 559.

32. These terms are from Suzan-Lori Parks's *The American Play.* See N. Franklin 86.

33. Father Ford provides young black men with a sense of self that the educational, judicial, and familial system failed to give them. Sonny is somewhat different. Never a "head-nodder" (his name for dope addicts), the correctional schools eventually did work for him, judging by his dedication of *Manchild.*

34. Aziz S. Atiya says that the Coptics are ethnically neither Semitic nor Hamitic peoples "but may be described as the descendants of a Mediterranean race that entered the Nile valley in unrecorded times." See Aziz S. Atiya, *The Copts and Christian Civilization* 2.

35. Edward Wakin, *A Lonely Minority* 5.

36. The *Encyclopedia Americana International Edition* says "Copt" is derived from the Greek word "Aigyptos" which means "Egyptian." After contact with the Arab world, "Aigyptos" became "Copt." See "Coptic Church" entry. According to the *Harper Collins Dictionary of Religion,* the Coptic Church is the autonomous Christian Church of Egypt, founded by Mark the Evangelist in the first century. It separated from Roman Christianity over theological differences, and after the Council of Chalcedon in A.D. 451, members who refused to accept the official Roman dogma established their own independent Coptic Church. Atiya says that after the Arab invasion in the seventh century, the Egyptian Copts solidified their ethnic and religious identity to distinguish themselves from Muslims (2). See "Coptic Church" entry.

37. The Coptic people make up the majority of the Christian minority population in Egypt. Muslims have been the majority since Arab Muslims invaded Egypt in the seventh century. There are relations between Coptics in Egypt and those of Ethiopia and other parts of Africa. See Wakin.

38. Haile Selassie is mentioned in *Manchild* by one of Ford's disciples. Haile Selassie emancipated the slaves and achieved greatness for Ethiopia when he defeated its Italian invaders in 1935. Ethiopia had defeated Italy once before at Adowa in 1896; see entry "Ethiopianism" in *The New Encyclopaedia Britannica,* vol. 4. Two books on the former ruler are Indrias Getachew, *Beyond the Throne;* Harold G. Marcus, *Haile Selassie I.*

39. Ethiopia was the first country in Africa to repel a European power, not once but twice. It is the only country in Africa that escaped colonization by Europe, an act that made it a leader in worldwide black liberation and power.

40. See Sundquist 553–554.

41. Meaning "Queen of the South." See Atiya, n. 28, 17. Father Ford never identifies this "son."

42. Pan-Africanism has roots in Marcus Garvey (1887–1940), mentioned elsewhere in the book. Of course, Garvey and Jamaica interconnect with the Rastafarians, a black Jewish movement and religion transplanted to the United States from Jamaica that derived its name from Haile Selassie. Ras (meaning "Prince") Tafari Makonnon was Haile Selassie's birth name. The name Haile Selassie means "Might of the Trinity." See entries "Haile Selassie" and "Rastafarians" in *Harper Collins Dictionary of Religion.*

43. Father Ford does not mention Ethiopianism in *Manchild.* I connect Father Ford's vision to Ethiopianism because of the strong presence of Ethiopia as leader of the black world in his story. Ethiopianism is a messianic philosophy that finds legitimacy in a key line already cited from Psalms 68:31: "Ethiopia shall soon stretch forth her hands unto God." The Coptic Church today extends into modern Ethiopia and includes other Africans. For more on Ethiopianism, see Fredrickson's discussion in *Black Liberation,* beginning on p. 61; Sundquist 551–563. Ethiopianism is also a religious movement linked to the rise of independence movements in Africa and to the rise of black independent churches in Africa at the end of the nineteenth century that sought freedom from white patronage and oppressive ties to institutionalized Western Christian religions.

44. The "Queen of Sheba" evokes one facet of a La Malinche construction, since she is the female component of *mestizaje* between two distinct peoples that originates a third hybrid people.

45. Though they may disagree on its meaning, Western Christian religions and Judaism accept the narrative of Adam and Eve's disobedience and their subsequent expulsion from the Garden of Eden in Genesis 3.

46. Refer to note 19 for the importance of First Lady Eleanor Roosevelt in *Manchild in the Promised Land.*

INTERLUDE 3

1. Chitterlings are the intestines of hogs that require extensive cleaning and long hours of cooking before they can be eaten.

2. See the introduction and chapter 1 for fuller discussions of La Chingada.

3. James Baldwin captured the "uncontrollable note of fear" in a parent who perceives "the child ... challenging the white world's assumptions ... [and] putting himself in the path of destruction." See Baldwin, *The Fire Next Time* 41.

4. Thousands of people, overwhelmingly men, black, white, Mexican, and other, were lynched in the United States. Although lynchings took place in the West and Midwest, the numbers were highest in the South, of which the vast majority were black men killed by white lynch mobs, especially between 1880 and 1932. See Schwarz, Rev. of *Without Sanctuary* 1, 4–5. To be sure, African Americans who migrated North and West took images of black mutilated bodies with them. Claude Brown makes reference to Emmett Till, a Chicago youth visiting Mississippi who was killed—mutilated, shot, and dumped in a river—in 1955 after whistling at a white storekeeper's wife (299).

5. See chap. 1.

6. The formation of the concept of a nuclear family household, as opposed to an extended-family household, is a relatively modern phenomenon. For two studies that examine the development of the family in relation to capitalism and nation building, see Leonore Davidoff and Catherine Hall, *Family Fortunes;* Shirley Samuels, *Romances of the Republic.*

7. See chap. 1.

8. Richard Terdiman, *Discourse/Counter Discourse* 61.

9. In retrospect, it is ironic that as Moynihan wrote his report, with its curiously rosy picture of white middle-class mothers, and as the government published and released it, white women such as Betty Freidan and Kate Millet were "cooking" up revolution. According to Abbey Lincoln, at this time "the dominion of the kitchen and the welfare apartment [were] hardly powerful vantage points" (Cade Bambara, ed., *The Black Woman* 89).

10. See chap. 3, p. 80.

11. The dictionary gives for its second meaning "hymen [LL, from Gk *hymen* membrane]: a fold of mucous membrane partly closing the orifice of the vagina." Philip Babcock Gove, ed., *Webster's Third New International Dictionary.*

12. Barbara Johnson, writing in the context of Nathaniel Hawthorne's story "The Birth-Mark." Johnson, *The Feminist Difference* 19.

13. Farah Jasmine Griffin, "*Who Set You Flowin'?*"

14. See Amiri Baraka, *Home* 91.

15. Jean Carey Bond and Patricia Peery, speaking in the context of the Moynihan Report, state, "The matriarchal fairy tale is part of a perennial tendency among whites to employ every available device in *their* ongoing effort to demasculinize the Black male." See Bond and Peery, "Is the Black Male Castrated?" 116.

16. I think what Angela Davis says is fitting here: "What is frequently implied by evocations of 'queens,' . . . is that the ultimate authority rests with the 'kings.'" Angela Davis, *Blues Legacies and Black Feminism* 122. The term "welfare queen," referring to a single woman, usually black, one who grew rich on tax-funded welfare checks and drove a "welfare Cadillac," was first used in a speech in the 1980s by then President Ronald Reagan.

17. La Malinche, who served as translator between the varying indigenous peoples and the Spaniards, is also known as La Lengua. In Spanish *la lengua*

means both "tongue" and "language," as it does in English (i.e., the phrase "one's mother tongue" to refer to one's native language). See del Castillo 124–149.

18. The word's primary meanings and perlocutionary effects in a specific situation, of course, will depend on who speaks it, to whom, and who overhears it. The history of the term has enormous racial volatility when used by whites to designate blacks but takes on a whole range of different meanings when spoken by blacks to blacks, as Sonny often does in the company of his black friends. However, no matter its primary meaning in a given situation, no matter how clear a speaker's intent, the word will resonate its other meanings. For example, when Sonny uses "bad-ass nigger" to refer to the kind of black man he aspires to be—courageous, no pushover for anyone—the term may be understood by his black buddies to mean what Sonny intends, as long as blacks are the interlocutors. However, the word also retains its degrading racist potency. Consequently, we are probably hard-pressed to understand why Sonny would want, under any circumstances, to use a word that Christopher Darden, the deputy district attorney and prosecutor in the O. J. Simpson case, called the "dirtiest, filthiest, nastiest word in the English language." See Jim Newton and Andrea Ford, "Lawyers Bitterly Debate Race in Simpson Case." The word has been a powder keg in many instances in the contemporary world. By the same token, when its white supremacist meaning is the one intended or understood, those of us reading *Manchild* will have learned the term is malleable for black Americans and that its usage is sometimes ironic and playful. My point is that though the context always determines its primary meaning, the residual meanings of this term are present. For an interesting study of the history of the word's role in American life and law, see Randall Kennedy, *Nigger: The Strange Career of a Troublesome Word.*

19. Different consequences result when Sonny uses the word in front of his Italian friend Minetti. See end of *Manchild*'s chapter 4. If anything, Sonny qualifies as a La Malinche figure in its empowering sense. While his mother had no choice but to undergo the humiliation in front of the white man, having no control over the word "nigger," Sonny chooses consciously to use the word and to control its meaning. "It was real wrong to call somebody [a black person] a nigger in front of a paddy [white Italian] boy. . . . But saying 'nigger' wasn't the main thing to me. The main thing was that these [black] cats were trying to fuck over this paddy boy. And this paddy boy was more man than any of those [black] cats there" (137). Sonny chooses to defy his culture's limitations by choosing when to say "the word" and under what circumstances.

20. Moynihan understood the gendered connotation of "nigger" when he ironically used it to highlight what happened to black men who asserted themselves, or tried to. One wrong step or response, and the black man was lynched, sometimes actually castrated and mutilated. Moynihan was looking for ways that would allow the black man to "strut," on Moynihan's terms of course. From his viewpoint, Mrs. Brown injures her son by not allowing him to act manly.

21. W. E. B. Du Bois, *The Souls of Black Folk* 3.

22. What Brown means by "the most soulful word" is that "nigger" is the epitome of "soul" among some black folk: real, authentic, and inassimilable by the white mainstream. See Claude Brown, "The Language of Soul" 230–237.

23. The debates of black and Chicano women with men of their cultural groups on male-female relationships are complex and passionate. Black and Chicano women scholars and writers in their separate cultural contexts testify that some African American and Chicano men participated in perpetuating the view of "the matriarch" and La Malinche as controlling stereotypes. Michelle Wallace, Toni Cade Bambara, and Patricia Hill Collins make these claims. Wallace has suggested that some black men accepted the terms of Moynihan's rhetorical model. She argues: "Just as black men were busiest attacking Moynihan, they were equally busy attacking the black woman for being a matriarch"; Michelle Wallace, *Black Macho and the Myth of the Superwoman* 110. Cade Bambara puts it more generally: "There is a dangerous trend observable in some quarters of the Movement to program Sapphire [the caricature of the iron-willed, treacherous black woman with contempt for black men] out of her 'evil' ways into a cover-up, shut-up, lay-back-and-be-cool obedience role" (102). Collins says that black men who foster views of "superstrong Black mothers" or self-sacrificing women, "richly endowed with devotion . . . and unconditional love," avoid seeing the "very real costs of mothering to African-American women" (116). Alma M. García discusses and offers examples of how Chicano women "challenged the portrait of the so-called 'Ideal Chicana'" that some male Chicano cultural nationalists created; they either glorified Chicano women for sustaining traditional gender roles or baited them as traitors if they critiqued the sexism in the Chicano movement (*Chicana Feminist Thought* 5–6). The early movement writings by women in García are also instructive. Voicing criticism, some black and Chicano women claimed that "family" in the debates of the previous decade had been a way of talking about masculinity because gender had mattered only as it related to the emasculation of black men.

24. The two gender systems are inflected differently. Whereas Moynihan assumes a patriarchal genealogical line, Paz emphasizes a matriarchal genealogical line. For the difference in nuance in Moynihan's and Paz's way of thinking of feminization, see chapter 1.

25. I think of Sherley Anne Williams's fictional runaway slave who shouts to her white mistress Rufel: "mammy's nobody's name." See Williams, *Dessa Rose*.

CHAPTER 4

1. Because Acosta's book, like Piri Thomas's *Down These Mean Streets* and Claude Brown's *Manchild in the Promised Land*, has the atmosphere of the traditional autobiography, hinting at events in the author's life, I use "Acosta" for the author and "Oscar" for the protagonist. Acosta gives a straightforward account of

his life in "Autobiographical Essay" and "From Whence I Came" in *Oscar "Zeta" Acosta: The Uncollected Works* (1996).

2. I believe this strategy was to some extent necessary in the Chicano movement years. It is all too easy now to criticize what occurred then, but we have to remember that this was probably the most constructive strategy open to the movement, given the history of racism and discrimination against ethnic minorities. We also have to allow that audience expectations change with time. We are ready to interpret Acosta's phrasing differently now than we would have thirty years ago.

3. Elizabeth Ammons, "Introduction" xi.

4. Turner, *The Forest of Symbols.*

5. Although we do not see the results of this choice in the *Autobiography,* Oscar's decision comes just in time for the Chicano Moratorium protest march against the war in East Los Angeles in summer 1970. For the results of Oscar/ Acosta's choice, presented in novelized form, see Oscar Zeta Acosta, *Revolt of the Cockroach People* (1973).

6. Thompson casts Acosta in various identities in this book: "Dr. Gonzo," the "Samoan," the "Brown Buffalo." Thompson is known as the creator and practitioner of Gonzo journalism, a term he, Tom Wolfe, and Norman Mailer popularized in the 1960s—meaning "wild," "crazy," an uninhibited style of writing and living.

7. Several early reviews mentioned Acosta's connection to Thompson. The book received short reviews in *Saturday Review, Publisher's Weekly, Library Journal Book Review,* and *Choice.* The early reviews from a Chicano perspective came from Arthur Ramírez in *Revista Chicano-Riqueña* (1975) and Oswaldo Romero in *Mester* (1974). More extensive articles by Chicano scholars began to appear in 1979. One example is by Ramón Saldívar, "A Dialectic of Difference." Another important article is Genaro Padilla, "The Self as Cultural Metaphor in Acosta's *Autobiography of a Brown Buffalo.*"

8. Most, possibly all, reviews in the ten-year period following the book's publication were written by Chicano men. Chicano women kept their distance. The Chicano poet Raúl Salinas, who met Acosta in 1972, gives us a taste of some Chicano women's reaction to Acosta: "Some Chicanas detested him. I remember some of them in San Diego telling me, 'This *vato* is grouse [*sic*]!' A sexist, they said. They thoroughly disliked his treatment of women in *The Autobiography of a Brown Buffalo.*" Quoted in Ilan Stavans, *Bandido* 115.

9. Stavans tells of how angry Acosta was on reading *Fear and Loathing in Las Vegas.* Acosta felt that Thompson had used the experiences and ideas he had shared with him on their Las Vegas trip and that Thompson had not given him due credit. After threatening Thompson's New York publisher with a lawsuit for libel, Random House and Acosta struck a bargain. Random House would secure a contract to publish Acosta's first book and Acosta would refrain from suing. Stavans, *Bandido* 99–100.

10. Thompson was researching a piece for *Rolling Stone* on police brutality in

East Los Angeles. Paul Perry, in *Fear and Loathing,* tells of Acosta's friends resenting Thompson at get-togethers in East Los Angeles. Perry quotes them as saying, "What the hell is this goddamn *gabacho* pig writer doing here?" (156).

11. It is worth making the distinction that Oscar never acts on his offensive judgments about various racial groups and women. He thinks the thoughts but never expresses them directly to the people involved. One of the few exceptions is when Oscar burns the hand of the man he categorizes as a homosexual and who seems to offend Oscar for no real reason in the scene at Trader JJ's (68).

12. Acosta is true to the impulses of a generation of "psychic outlaws," a term coined by Norman Mailer. See Barry H. Leeds, *Ken Kesey* 7–8. Not for them the gray-flannel suits or the eight-to-five office jobs of the 1950s. Kerouac's *On the Road* captured the heartbeat of this "crazy," psychedelic drug-taking generation who knew no rules and for whom, according to Hunter S. Thompson, "sleep was out of the question" (Perry, *On the Bus* xv). Ken Kesey, one of these iconic counterculture writers, did not write a road narrative per se, but *One Flew Over the Cuckoo's Nest* (1962) might qualify as an anti–road novel, about men confined to a mental institution who cannot be "natural" men. Of course, Kesey and the Merry Pranksters took the legendary, very visible bus trip across the country in summer 1964. Tom Wolfe made this "freaking lurid" bus trip the subject of his best-selling *The Electric Kool-Aid Acid Test* (1968).

13. Once free to roam, unbridled, the buffalo was hunted, killed, skinned, and sold. The killing of the buffalo also meant the destruction of the Indian peoples for whom the buffalo was a kind of "commissary," a cornucopia. As the buffalo were pushed westward, so were the Indian peoples. According to Art Raymond, an interviewee in the PBS video documentary *Sacred Buffalo People,* "General Sheridan said that in order to get to the root of the problem we must exterminate Indian men, women and children. That's what he said. And later on, in order to help bring about the extermination, the word was put out by the military to kill off all the buffalo, to encourage the slaughter of the buffalo at every turn." The buffalo image is appropriate for Oscar, not only because he is big and heavy, but also because he is symbolically the "hunted game" of the "Okies" and "Texas Ranger" policeman of Riverbank. See *Sacred Buffalo People.* "Okie," of course, is a pejorative term used during the Great Depression to refer to the migrant workers from Oklahoma and environs.

14. In Spanish "flesh" is *carne,* and evokes Bakhtin's *carni*valesque, which fits in with Oscar's theatrics. See Bakhtin, *Rabelais and His World.*

15. San Francisco was the adopted home of the Beats—Jack Kerouac, Allen Ginsberg, Neal Cassady. In a sense, these white ethnic men were "migrants" who came out West from New York in the 1950s—and San Francisco's 1960s "fame" was due to Haight-Ashbury, the West Coast Greenwich Village of the period.

16. That is, Colorado, Idaho, Montana, Nevada, Utah, and Wyoming. Oscar also passes through Taos, where toward the end of the book he says he lost his wallet (*Brown Buffalo* 187).

17. Just in time for the East Los Angeles school walkouts, the event that opens *The Revolt of the Cockroach People.*

18. In a 1998 *Los Angeles Times* article, Yvette C. Doss reported that Acosta had "subpoenaed every member of the Los Angeles County grand jury to prove a pattern of discrimination against Mexican Americans." In *Fear and Loathing,* Perry also mentions that Acosta "subpoenaed every superior court judge in Los Angeles, 109 in all, and cross-examined them about racism in the court system to prove that no Chicano could possibly get a fair trial" (164). In 1970 Acosta also defended Mexican Americans charged with setting fires at the Biltmore Hotel in Los Angeles when Governor Ronald Reagan delivered a speech there in the late 1960s. According to Doss, this case was known as the "Biltmore Seven." Ian F. Haney López in *Racism on Trial* tells us that *six* defendants stood trial (36) and gives additional details about the legal cases argued by Acosta.

19. Turner connects his category "liminality" to Mary Douglas's concept of the unclean in cultural rituals. Turner says, "In fact, in confirmation of Dr. Douglas's hypothesis, liminal *personae* nearly always and everywhere are regarded as polluting to those who have never been, so to speak, 'inoculated' against them." See Mary Douglas, *Purity and Danger;* Turner 97.

20. Oscar corrects Hunter Thompson's attribution to him of 300 pounds. In any case, his abundant "belly" leads Stavans to cast him, humorously and redundantly, a "chubby *panzón.*" Stavans, *Bandido* 18. The textual image of a man with hand on hips and "sandbaked" elbows spread "like wings" matches the image of the real Acosta in one of the few photographs of him that survive.

21. See end of note 13 for explanation of "Okie."

22. In addition to the two "Miss Its," Jane Addison and Alice Brown, there are the "Swedish babe from Minnesota" (16), the "voluptuous Armenian nurse" (51), and the "Rumanian lass from South Carolina" (47).

23. In giving this police official, someone Oscar types as a "Texas Ranger," a feminine name, Acosta is "rewriting" and obtaining revenge by feminizing those who have feminized him.

24. I am not attributing to Acosta a conscious intertextuality with Lewis. There is no direct connection, nor do I mean to suggest any, between Acosta and Lewis or between *The Autobiography of a Brown Buffalo* and *La Vida.*

25. Of course, the film was based on the 1957 broadway musical by the same title. For a thorough analysis of *West Side Story,* the film, see Arturo Sánchez-Sandoval, "A Puerto Rican Reading of the America of *West Side Story.*"

26. One important reason for this silence was the absence of viable forums for discussion and debate about issues that affected the Puerto Rican community on the mainland. One of the first forums to appear was El Centro de Estudios Puertorriqueños in 1972, seven years after the publication of *La Vida.* See introduction, note 21. In note 8 of the introduction, I point to one review of Lewis's book in 1967. However, just as *Down These Mean Streets* attracted the attention of African American readers, so did *La Vida.* Luther P. Jackson reviewed both *Down These*

Mean Streets and *La Vida* for the black journal *Crisis*. He noted that *La Vida* "is mute about color prejudice as a poverty factor"; see Luther P. Jackson, "Culture or Color" 192.

27. In interlude 4, I focus on Oscar and *The Autobiography of a Brown Buffalo* in relation to Octavio Paz's La Malinche and the pachuco. These are not far-fetched connections given the historical relationship between Mexicans and Chicanos.

28. The term "the poor" has serious limitations because it implies moral deficiency, not only absence of economic stability.

29. I explain the "culture of poverty" in detail in chapter 1, section 6. Here I add that it was a tidy, unified statement about poverty and its causes, a popular, elastic model and umbrella term with transferable value to include other groups. Rigdon notes that the "culture of poverty" was "a dramatic yet conveniently vague phrase that helped to call attention to the problems of the poor—or . . . to the *problem* of the poor. The convenience of the phrase is that it contains something for everyone; in using it to describe the life-style of the poor, one can attach to it the causation of one's choice" (Rigdon 87). A case in point involves African Americans. Though Lewis specifically stated that he did not consider African Americans to exemplify the traits of the "culture of poverty" (*La Vida* xlvii; see Valentine 71), other social scientists ascribed the same characteristics Lewis specifically extrapolated from his work with lower-class Mexicans and Puerto Ricans—for example, fatherless children and self-generating destitution—to African Americans living in inner cities. The Moynihan report is one example.

30. By this time Lewis had written *Five Families* (1959), *Tepotzlán* (1960), and *Pedro Martínez* (1964). *Children of Sánchez* was published in 1961.

31. See chapter 1 for the controversy created in Mexico by the Spanish translation of *The Children of Sánchez*.

32. Of course, this assumes that they were in it to begin with. Whether the Sánchez children were ever in the "culture of poverty" is a debatable point, since several critics of the concept have noted a disconnection between Lewis's conceptual statements and the facts of his descriptions. See Valentine 59–67. See also the many responses to *The Children of Sánchez*, *Pedro Martínez*, and *La Vida* in *Current Anthropology* 1967, and the debate surrounding the subject of culture and poverty in response to Valentine. Among others, see Maldonado-Denis.

33. In this sense, Consuelo herself was "author" and "ethnographer." Most likely her work provided raw material for Lewis's book. For a discussion of how Consuelo is "author" of her own story in relation to *The Children of Sánchez*, see Franco 159–174.

34. This quote is from Lewis's correspondence in 1966 with one associate on the Puerto Rican project in the slum of Esmeralda. See Rigdon 253.

35. Lewis did not really think that the "culture of poverty" he had set out to explain fit the Ríos family. See Rigdon 256 for Lewis's thinking on the "culture of poverty" and the behavior of the Ríos family. Despite his own reservations about

the lack of fit between the phrase "culture of poverty" and his intended meaning, on the one hand, and the specifics of the "deviant" behavior of the extended Ríos family, on the other, he nonetheless chose to include a comprehensive explanation of the "culture of poverty" in his introduction to *La Vida* and used the phrase in the book's subtitle: *A Puerto Rican Family in the Culture of Poverty—San Juan and New York.*

36. See chap. 1, n. 46.

37. Letter to Muna Muñoz Lee, principal translator for the Puerto Rico and Cuba projects, dated May 24, 1965. See Rigdon 245.

38. Valentine points to several inconsistencies between Lewis's abstractions and the actual behavior he describes about the Ríoses (60–61). Another important critic of the "culture of poverty" was Eleanor Leach. See Eleanor Leach, *The Culture of Poverty: A Critique.*

39. While men were men and women were women in Mexico, there was in Puerto Rico, according to Lewis, "confusion of sexual identification," (*La Vida* xlviii). The strong woman–weak man opposition coincides with Moynihan's discussion of the structure of the lower-class Negro family. Lewis's Ríos family and Moynihan's generic Negro family were matriarchal and hence social units in disintegration.

40. Lewis worried that the Ríoses' crude language and behavioral patterns would lead middle-class audiences to misjudge them, to think them "animal-like" (Rigdon 253). They made an impression he preferred to avoid since he felt committed to them for having confided in him about their lives. Yet *La Vida* is full of sordid activities and language. For a study of the "unclean" as an anthropological notion, see Mary Douglas. In *Purity and Danger,* Douglas puts it this way: "Dirt is the by-product of a systematic ordering and classification of matter, in so far as ordering involves rejecting inappropriate elements" (35). See note 19 above.

41. The policy-making process did not interest Lewis, but he wanted his ideas to effect policy. Lewis had access to government officials with power to make policies, and he was known to have sent copies of his work to them. His 1967 conversation with Senator Robert Kennedy appeared in *Redbook* (Rigdon 152, 170). Lewis may have had no direct involvement with Johnson's War on Poverty, but he was assigned "part of the credit—or blame—for the poverty program adopted by the Johnson administration, because of frequent use by some policy advisers of the culture of poverty explanation" (Rigdon 152). Valentine, for example, held Lewis and his "culture of poverty" partly responsible for the failure of Johnson's War on Poverty. Lewis called Valentine's accusation nonsense. Rather it was, he said, "the failure of the President and the Congress . . . to understand the degree of national commitment necessary to cope with the problems" (Rigdon 152). Rigdon herself adds that "[i]n fact Kennedy's and Johnson's advisers had picked up the concept [of the "culture of poverty"] *not* from Lewis, who had as yet written nothing on poverty in the United States, but from Michael Harrington's *The Other America.*" Rigdon's statement ("nothing on poverty in the United States") highlights the

contradictory status of Puerto Rican citizenship, because from one perspective, Puerto Rico *is* the United States. Harrington reviewed *La Vida* in the *New York Times Book Review*.

42. Valentine says: "The phrase 'culture of poverty' was coined by Oscar Lewis . . . and popularized by Harrington" (191). Lewis himself said that "Michael Harrington used [the phrase] extensively in his book *The Other America* (1961), which played an important role in sparking the national anti-poverty program in the United States" (xlii). Rigdon agrees with Valentine that Harrington borrowed the phrase, and adds "without citation, from *Five Families*" (151). Harrington, a Socialist, argued: "tens of millions of Americans are, at this moment, maimed in body and spirit" (9). Harrington used the expression "culture of poverty" in his Appendix; see Harrington 171–172.

43. From Allen J. Matusow, *The Unraveling of America* 119. Quotations from various mainstream print media that appeared on the back cover of the 1963 Penguin edition of Harrington's book pointed to Kennedy's awareness of *The Other America*: "It impressed Jack Kennedy . . . it is clear that [this] book contributed to Johnson's new drive" (*Time*); "The late President asked Walter Heller, chairman of the Council of Economic Advisers, for a copy of Michael Harrington's newly published, non-technical report on poverty, *The Other America* . . . Heller recommended that the war on poverty be declared, and just three days before his death last November, the President gave his chief economic aide the go-ahead to rough out the orders" (*Newsweek*); "*The Other America* has been credited with helping to open the Administration drive on poverty" (*New York Times*).

44. Johnson's war against poverty did not happen only because Harrington wrote a book bearing the influence of Lewis's fieldwork and ideas on poverty. As Matusow pointed out, it was crucial here that an aggrieved and vocal constituency demanded action to address unemployment and low wages (119, 24).

45. Bakhtin, *Rabelais and His World*.

46. Tomás Ybarra-Frausto, "Rasquachismo: A Chicano Sensibility" in *Chicano Art* 155. See also Yolanda Broyles-González, *El Teatro Campesino* 10, 35–38.

47. Stavans, *Race and Mercy*.

INTERLUDE 4

1. The word "pachuco" belongs to a subdialect of Spanish called *caló*. The pachucos of the 1940s spoke a *caló* dialect and Mexican and Mexican American urban youth speak it to this day. The phenomenon of the pachuco is primarily associated with Los Angeles due to the Zoot Suit Riots that took place there in July 1943. There were female *pachucas* known as "Black Widows." See Stuart Cosgrove, "The Zoot-Suit and Style Warfare" 83–85.

2. In the print media about the Zoot Suit Riots of 1944, when white sailors battled in the streets of Los Angeles with Mexican American pachucos, the lat-

ter were represented as the antithesis to the masculine sailors. The sailors were known to strip them of their vestments, a symbolic source of their power and energy.

3. See Ammons; also see Gates. Tiffany Ana López has applied a trickster figure framework to Chicano literature. See López, "María Cristina Mena."

4. The negative side of the spectrum of symbolic descriptors attributed to the pachuco and zoot-suiter included "bizarre creature," "social pariah," a sinister, dangerous, anarchistic figure. What is certain is that their symbolic meaning was inseparable from the war effort. As Mazón argues, "Zoot-suiters transgressed the patriotic ideals of commitment, integrity, and loyalty with noncommitment, incoherence, and defiance." See Mauricio Mazón, *The Zoot-Suit Riots* 9. More recently, Tovares's film, *The Zoot Suit Riots,* provides an in-depth view of the zoot-suiter and the riots of the 1940s.

5. The title of Paz's chapter is "The *Pachuco* and Other Extremes."

6. While "pachuco" is culturally specific to Mexican American communities, "zoot-suiter" is a cross-racial term that embraces working-class African Americans, Mexican Americans, and ethnic whites who wore that apparel. The term "zoot suit" has been linked to jazz culture and plays on rhyme. It connotes the expression to "suit" or "zoot" up, leading to this pun: "Does the 'suit' zoot you?"

7. Horace Cayton made such an accusation of African American zoot-suiters in 1943, the years of most intense scrutiny of the zoot-suiter. See Shane White and Graham White, *Stylin'.*

8. Ralph Ellison, "Change the Joke and Slip the Yoke" 55.

9. Marcos Sánchez-Tranquilino and John Tagg, in "The Pachuco's Flayed Hide," offer examples of the southern dandy, the western gambler, the modern urban gangster. Indeed, Oscar identifies with the cinematic image of the white ethnic cultural outlaws, played by Edward G. Robinson, James Cagney, and, of course, Humphrey Bogart. These were the hard-drinking, shadowy types who bucked the system and "out-copped the cops." See Sánchez-Tranquilino and Tagg 559.

10. Male Chicano academics who were the first generation in families from either rural or working-class environments to enter the educational citadel wrote about this prototypic figure. Arturo Madrid and Lauro Flores, for example, wrote research essays, José Montoya and Tino Villanueva poetry, and Luis Valdez drama about the pachuco. Some of these academics had been or knew pachucos firsthand. Paz was a cosmopolitan Mexican who enjoyed celebrity in the United States. See Lauro Flores, "La Dualidad del Pachuco." For poetic responses, see José Montoya, "El Louie"; Tino Villanueva, "Pachuco Remembered."

11. The phrase is Turner's.

12. For example, Oscar in the text does not don the zoot suit, or anything close to it. In fact, he does the direct opposite. When schoolboys growing up in the 1940s in Riverbank, Oscar and his brother wear short pants, a mode of dress that earned praise from their patriotic teacher because she credited them with

supporting the war effort by preserving material needed to clothe the soldiers. The zoot suit, on the contrary, represented "excess"—a defiant stance against the streamlined military suits sanctioned by Uncle Sam and an antipatriotic symbol against the rationing of material and goods of the government.

13. See chapter 2 for a lengthier discussion of the uses of blackface. Also see Lott, *Love and Theft;* Rogin.

14. Brew is Piri's friend and fellow traveler in *Down These Mean Streets.*

15. I cover these responses in chapter 1.

16. Oscar's metaphor for the border town of Juárez.

17. This scene plays on the ambiguity of the term *mexicano,* which may refer, depending on the context, to "nationality" but also to "ethnicity." Mexican nationals are, of course, *mexicanos,* but some people of Mexican descent, even though born and raised in the United States, prefer to use this term to refer to themselves.

EPILOGUE

1. On publishing my article "*La Malinche* at the Intersection: Race and Gender in *Down These Mean Streets,*" *PMLA,* (January 1998), I received an e-mail from Jack Yeager (September 15, 1998), who graciously informed me that the trope of La Malinche appears in the writings of Kim Lefevre, a contemporary writer of Vietnamese origin who publishes in French. In one of her narratives, Lefevre recounts growing up the child of a Vietnamese mother and French father in Indochina during the colonial period. The title of her narrative is *Moi, Marina la Malinche* (1994). I am grateful to Yeager for making me aware of Lefevre's text.

BIBLIOGRAPHY

Aaron, Daniel. "Out of the Closet." Review of *Manchild in the Promised Land,* by Claude Brown. *New Statesman,* August 5, 1966: 204.

Acosta, Oscar Zeta. *The Autobiography of a Brown Buffalo.* 1972. New York: Vintage, 1989.

———. *Oscar "Zeta" Acosta: The Uncollected Works.* Ed. Ilan Stavans. Houston: Arte Público, 1996.

———. *Revolt of the Cockroach People.* New York: Bantam, 1974.

Acosta-Belén, Edna. "Beyond Island Boundaries: Ethnicity, Gender, and Cultural Revitalization in Nuyorican Literature." *Callaloo* 15 (1992): 979–998.

———. "Conversations with Nicholasa Mohr." *Revista Chicano-Riqueña* 8.2 (1980): 35–41.

———. *The Puerto Rican Woman.* New York: Praeger, 1979.

Alarcón, Norma. "Chicana Feminist Literature: A Re-Vision through Malintzin/or Malinche: Putting Flesh Back on the Object." Anzaldúa and Moraga 182–190.

———. "Traddutora, Traditora: A Paradigmatic Figure of Chicana Feminism." *Cultural Critique* 13 (1989): 57–87.

Almaguer, Tomás. "Chicano Men: A Cartography of Homosexual Identity and Behavior." *differences* 3.2 (1991): 75–100.

———. *Racial Fault Lines: The Historical Origins of White Supremacy in California.* Berkeley: University of California Press, 1994.

Roberto Alvarez v. the Board of Trustees of the Lemon Grove School District. 66625. Cal. Super. Ct. San Diego County. April 16, 1931.

Ammons, Elizabeth. "Introduction." *Tricksterism in Turn-of-the-Century American Literature: A Multicultural Perspective.* Ammons and White-Parks vii–xiii.

Ammons, Elizabeth, and Annette White-Parks. *Tricksterism in Turn-of-the-Century American Literature: A Multicultural Perspective.* Hanover: University Press of New England, 1994.

Anaya, Rudolfo. *Bless Me Ultima.* Berkeley: Quinto Sol Publications, 1972.

Anzaldúa, Gloria. "La Prieta." *This Bridge Called My Back: Writings by Radical Women of Color.* Anzaldúa and Moraga 198–209.

Anzaldúa, Gloria, and Cherríe Moraga, eds. *This Bridge Called My Back: Writings by Radical Women of Color*. Watertown, MA: Persephone Press, 1981.

Aparicio, Frances R. "From Ethnicity to Multiculturalism: An Historical Overview of Puerto Rican Literature in the United States." *Handbook of Hispanic Cultures in the United States: Literature and Art*. Ed. Francisco Lomelí. Houston: Arte Público, 1993. 19–39.

Atiya, Aziz S. *The Copts and Christian Civilization*. Salt Lake City: University of Utah Press, 1979.

Austin, Regina. "Sapphire Bound." *Wisconsin Law Review* (1989): 539–578.

Baca Zinn, Maxine. "Political Familism: Toward Sex-Role Equality in Chicano Families." *Aztlán* 6 (1975): 13–26.

Baker, Houston A. "Environment as Enemy in a Black Autobiography: *Manchild in the Promised Land*." *Pylon* 32 (1971): 53–59.

Bakhtin, M. M. [Mikhail Mikhailovich]. *Rabelais and His World*. Trans. Helene Iswolsky. Cambridge, MA: MIT Press, 1968.

Baldwin, James. *The Fire Next Time*. New York: Dell, 1962.

———. "Negroes Are Anti-Semitic Because They're Anti-White." *Collected Essays*. New York: Library of America, 1998. 744–745.

Bannerman, Helen. *The Story of Little Black Sambo*. Bedford, MA: Appleton Books, 1995.

Baraka, Amiri. *Home*. New York: William Morrow, 1966.

Baskir, Lawrence M., and William A. Strauss. *Change and Circumstance: The Draft, the War, and the Vietnam Generation*. New York: Vintage, 1978.

Bendiner, Elmer. "Machismo." *Nation* Sept. 25, 1967: 283–284.

Benjamin, Walter. *Illuminations*. Trans. Harry Zohn. New York: Schocken, 1968.

Berger, James. "Ghosts of Liberalism: Morrison's *Beloved* and *The Moynihan Report*." *PMLA* 3 (1996): 408–420.

Berman, Paul. "The Other and the Almost the Same." *New Yorker* 18 (February 1994): 63.

Binder, Wolfgang. "An Interview with Piri Thomas." *Minority Voices* 4.1 (1980): 63–78.

Bohme, Frederick G. *200 Years of U.S. Census Taking: Population and Housing Questions, 1790–1990*. Washington, D.C.: U.S. Dept. of Commerce, Bureau of the Census, 1989.

Bond, Jean Carey, and Patricia Peery. "Is the Black Male Castrated?" Cade Bambara 113–118.

Bonilla, Frank. *The Failure of Elites*. Cambridge, MA: MIT Press, 1970.

Bonilla, Frank, Edwin Meléndez, Rebecca Morales, and María de los Angeles Torres, eds. *Borderless Borders: U.S. Latinos, Latin Americans, and the Paradox of Interdependence*. Philadelphia: Temple University Press, 1998.

Bordo, Susan. *Unbearable Weight: Feminism, Western Culture, and the Body*. Berkeley: University of California Press, 1993.

Brown, Claude. *The Children of Ham*. New York: Stein and Day, 1976.

————. "The Language of Soul." *Mother Wit from the Laughing Barrel: Readings in the Interpretation of Afro-American Folklore*. Ed. Alan Dundes. New York: Garland, 1981.

————. *Manchild in the Promised Land*. New York: Signet, 1965.

Brown v. Board of Education. 349 U.S. 249 (1955).

Broyles-González. Yolanda. *El Teatro Campesino: Theater in the Chicano Movement*. Austin: University of Texas Press, 1994.

Bruce-Novoa, Juan. "Canonical and Non-Canonical Texts." *The Américas Review* 14.3–4 (1986): 11–35.

Cade Bambara, Toni. "On the Issue of Roles." *The Black Woman*. Cade Bambara 101–110.

————, ed. *The Black Woman*. New York: Mentor, 1970.

Candelaria, Cordelia. "La Malinche: Feminist Prototype." *Frontiers* 2 (1980): 1–6.

Castañeda, Jorge G. *Utopia Unarmed: The Latin American Left after the Cold War*. New York: Knopf, 1993.

Chabram-Dernersesian, Angie. "I Throw Punches for My Race, but I Don't Want to Be a Man: Writing Us—Chica-nos (Girl, Us)/Chicanas—into the Movement Script." *Cultural Studies*. Ed. Lawrence Grossberg, Cary Nelson, and Paula Treichler. New York: Routledge, 1992. 81–95.

Choice. Review of *Autobiography of a Brown Buffalo*, by Oscar Zeta Acosta. 10 (May 1973): 538.

Clark, Kenneth. *The Dark Ghetto*. New York: Harper, 1965.

Collins, Patricia Hill. *Black Feminist Thought: Knowledge, Consciousness, and the Politics of Empowerment*. New York: Routledge, 1991.

"Coptic Church." *The Encyclopedia Americana International Edition*. Danbury, CT: Grolier, 2002.

"Coptic Church." *Harper Collins Dictionary of Religion*. San Francisco: HarperSan Francisco, 1995.

Cosgrove, Stuart. "The Zoot-Suit and Style Warfare." *History Workshop Journal* 18 (Autumn 1984): 77–91.

Cotera, Marta. *The Chicana Feminist*. Austin, TX: Austin Information Systems Development, 1977.

————. *Diosa y Hembra: The History and Heritage of Chicanas in the U.S*. Austin, TX: Austin Information Systems Development, 1976.

Cruz-Malavé, Arnaldo. "Toward an Art of Transvestism: Colonialism and Homosexuality in Puerto Rican Literature." *Entiéndes? Queer Readings, Hispanic Writings*. Ed. Emilie L. Bergmann and Paul Julian Smith. Durham: Duke University Press, 1995. 137–167.

————. "'What a Tangled Web . . . !': Masculinity, Abjection, and the Foundations of Puerto Rican Literature in the United States." *differences* 8.1 (1997): 132–151.

Cypess, Sandra Messinger. *La Malinche in Mexican Literature: From History to Myth*. Austin: University of Texas Press, 1991.

Davidoff, Leonore, and Catherine Hall. *Family Fortunes: Men and Women of the English Middle Class, 1780–1850*. Chicago: University of Chicago Press, 1987.

Davis, Angela. *Blues Legacies and Black Feminism*. New York: Vintage, 1999.

Davis, Charles T., and Henry Louis Gates Jr., eds. *The Slave's Narrative*. New York: Oxford University Press, 1985.

Davis, David Brion. "Jews and Blacks in America." *New York Review of Books*, December 2, 1999: 57–63.

Davis, F. James. *Who Is Black? One Nation's Definition*. University Park: Pennsylvania State University Press, 1991.

Davis, Thulani. "We Need to Do Some Work." *Time*, February 28, 1994: 29–30.

de Coll, Josefina Oliva. *La resistencia indígena ante la conquista*. Mexico, D.F.: Siglo Veintiuno Editores, 1974.

de la Cadena, Marisol. *Indigenous Mestizos: The Politics of Race and Culture in Cuzco, Peru, 1919–1991*. Durham: Duke University Press, 2000.

del Castillo, Adelaida. "Malintzin Tenepal: A Preliminary Look into a New Perspective." Sánchez and Cruz 124–149.

Díaz, Bernal. *The Conquest of New Spain*. Trans. J. M. Cohen. Middlesex, England: Penguin, 1963.

Díaz Quiñones, Arcadio. "Racismo, Historia, Esclavitud." Estudio Preliminar. *El prejuicio racial en Puerto Rico*. By Tomás Blanco. Río Piedras: Ediciones Huracán, 1985. 15–91.

Diner, Hasis. *Almost Promised Land: American Jews and Blacks, 1915–1935*. 1977. Rev. ed. Baltimore: John Hopkins University Press, 1995.

Doss, Yvette C. "The Lost Legend of the Real Dr. Gonzo." *Los Angeles Times*, June 5, 1998: F2.

Douglas, Mary. *Purity and Danger: Concepts of Pollution and Taboo*. London: Routledge, 1966.

Du Bois, W. E. B. *The Souls of Black Folk*. 1903. New York: Bantam, 1989.

Edelman, Lee. "The Part for the (W)hole." *Homographesis: Essays in Gay Literary and Cultural Theory*. New York: Routledge, 1994. 42–75.

"Eleanor Roosevelt National Historic Site—The Wiltwyck School." *International Coalition of Historic Site Museums of Conscience*. May 20, 2004. http://www.sitesofconscience.org/eng/roosevelt_wiltwyck.htm.

Ellison, Ralph. "Change the Joke and Slip the Yoke." *Shadow and Act*. New York: Random House, 1964.

Espinosa, Paul, dir. *The Lemon Grove Incident*. Espinosa Productions, 1985.

"Ethiopia." *The New Interpreter's Bible*. Nashville: Abingdon Press, 1994.

"Ethiopianism." *The New Encyclopaedia Britannica*. Chicago: Encyclopaedia Britannica, 2002.

Fanon, Frantz. "The Man of Color and the White Woman." Trans. Charles Lam Markmann. *Black Skin, White Masks*. New York: Grove, 1967. 63–82.

Fernández Cintrón, Celia, and Marcia Rivera Quintero. "Bases de la sociedad sexista en Puerto Rico." *Revista/Review Interamericana* 4.2 (1974): 239–245.

Flores, Juan. "Back Down These Mean Streets: Introducing Nicholasa Mohr and Louis Reyes Rivera." *Revista Chicano-Riqueña* 8.2 (1980): 51–56.

Flores, Lauro. "La dualidad del Pachuco." *Revista Chicano-Riqueña* 6.4 (1978): 51–58.

Flores, William V., and Rina Benmayor. *Latino Cultural Citizenship: Claiming Identity, Space, and Rights.* Boston: Beacon, 1977.

Foley, Neil. *The White Scourge: Mexicans, Blacks, and Poor Whites in Texas Cotton Culture.* Berkeley: University of California Press, 1997.

Franco, Jean. *Plotting Women: Gender and Representation in Mexico.* New York: Columbia University Press, 1989.

Franklin, Nancy. "Double Dealing." Rev. *Topdog/Underdog. New Yorker,* August 6, 2001: 86–87.

Frazier, E. Franklin. *The Negro Family in the United States.* 1939. Chicago: University of Chicago Press, 1967.

Fredrickson, George M. *Black Liberation: A Comparative History of Black Ideologies in the United States and South Africa.* New York: Oxford University Press, 1995.

———. *White Supremacy: A Comparative Study in American and South African History.* New York: Oxford University Press, 1981.

Freidan, Betty. *The Feminine Mystique.* New York: Norton, 1963.

Friedman, Murray. *What Went Wrong? The Creation and Collapse of the Black Jewish Alliance.* New York: Free Press, 1995.

Galbraith, John Kenneth. *The Affluent Society.* 40th Anniversary Edition. Boston: Houghton Mifflin, 1998.

García, Alma M., ed. *Chicana Feminist Thought: The Basic Historical Writings.* New York: Routledge, 1997.

———. "Introduction." *Chicana Feminist Thought: The Basic Historical Writings.* García 1–16.

Garvey, Marcus. *Philosophy and Opinions of Marcus Garvey.* Ed. Amy Jacques-Garvey. New York: Atheneum, 1969.

Gaspar de Alba, Alicia. "Malinchista, a Myth Revised." *Infinite Divisions: An Anthology of Chicana Literature.* Ed. Tey Diana Rebolledo and Eliana S. Rivero. Tucson: University of Arizona Press, 1993. 212–213.

Gates, Henry Louis, Jr. "The Blackness of Blackness: A Critique of the Sign and the Signifying Monkey." *Black Literature and Literary Theory.* Ed. Henry Louis Gates Jr. New York: Methuen, 1984.

———. *The Signifying Monkey: A Theory of Afro-American Literary Criticism.* New York: Oxford University Press, 1988.

Geertz, Clifford. *After the Fact: Two Countries, Four Decades, One Anthropologist.* Cambridge, MA: Harvard University Press, 1995.

———. "Life among the Anthros." *New York Review of Books* 48.2 (February 8, 2001): 18–22.

Getachew, Indrias. *Beyond the Throne: The Enduring Legacy of Emperor Haile Selassie I.* Ed. Richard Pankhurst. Addis Ababa, Ethiopia: Shama, 2001.

Gilroy, Paul. *The Black Atlantic: Modernity and Double Consciousness*. Cambridge, MA.: Harvard University Press, 1993.

Ginsburg, Carl. *Race and Media: The Enduring Life of the Moynihan Report*. New York: Institute for Media Analysis, 1989.

Gitlin, Todd. *The Sixties: Years of Hope, Days of Rage*. 1987. New York: Bantam, 1993.

Glazer, Nathan, and Daniel Patrick Moynihan. *Beyond the Melting Pot: The Negroes, Puerto Ricans, Jews, Italians, and Irish of New York City*. Cambridge, MA: MIT Press, 1963.

Gonzales, Rodolpho (Corky). *I am Joaquín. Yo soy Joaquín; an Epic Poem. With a Chronology of People and Events in Mexican and Mexican American History*. New York: Bantam, 1972.

González, Deena. "*Malinche* as Lesbian." *California Sociologist* 14 (1991): 91–97.

Gove, Philip Babcock, ed. *Webster's Third New International Dictionary*. Springfield, MA: Merriam-Webster, 1969.

Griffin, Farah Jasmine. "*Who Set You Flowin'?*" *The African American Migration Narrative*. New York: Oxford University Press, 1995.

Griffith, Beatrice. *American Me*. Boston: Houghton Mifflin, 1948.

Gutiérrez, Ramón, and Genaro Padilla, eds. *Recovering the U.S. Hispanic Literary Heritage*. Houston: Arte Público Press, 1993.

Gutman, Herbert. *The Black Family in Slavery and Freedom 1750–1925*. New York: Pantheon, 1976.

Gutmann, Matthew C. *The Meanings of Macho: Being a Man in Mexico City*. Berkeley: University of California Press, 1996.

"Haile Selassie." *Harper Collins Dictionary of Religion*. San Francisco: HarperSan Francisco, 1995.

"Ham." *The New Interpreter's Bible*. Nashville: Abingdon Press, 1994.

Handlin, Oscar. *The Newcomers: Negroes and Puerto Ricans in a Changing Metropolis*. Cambridge, MA: Harvard University Press, 1959.

Harper Collins Dictionary of Religion. Gen. ed. Jonathan Z. Smith et al. San Francisco: HarperSan Francisco, 1995.

Harrington, Michael. "Everyday Hell." Rev. of *La Vida: A Puerto Rican Family in the Culture of Poverty*, by Oscar Lewis. *New York Times Book Review*, November 20, 1966, sec. 7: 1+.

———. *The Other America: Poverty in the United States*. 1963. New York: Macmillan, 1969.

Hartshorn, Thomas L. "Horatio Alger in Harlem: *Manchild in the Promised Land*." *Journal of American Studies* 24.2 (1990): 243–248.

Hearings. Subcommittee on Executive Reorganization of the Committee on Government Operations. U.S. Senate, 89th Cong., 2d sess. 1966.

Hedrick, Trace. "Spik in Glyph? Translation, Wordplay, and Resistance in Chicano Bilingual Poetry." *The Translator* (1996): 141–160.

Hill, Robert A. "Black Zionism." *African Americans and Jews in the Twentieth Cen-*

tury: Studies in Convergence and Conflict. Ed. V. P. Franklin, Nancy L. Grant, Harold M. Kletnick, and Genna Rae McNeil. Columbia: University of Missouri Press, 1998.

hooks, bell. "Race and Sex." *Yearning: Race, Gender, and Cultural Politics.* Boston: South End Press, 1990. 57–64.

Hughes, Langston. *The Big Sea: An Autobiography.* New York: Thunder's Mouth, 1986.

Ignatiev, Noel. *How the Irish Became White.* New York: Routledge, 1995.

Jackson, Luther P. "Culture or Color." *Crisis* (June-July 1968): 189–193.

Jackson, Walter. *Gunnar Myrdal and America's Conscience: Social Engineering and Racial Liberalism, 1938–1987.* Chapel Hill: University of North Carolina Press, 1990.

Johnson, Barbara. *The Feminist Difference.* Cambridge, MA: Harvard University Press, 1998.

Johnson, Lyndon B. "To Fulfill These Rights." Commencement Address. Howard University. June 4, 1965.

"Justine Wise Polier—The Wiltwyck School." *Jewish Women's Archive.* May 20 2004. http://www.jwa.org/exhibits/wise/jp7.htm.

Kaplan, Amy, and Donald Pease, eds. *Cultures of United States Imperialism.* Durham: Duke University Press, 1993.

Kelley, Robin D. G. *Hammer and Hoe: Alabama Communists during the Great Depression.* Chapel Hill: University of North Carolina Press, 1990.

Kennedy, Randall. *Nigger: The Strange Career of a Troublesome Word.* New York: Pantheon, 2002.

Kerouac, Jack. *On the Road.* 40th Anniversary Ed. New York: Viking, 1997.

Kesey, Ken. *One Flew Over the Cuckoo's Nest.* 1962. New York: Viking, 1969.

Killens, John O. "On *El Barrio* and Piri Thomas." Review of *Down These Mean Streets,* by Piri Thomas. *Negro Digest* (1968): 94–97.

Kingston, Maxine Hong. *The Woman Warrior: Memoirs of a Girlhood Among Ghosts.* 1975. New York: Vintage, 1989.

Kinsbruner, Jay. *Not of Pure Blood: The Free People of Color and Racial Prejudice in Nineteenth-Century Puerto Rico.* Durham: Duke University Press, 1996.

La Gaceta. 12.127 (marzo 1965).

Ladmer, Joyce. *Tomorrow's Tomorrow: The Black Woman.* Garden City, NY: Doubleday, 1971.

Lancaster, Roger. *Life Is Hard: Machismo, Danger, and the Intimacy of Power in Nicaragua.* Berkeley: University of California Press, 1992.

Leach, Eleanor. *The Culture of Poverty: A Critique.* New York: Simon and Schuster, 1971.

Leeds, Barry H. *Ken Kesey.* New York: F. Ungar, 1981.

Lefevre, Kim. *Moi, Marina la Malinche.* Paris: Stock, 1994.

Lerner, Michael, and Cornel West. *Jews and Blacks: Let the Healing Begin.* New York: Putnam, 1995.

Levine, Lawrence W. *Black Culture and Black Consciousness: Afro-American Folk Thought from Slavery to Freedom*. New York: Oxford University Press, 1977.

Lewis, Oscar. *The Children of Sánchez: Autobiography of a Mexican Family*. New York: Random House, 1961.

———. *Five Families*. New York: New American Library, 1959.

———. *La Vida: A Puerto Rican Family in the Culture of Poverty—San Juan and New York*. New York: Oxford University Press, 1965.

Library Journal Book Review. Review of *Autobiography of a Brown Buffalo*, by Oscar Zeta Acosta. 98 (March 1973): 734.

Limerick, Patricia Nelson. *The Legacy of Conquest*. New York: Norton, 1987.

Lincoln, Abbey. "Who Will Revere the Black Woman?" Cade Bambara 80–89.

Lipsitz, George. *Dangerous Crossroads: Popular Music, Postmodernism, and the Poetics of Place*. 1994. New York: Verso, 1997.

———. *The Possessive Investment in Whiteness: How White People Profit from Identity Politics*. Philadelphia: Temple University Press, 1998.

López, Ian F. Haney. *Racism on Trial*. Cambridge, MA: Harvard University Press, 2003.

López, Tiffany Ana. "María Cristina Mena: Turn-of-the-Century La Malinche, and Other Tales of Cultural (Re)Construction." Ammons and White-Parks 21–45.

Lott, Eric. *Love and Theft: Blackface Minstrelsy and the American Working Class*. New York: Oxford University Press, 1995.

———. "White Like Me: Racial Cross-Dressing and the Construction of American Whiteness." Kaplan and Pease 474–495.

Loving v. Virginia. 388 U.S. 1 (1967).

MacPherson, Myra. *Long Time Passing: Vietnam and the Haunted Generation*. New York: Doubleday, 1984.

Maddocks, Melvin. "The Knuckle-Hard Code of the Barrio." Review of *Down These Mean Streets*, by Piri Thomas. *Life Book Review* (1967): 8.

Madrid, Arturo. "In Search of the Authentic Pachuco." *Aztlán* 4.1 (1973): 31–60.

Mailer, Norman. *Advertisements for Myself*. New York: Putnam, 1959.

Maldonado-Denis, Manuel. "Book Review of *The Children of Sánchez, Pedro Martínez*, and *La Vida* by Oscar Lewis." *Current Anthropology* 8.5 (1967): 496–497.

Marable, Manning. *Beyond Black and White: Transforming African-American Politics*. New York: Verso, 1995.

Marcus, Harold G. *Haile Sellassie I: The Formative Years, 1892–1936*. Berkeley: University of California Press, 1987.

Mariscal, George, ed. *Aztlán and Viet Nam: Chicano and Chicana Experiences of the War*. Berkeley: University of California Press, 1999.

Martínez-Echazábal, Lourdes. *Para una semiótica de la mulatez*. Madrid: José Porrúa Turanzas, 1990.

————. "*Mestizaje* and the Discourse of National/Cultural Identity in Latin America, 1845–1959." *Latin American Perspectives* 25.3 (May 1998): 21–42.

Massey, Douglas. "Explaining the Paradox of Puerto Rican Segregation." *Social Forces* (1985): 306–331.

Matusow, Allen J. *The Unraveling of America: A History of Liberalism in the 1960s.* New York: Harper, 1984.

Mazón, Mauricio. *The Zoot-Suit Riots.* Austin: University of Texas Press, 1984.

Menand, Louis. "College: The End of the Golden Age." *New York Review of Books,* October 18, 2001: 44–47.

Mirandé, Alfredo, and Evangelina Enríquez. *La Chicana: The Mexican American Woman.* Chicago: University of Chicago Press, 1979.

Mitchell, Loften. "Growing Up Ghetto." Review of *Manchild in the Promised Land,* by Claude Brown. *The Crisis,* October 1965: 511+.

Mohr, Eugene V. *The Nuyorican Experience: Literature of the Puerto Rican Minority.* Westport, CT: Greenwood Press, 1982.

Mohr, Nicholasa. *Nilda: A Novel.* Houston: Arte Público, 1986.

Monge, José Trías. *Puerto Rico: The Trials of the Oldest Colony in the World.* New Haven: Yale University Press, 1997.

Montiel, Miguel. "The Social Science Myth of the Mexican American Family." *Voices: Readings from El Grito.* 2d ed. Berkeley: Quinto Sol Publications, 1973.

Montoya, José. "El Louie." *Fiesta in Aztlán: Anthology of Chicano Poetry.* Ed. Toni Empringham. Santa Barbara, CA: Capra, 1982.

Moraga, Cherrie. "A Long Line of Vendidas." *Loving in the War Years.* Boston: South End Press, 1983. 90–144.

————. "La Güera." *Loving in the War Years.* Boston: South End Press, 1983. 50–59.

Moran, Rachel. "Unrepresented." *Representations* 55.957 (1996): 139–154.

Morrison, Toni. "Rootedness: The Ancestor as Foundation." *Black Women Writers* (1950–1980). Ed. Mari Evans. New York: Anchor, 1984. 339–345.

Moynihan, Daniel Patrick. *The Negro Family: The Case for National Action. The Moynihan Report and the Politics of Controversy.* Rainwater and Yancey 41–124.

————. *Understanding Poverty: Perspectives from the Social Sciences.* New York: Basic Books, 1969.

Mullen, Edward J., ed. *Langston Hughes in the Hispanic World and Haiti.* Hamden, CT: Archon, 1977.

Myrdal, Gunnar. *An American Dilemma: The Negro Problem and Modern Democracy.* New York: Harper, 1944.

Naeem, Abdul Basit. "Comment on First Novel by Black Harlem Writer." *Muhammed Speaks* (1965): 10.

Neco, Luis M. Review of *Down These Mean Streets,* by Piri Thomas. *Crime and Delinquency* 15.2 (1969): 308–310.

Nelson, Dana. *The Word in Black and White: Reading "Race" in American Literature, 1638–1867.* New York: Oxford University Press, 1992.

Newton, Jim, and Andrea Ford. "Lawyers Bitterly Debate Race in Simpson Case." *Los Angeles Times,* January 14, 1995: 1+.

Nieto-Gómez, Ana. "La Feminista." *Encuentro Femenil* 1 (1973): 34–47.

Omi, Michael, and Howard Winant. *Racial Formation in the United States: From the 1960s to the 1990s.* New York: Routledge, 1994.

Omolade, Barbara. "Hearts of Darkness." *Powers of Desire: The Politics of Sexuality.* Ed. Ann Snitow, Christine Stansell, and Sharon Thompson. New York: Monthly Review Press, 1983. 350–367.

Ostaloza Bey, Margarita. *Política sexual en Puerto Rico.* Río Piedras: Huracán, 1989.

Padilla, Elena. Rev. of *La Vida: A Puerto Rican Family in the Culture of Poverty-San Juan and New York,* by Oscar Lewis. *Political Science Quarterly* 82 (1967): 651–652.

Padilla, Genaro. "The Self as Cultural Metaphor in Acosta's *Autobiography of a Brown Buffalo.*" *Journal of General Education* 35.4 (1984): 242–258.

Paredes, Américo. *With a Pistol in His Hand, a Border Ballad and Its Hero.* Austin: University of Texas Press, 1958.

Parker, Andrew, Mary Russo, Doris Sommer, and Patricia Yaeger, eds. *Nationalisms and Sexualities.* New York: Routledge, 1992.

Parks, Suzan-Lori. *Topdog/Underdog.* New York: Theatre Communications Group, 2001.

Paz, Octavio. *The Labyrinth of Solitude.* 1950. Trans. Lysander Kemp. New York: Grove, 1961.

Perry, Paul. *Fear and Loathing: The Strange and Terrible Saga of Hunter S. Thompson.* New York: Thunder's Mouth, 1993.

———. *On the Bus: The Complete Guide to the Legendary Trip of Ken Kesey and the Merry Pranksters and the Birth of the Counterculture.* New York: Thunder's Mouth, 1990.

Plessy v. Ferguson. 163 U.S. 538 (1896).

Pratt, Mary Louise. "Arts of the Contact Zone." *Profession* 91 (1991): 33–40.

———. *Imperial Eyes: Travel Writing and Transculturation.* New York: Routledge, 1992.

———. " 'Yo Soy La Malinche': Chicana Writers and the Poetics of Ethnonationalism." *Callaloo* 16 (1993): 859–873.

Publisher's Weekly. Rev. of *Autobiography of a Brown Buffalo,* by Oscar Zeta Acosta. July 31, 1972: 67.

Rainwater, Lee, and William L. Yancey. *The Moynihan Report and the Politics of Controversy.* Cambridge, MA: MIT Press, 1967.

Rama, Angel. *Transculturación narrativa en América Latina.* México, D.F.: Siglo Veintiuno, 1982.

Ramirez, Arthur. Rev. of *Autobiography of a Brown Buffalo*, by Oscar Zeta Acosta. *Revista Chicano-Riqueña* 3.3 (1975): 46–53.

Ramirez, Deborah. "Multicultural Empowerment: It's Not Just Black and White Anymore." *Stanford Law Review* 47 (1996): 957–992.

Ramos, Samuel. *El perfil del hombre y la cultura en México/Profile of Man and Culture in Mexico*. 1934. Trans. Peter G. Earle. 2d ed. Austin: University of Texas Press, 1972.

Raphael, Lennox. "What's Happening Here." Rev. of *Down These Mean Streets*, by Piri Thomas. *Freedomways* 7 (1967): 358–359.

"Rastafarians." *Harper Collins Dictionary of Religion*. San Francisco: HarperSan Francisco, 1995.

Rendón, Armando. *The Chicano Manifesto*. New York: Macmillan, 1971.

Rich, Adrienne. *Blood, Bread, and Poetry*. New York: Norton, 1986.

Rigdon, Susan. *The Culture Facade: Art, Science, and Politics in the Work of Oscar Lewis*. Urbana: University of Illinois Press, 1988.

Roach, Joseph R. *Cities of the Dead: Circum-Atlantic Performance*. New York: Columbia University Press, 1996.

Rodríguez, Clara E. "Puerto Ricans in Historical and Social Science Research." *Handbook of Research on Multicultural Education*. Ed. Cherry A. McGee Banks. New York: Macmillan, 1995. 223–244.

———. *Puerto Ricans: Born in the U.S.A.* Boston: Unwin Hyman, 1989.

Rodriguez, Richard. *Hunger of Memory: The Education of Richard Rodriguez: An Autobiography*. 1982. New York: Bantam, 1988.

Roediger, David. *The Wages of Whiteness: Race and the Making of the American Working Class*. London: Verso, 1991.

Rogin, Michael. *Blackface, White Noise: Jewish Immigrants in the Hollywood Melting Pot*. Berkeley: University of California Press, 1996.

Romano-V, Octavio I. "The Historical and Intellectual Presence of Mexican-Americans." *El Grito* 2.2 (1969): 32–46.

Romero, Oswaldo. Rev. of *The Autobiography of a Brown Buffalo*, by Oscar Zeta Acosta. *Mester* 4.2 (1974): 141.

Rotello, Carlos. "The Box of Groceries and the Omnibus Tour: *Manchild in the Promised Land*." *October Cities: The Redevelopment of Urban Literature*. Berkeley: University of California Press, 1998. 269–292.

S. M. "In the Arms of Lady Snow." Rev. of *Down These Mean Streets,* by Piri Thomas. *Newsweek* May 29, 1967: 96–97.

Sacred Buffalo People: The Bison in Plains Indian Culture. Red Eye Television. Native American Public Broadcasting Consortium, 1992.

Saldívar, Ramón. "A Dialectic of Difference: Toward a Theory of the Chicano Novel." *MELUS* 6.3 (1979): 78–89.

Salzman, Jack, and Cornel West, eds. *Struggles in the Promised Land*. New York: Oxford University Press, 1997.

Samuels, Shirley. *Romances of the Republic: Women, the Family, and Violence in the Literature of the Early American Nation.* New York: Oxford University Press, 1996.

Sánchez, Luis Rafael. "La guagua aérea." *La guagua aérea.* San Juan: Editorial Cultural, 1994. 11–22.

Sánchez, Marta E. "Calibán: The New Latin American Protagonist of the Tempest." *Diacritics* 6.1 (1976): 54–61.

———. *Contemporary Chicana Poetry: A Critical Approach to an Emerging Literature.* Berkeley: University of California Press, 1985.

———. "*La Malinche* at the Intersection: Race and Gender in *Down These Mean Streets.*" *PMLA* 113 (1998): 117–128.

Sánchez, Rosaura. "Reconstructing Chicana Gender Identity." *American Literary History* 9 (1997): 350–363.

Sánchez, Rosaura, and Rosa Martínez Cruz, eds. *Essays on La Mujer.* Los Angeles: UCLA Chicano Studies Center Publications, 1977.

Sánchez-Korrol, Virginia E. *The Puerto Rican Struggle: From Colonia to Community. The History of Puerto Ricans in New York City, 1917–1948.* Westport, CT: Greenwood Press, 1983.

Sánchez-Sandoval, Arturo. "A Puerto Rican Reading of the America of *West Side Story.*" *José, Can You See? Latinos On and Off Broadway.* Madison: University of Wisconsin Press, 1999. 62–82.

Sánchez-Tranquilino, Marcos, and John Tagg. "The Pachuco's Flayed Hide: Mobility, Identity, and *Buenas Garras.*" *Cultural Studies.* Ed. Lawrence Grossberg, Cary Nelson, and Paula A. Treichler. New York: Routledge, 1992.

Saturday Review. Review of *Autobiography of a Brown Buffalo,* by Oscar Zeta Acosta. November 11, 1972: 67–69.

Saxton, Alexander. *The Rise and Fall of the White Republic: Class Politics and Mass Culture in Nineteenth-Century America.* New York: Verso, 1990.

Schwarz, Benjamin. Rev. of *Without Sanctuary: Lynching Photography in America,* by James Allen. *Los Angeles Times Book Review* Feb. 13, 2000: 1+.

Silberman, Charles E. "Beware the Day They Change Their Minds!" *Fortune* Nov. 1965: 150+.

———. "The City and the Negro." *Fortune,* March 1962: 88+.

Sollors, Werner. *Neither Black nor White Yet Both: Thematic Explorations of Interracial Literature.* New York: Oxford University Press, 1997.

Spicer, Edward H. *Cycles of Conquest.* Tucson: University of Arizona Press, 1962.

Stack, Carol B. *All Our Kin: Strategies for Survival in a Black Community.* New York: Harper & Row, 1974.

Stavans, Ilan. *Bandido: Oscar 'Zeta' Acosta and the Chicano Experience.* New York: Harper, 1995.

———. *Race and Mercy: A Conversation with Piri Thomas.* 1995. Available at http://www.cheverote.com/reviews/stavansinterview.html. Sept. 14, 2003.

Stern, Daniel. "One Who Got Away." *New York Times Book Review,* May 21, 1967: 45–46.

Sundquist, Eric. *To Wake the Nations: Race in the Making of American Literature.* Cambridge, MA: Belknap, 1993.

Terdiman, Richard. *Discourse/Counter Discourse: The Theory and Practice of Symbolic Resistance in Nineteenth-Century France.* Ithaca: Cornell University Press, 1985.

Thernstrom, Stephan, Ann Orlov, and Oscar Handlin, eds., *Harvard Encyclopedia of American Ethnic Groups.* Cambridge, MA: Belknap, 1980.

Thomas, Piri. *Down These Mean Streets.* 1967. New York: Vintage, 1974.

Thompson, Hunter S. *Fear and Loathing in Las Vegas: A Savage Journey to the Heart of the American Dream.* 1971. New York: Vintage, 1989.

Tovares, Joseph, dir. *Zoot Suit Riots.* WGBH Educational Foundation, PBS Home Video, 2002.

Traub, James. "Bleak House." Rev. of *The Lost Children of Wilder: The Epic Struggle to Change Foster Care,* by Nina Bernstein. *New York Review of Books,* May 17, 2001: 24–27.

Turner, Victor. *The Forest of Symbols.* Ithaca: Cornell University Press, 1967.

United States Senate. *Hearings before the Subcommittee on Executive Reorganization of the Committee on Government Operations.* 89th Cong., 2d sess. August 29 and 30, 1966.

United States v. Thind. 261 U.S. 204. U.S. Supreme Court (1923).

Urciuoli, Bonnie. *Exposing Prejudice: Puerto Rican Experiences of Language, Race, and Class.* Boulder, CO: Westview, 1996.

Valdés-Fallís, Guadalupe. "The Liberated Chicana: A Struggle against Tradition." *Women: A Journal of Liberation* 3 (1974): 20–21.

Valentine, Charles. *Culture and Poverty: Critique and Counter-Proposals.* Chicago: University of Chicago Press, 1968.

Valenzuela-Arce, José Manuel. *Impecable y diamantina: la deconstrucción del discurso nacional.* Tijuana, Mexico: Colegio de la Frontera Norte, 1999.

Vidal, Mirta. "Women: New Voice of La Raza." *Chicanas Speak Out.* New York: Pathfinder Press, 1971. 3–11.

Villanueva, Tino. "Pachuco Remembered." *Fiesta in Aztlán: Anthology of Chicano Poetry.* Ed. Toni Empringham. Santa Barbara, CA: Capra, 1982.

Wakin, Edward. *A Lonely Minority: The Modern Story of Egypt's Copts.* New York: William Morrow, 1963.

Wallace, Michelle. *Black Macho and the Myth of the Superwoman.* New York: Verso, 1979.

Warren, Kenneth W. *Black and White Strangers: Race and American Literary Realism.* Chicago: University of Chicago Press, 1993.

West Side Story. Dir. Robert Wise. s.n., 1961.

Westminister School District of Orange County v. Mendez. 161 F. 2d 774. 9th Circuit. 1947.

White, Shane, and Graham White. *Stylin': African American Expressive Culture from Its Beginning to the Zoot Suit*. Ithaca: Cornell University Press, 1998.

Williams, Sherley Anne. *Dessa Rose*. New York: William Morrow, 1986.

Wolfe, Tom. *The Electric Kool-Aid Acid Test*. New York: Bantam, 1968.

Ybarra-Frausto, Tomás. "Rasquachismo: A Chicano Sensibility." *Chicano Art: Resistance and Affirmation 1965–85*. Ed. Richard Griswold del Castillo, Teresa McKenna, and Yvonne Yarbro-Bejarano. Los Angeles: Wight Art Gallery, University of California, 1991. 155–162.

Yeager, Jack. E-mail to author. September 15, 1998.

Yetman, Norman R. *Life under the 'Peculiar Institution': Selections from the Slave Narrative Collection*. New York: Holt, Rinehart and Winston, 1970.

INDEX